MW00994612

The Rainbow
Bookshelf

Jack Sutherland

EVERY STEP ★OF THE★ WAY

Louisville's Road to the National Championship

Jock Sutherland's
EVERY STEP OF THE WAY
Louisville's Road
to the National Championship

Publisher: Lawrence C. Falk
Edited by: John Crawley
Editorial assistants: Jo Anna Arnott, Judi Hutchinson, Garry Jones, Suzanne Benish Kurowsky
Cover illustration: Jerry McKiernan
Printed by: Jostens, Printing and Publishing Division
Photographs courtesy of: Garry Jones, Angela Kapfhammer, Kevin Cooper, Tim Easley,
            Kenny Klein

Copyright © 1986, by Falsoft, Inc., publishers of SCORECARD Magazine, The Falsoft Building, 9509 U.S. Highway 42, Prospect, Kentucky 40059. Telex 750815

No part of this book may be reproduced or utilized in any form or by any means, electronic or mechanical, including photocopying, recording or by any information storage and retrieval system, without written permission from the publisher. All inquiries should be directed to: Falsoft, Inc., publishers of SCORECARD Magazine, The Falsoft Building, 9509 U.S. Highway 42, Prospect, Kentucky 40059.

Library of Congress Catalog Card Number: 86-61535
ISBN: 0-932471-04-8
Printed in the United States of America. All rights reserved.
1 2 3 4 5 6 7 8 9 10

Dedication

The dedication of this book is based on three words — encouragement, motivation and accomplishment — and shared by the three factors that made it possible.

I dedicate this book to my wife Phyllis Jo (P.J.) who is a terrific friend and a real companion. Her encouragement made it possible for me to undertake this project and make it a reality.

I dedicate this book to the fans of the University of Louisville basketball program for providing me with the motivation.

I dedicate this book to the seniors — Jeff Hall, Billy Thompson, Milt Wagner and Robbie Valentine — for the experiences of the past and for their accomplishments during the 1985-86 championship season. I wish them well.

Acknowledgements

The customary practice is for an author to thank all the people who helped him with his book. First, it takes someone to believe in you, someone willing to accept the publishing responsibility. For that, I owe a nod of thanks to Mr. Lawrence C. Falk of Falsoft, Inc.

Next, it takes someone to follow behind the author and straighten things up a little here and there, at least in my case it does. That nod of thanks goes to Mr. John Crawley, editor of SCORE**CARD**.

You've heard the old saying "a picture is worth a thousand words." For that, my thanks go to Garry Jones, assistant editor of SCORE**CARD** who just happens to be an accomplished photographer, and to the University of Louisville's sports information office and director Kenny Klein.

And last, but certainly not least, you have to have something to write about. My final thanks go to the 1985-86 Louisville Cardinal basketball team and coaching staff of Denny Crum, Jerry Jones, Wade Houston and Bobby Dotson. They created the story, I just put it on paper.

Introduction

How did a guy with my voice and ability to slaughter the English language ever get on the radio? It's a logical question, one worth answering.

I retired with 25 years of service in the public school system where I coached high school basketball in each of those years. My coaching and teaching days consisted of four years at Gallatin County High, seven years at Harrison County High, one year at Madisonville High and 13 years at Lexington Lafayette High. I spent three years in the U.S. Army and two years at the University of Alabama, so after 30 years I was ready to retire.

As for coaching, my claim to fame was that I was the only high school coach to win three regional championships at three different schools, and my 1979 Lafayette team won the Kentucky State Championship. It was after that 1979 team that I pulled the plug on my coaching. My accomplishments weren't much after 25 years of pain and suffering, but there were many, many good times that I'll always cherish.

But how did I get into the radio business? After I retired from coaching, I did some high school broadcasts for WVLK in Lexington. Later, Van Vance and WHAS radio asked me to do the state tournament broadcasts. Van and I really had a good chemistry between us. He was a lot of fun to work with and always gave me the perfect remarks to bounce off of. The opportunity to do the University of Louisville basketball broadcasts came when Van accepted me as his partner and U of L approved me just before the 1983-84 season. Even then, I hadn't been a stranger to the Louisville program. Before joining Van on radio, I spent two years with Dave Conrad on WHAS-TV as the color commentator for Cardinal games.

Van Vance is a pro. He's so smooth with that big, booming voice of his while I'm just the opposite. I have that "Dizzy Dean" quality so it's probably the contrast between us that makes up what I think is a very good broadcasting team. We seem to be with each other constantly and, between the laughs, there's a lot of basketball talk that goes on. We are both very familiar with the situations surrounding the game and have become familiar sights at various arenas around the country.

Those close to us while traveling on the road have nicknamed us Batman and Robin, Mo and Shmo, Nip and

Tuck, and just about any other names imaginable. But it has always been done in fun.

Both Van and I are ex-basketball players from many years ago. Van spent six seasons as the voice of the Kentucky Colonels. His background coupled with mine gives what I think is a pretty good foundation on which to build a team.

I consider myself very lucky to be a support person for Van Vance on WHAS and the color commentator for the Louisville Cardinal basketball team. It's one of the nicest things to ever come my way and I make every effort to be worthy of the position. Still, I have my critics. Two of my toughest critics are my sons, Charles and Glenn. Charles is an attorney and Glenn is a dentist, both in the Lexington area. They are avid basketball fans and keep me on my toes with their constant critiques. By the way, both of them picked the Cards to win the national championship before I did.

It was from my radio position and my job as a columnist for SCORECARD that I observed the Cardinals during the 1985-86 season, every step of the way. It was through my experiences of traveling with the team that made it possible to accumulate the information necessary in a project such as this.

Why would anybody in their right mind want to take on such a self-made assignment? I blame it on the U of L fans, the greatest fans in the world. It was their dedication during the 1985-86 season that got me going. The sacrifices made by the hundreds of Cardinal followers throughout the season and NCAA Tournament were astounding. The undying faith displayed by all motivated me. Those who made the trips to Ogden, Houston and Dallas suffered through personal inconveniences and burdens, but they weathered the storm. And those who didn't make the trips weren't forgotten as everyone knew their hearts were with the team. There was just something special about the U of L fans and I felt they all deserved something special in return. That's the reason for this book.

It was at the pep rally before the national semifinal game against LSU that I told P.J. that if the Cards won the national title, then I was going to write about it. I just felt every Cardinal fan should have the complete story of this beautiful season.

I tried to follow the example of the U of L players while writing this book, giving it a quality effort. It was a very challenging undertaking which required giving up just about everything except going to the bathroom. It was a sacrifice, but that's the way it was with all the Cardinal lovers, and, for sure, I'm one of them. I hope you'll enjoy it and that you'll put it somewhere after you're finished to let it gather some dust. Then later, as time passes (and it does very quickly), pick it up and dust it off, and, as you glance through the pages another time, say "I was there" or "I remember that." Remember it all over again.

I sincerely hope this book can become a treasure chest full of memories for you. Just like the coaching staff, the players and you, I gave it my best effort.

— *Jock Sutherland*

Table of Contents

1

Beginning at the End

The beginning of Louisville's drive for a national championship in 1985-86 actually started back in the cold of New York during the latter days of March, 1985. Four teams — Louisville, UCLA, Indiana and Tennessee — were trying to salvage what were otherwise disappointing seasons. It was the Final Four, not of the NCAA Tournament but the post-season National Invitation Tournament. U of L's semifinal opponent was UCLA.

First, let's go back a little to get the overall picture. The Cardinals and the Bruins had met one month earlier in Los Angeles. It was just another regular-season game for both, but a win over UCLA quite possibly would have been the little push needed for Louisville to get an invitation to the NCAA post-season tourney. But the Cards came up short at the buzzer, 75-65. It was a game that typified the entire 1984-85 season.

It was during this season that the Cardinals would come up short a gigantic total of 18 times. On the bright side of this picture, they had won a total of 19 times. But by Louisville's and Denny Crum's standards, that was way below par.

Despite playing one of the toughest schedules in the nation, Louisville was snubbed by the NCAA Selection Committee, and rightly so. Instead, the Cardinals managed to get a bid to play in the once-prestigious NIT. It was hard to imagine an NCAA Tournament going on with the University of Louisville nowhere to be found. Crum's teams had already made three trips to the Final Four since 1980 and had come away with the championship crown once.

The fact is, though, the Cards didn't merit a bid with a 16-16 record at the time. So, for the first time since 1976, they would have to settle for an invitation to the NIT. An NIT crown would salvage a little honor and soothe the wounds of the Cardinals' pride. The 16 losses were the most by a Louisville team since the 1939-40 season. Also by participating in the NIT, U of L had a chance to keep its string of 40 consecutive winning seasons (an NCAA record) alive and the opportunity to give Crum his 14th straight 20-win season. A lot was at stake, at least in the minds of the U of L fans and the record-keepers, and after all, it was March and everyone is well aware of the reputation the Cards had established with their quality of play during that particular month.

Louisville opened NIT action against tiny Alcorn State in the 7,000-seat Broadbent Arena (Freedom Hall was already booked for another event at the time). They had no easy task in eliminating Davey Whitney's NAIA school. The Cardinals got out alive with a paltry two-point victory, 77-75.

The next opponent was South Florida of the Sun Belt Conference, coached by Kentucky-bred Lee Rose. This game was played in the more familiar surroundings of Freedom Hall. Again the Cards escaped with a win, 68-61, and assured themselves of at least another winning season.

Louisville followed that win with another victory in Freedom Hall over Tennessee-Chattanooga, 71-66, which advanced them to the NIT Final Four in New York. That, in itself, was some sort of redemption for an otherwise poor season. At least a winning season was assured and they were just one game short of keeping Crum's string of 20-win seasons intact. They'd have two chances left to win just one game.

Athletic director Bill Olsen received word that UCLA would be the team Louisville would have to beat to reach the finals of the NIT. But as fate would have it, it didn't happen. The Bruins won the semifinal game by defeating the Cardinals 75-66.

Then came the dreaded consolation game, a game that's sort of like eating leftovers all the time. What's the use of a consolation game? Coach Crum even made the remark that the NIT should take a lesson from the NCAA and eliminate this totally useless waste of time, even though he wasn't that blunt about it.

Still, the game had to be played. As it turned out, it was just barely played by the disappointed Louisville team. Tennessee, which had been beaten by Indiana, registered 100 points on the scoreboard against the Cardinals and easily won by the score of 100-84. That score obviously indicated that there wasn't a lot of defense being played.

It was a real bad feeling watching that happen to the Cardinals. It just didn't seem possible that a mediocre team, or anybody else, could do that against Louisville.

"To score 100 points against a team that has such a great tradition of winning basketball, in Madison Square Garden, will always be a game that I'll remember," said Volunteer coach Don DeVoe.

Well, for me, it will always be a game that I've already forgotten. My radio partner at WHAS, Van Vance, and I

Player injuries contributed to the disappointing 19-18 record in 1984-85.

The new freshmen recruiting class was tabbed as the best in the nation by many of the experts.

usually talk and joke around while we are packing the equipment up after a game but this time it was a different feeling. Nothing was said and there were no laughs. We just packed up and got out of there as quickly as possible.

I think what happened to the championship team of 1985-86 began back on that night in New York, March 29, when Tennessee had everything its way against Louisville. It was a nasty way to spend an evening and end a season.

When the Cardinal players returned to Louisville and tried to become normal students without the rigors of being athletes in a big-time basketball program, they found a feeling within themselves they didn't like. These same athletes had walked Belknap Campus many times, always proud and very special. Not any more. That wasn't what they were feeling.

These athletes had come to Louisville on the heels of the 1980 national championship team. Louisville was a great basketball program and the players on the 1984-85 team had inherited this greatness. It was their role to carry it forward. Obviously, that hadn't been accomplished.

On the days that followed the loss to Tennessee, it didn't seem so great anymore. These athletes felt the pain deep inside themselves because the greatness had slipped away during that 1984-85 season and they realized it had been their group which allowed it to happen. Sure, there were plenty of excuses, mostly key injuries, but the bottom line was that it did happen.

Knowing the upcoming seniors as I did, I was sure they'd make a new commitment within themselves. In the days that followed, the recruiting rumor-mill got hot and heavy. Those rumors became facts when the U of L coaching staff signed Tony Kimbro, Pervis Ellison, Avery Marshall, David Robinson, Keith Williams and Kenny Payne to national letters-of-intent. There were also rumors floating around concerning the healing of Milt Wagner's injury. Kevin Walls' situation was looking better. They were all little signs that things would be different in 1985-86.

That feeling of being special found its way back to the Louisville campus.

There were some other things beginning to happen worth mentioning. Denny Crum had changed his way of thinking in regards to strength and conditioning. Assistant football coach Doug Semenick had tried to sell him on the fairly new procedure as far as basketball was concerned after the 1980 championship year. Some of the top schools like North Carolina were using a strength program, but Denny probably felt like "who needs it?" His team had just won all the marbles so why try to fix something that wasn't broken? Whatever his reasons, Coach Crum didn't buy it.

But things change and so did the head coach. At the banquet following the disappointing 1984-85 season, Denny surprised everyone when he introduced his new weight and agility coordinator, Semenick. Crum told the large crowd that Semenick would be the person who would immediately begin putting all the basketball players through a tough conditioning program.

Actually, it was the beginning of Denny's new get-tough policy. Most of Crum's former players who had gone on to the professional ranks believed in that type of training, and Denny was serious about it. "Next fall we will be over our scholarship limit by two people," Crum told the audience. "I will look at Coach Semenick's records and the ones who have been working hard won't have to worry. But the ones who aren't working hard will have plenty to worry about."

I'm sure that got the attention of his players.

The warm weather rolled around and a new summer league popped up — The Louisville Developmental Summer League. It was a very, very good league and just what the players needed. All the Louisville players participated and one team in particular, The Future Stars (aptly named because all the incoming freshmen were on the team), caught the eyes of the many thousands that watched. The younger players did more than hold their own against the likes of Derek Smith, Rodney McCray and Rick Wilson.

The league sort of got the basketball spirit recharged. Many superlatives began being tossed around from people who had seen the summer action, and the basketball interest of Cardinal fans seemed to fire up a little earlier than normal in the fall of 1985. Yes, sirree, those Cardinal fans could barely wait for the new season's opener in Cincinnati on Nov. 26, 1985, kicking off the first-ever Big Apple National Invitation Tournament.

Kenny Payne, interviewed by AP's Jane Gibson on picture day, quickly found out how important basketball at U of L really is.

4

This time, however, the NIT had a totally different meaning to the Cardinals. Instead of it being a place to end it all like it was back in March, it was a place to start over again. Louisville was going back to the scene of the crime, New York City, where Tennessee had embarrassed them by scoring 100 points and put Louisville out of its misery with two straight defeats.

This time it was a totally different trip to New York. With Louisville in the final foursome were three of the nation's best teams — Kansas, Duke and St. John's. All four had the ability to be considered legitimate NCAA Final Four contenders and, as it turned out, only St. John's failed to make the big party in Dallas.

As far as the record was concerned, Louisville didn't fare much better than it did the year before. They lost games to Kansas and St. John's, but it was a different story now. Against such highly respected opponents, Louisville showed all New Yorkers and the rest of the nation that "what you are seeing now is a lot different than what you saw the last time we were in town." And you can take that to the bank. It was in these games that it became obvious to all that Denny Crum had begun to put it all back together again, despite the losses. His assistants, Bobby Dotson and Wade Houston, had been on the road and brought back to Louisville all Crum had needed. Everyone had done what it took to get back off the canvas after being pretty-well punched out. It was time for the final blow that would eliminate team after team down the stretch until there would be no one left to beat.

For sure, all the great things that happened to the Cardinals and their fans during the 1985-86 season really began back on that cold night in New York, in late March of 1985, when the Cardinal family of players, fans and coaches looked up at the scoreboard in Madison Square Garden and saw Tennessee 100, Louisville 84. It was an awful sight, but one worth remembering!

Weight and agility coordinator Doug Semenick put Herbert Crook through some preseason conditioning drills.

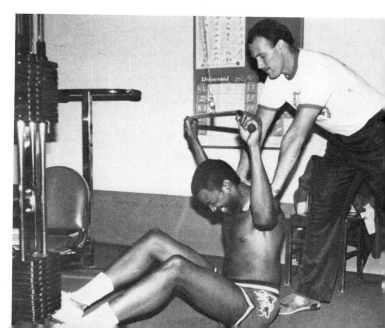

CHAPTER

2

The 'Fat Lady' Sings

The National Invitation Tournament — that's where it all began for the 1985-86 season. Ironically, that's where it all ended in 1984-85.

For the record, it wasn't a very memorable ending. Tennessee had handled the Cardinals without any problem. In fact, the Volunteers broke the century mark in that consolation game, 100-84, the first time that had happened against Louisville since 1974. A winning season (Louisville's 41st consecutive) was salvaged, but Crum's streak of 13 seasons with 20 or more wins had come to a screeching halt.

That final game against Tennessee pretty well summed up the entire 1984-85 season for Louisville. The year had been one constant struggle after Milt Wagner had injured himself against Virginia Commonwealth in just the second game of the year.

But now it was time to make amends. It was the opening of a new season with new hopes and new faces. It was the first-ever Big Apple NIT. Maybe, just maybe, this time things would be different.

When it comes to scheduling, the Cardinals take on whomever, whenever and wherever. For that reason, opening in the Big Apple NIT didn't come as a surprise.

Back in my coaching days, I always made it a point to open the season against someone I thought I could beat. Denny Crum doesn't think like that.

Here Louisville was, starting its season in New York with a freshman at center; a guard, Wagner, who had sat out an entire year because of an injury and was unproven after the long layoff; a solid player in Hall, but not a true point guard; a forward, Thompson, who hadn't lived up to fan expectations; Crook, a player nobody expected would win the starting job, except Herbert; and a bench where at least half the players were freshmen, untested and untried.

With these facts it was off to the NIT for a chance at glory as well as a chance to go el-floppo. The team bus loaded up and headed to Cincinnati, site of the first round for the Cardinals. The first opponent would be Miami of Ohio. Louisville checked into the Clarion Hotel, a place that would be headquarters for the Cards during opening-round action.

Lesson No. 1 for freshmen is how to live on the road. You can just imagine how excited a freshman would be going from a school bus and a high school game to a big Greyhound-type bus (with Louisville painted on each side), a nice hotel and a chance to play in the Big Apple NIT. That's coming a long way, baby, in a very short time — seven months to be exact. For sure, all these freshmen had the ability to become excellent Division I players or they wouldn't have been recruited, but there's a learning process that 99 percent of all freshmen have to pass through. Playing on the road is one step in the process.

How about Miami of Ohio? What type of opponent would they be? They would put one of the nation's better players, Ron Harper, on the court against the Cards. This guy could do it all and was good enough after his junior year to enter the NBA draft, but he chose to finish his senior year. He's tough both inside and out, has good shooting range and all the moves.

It's a common fact that Crum's teams play a team defense and don't really concentrate on one player. It's his theory that

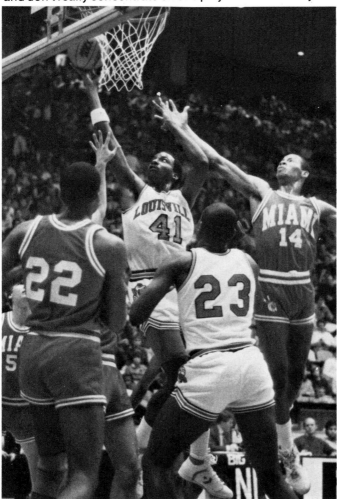

Herbert Crook was a surprise starter in the season opener against Miami of Ohio.

you play everyone tough and you'll come out ahead. Sure, his teams will shade to a tough player for help but all the players are defended.

Would this do the job against a player like Harper? What kind of supporting cast did he have? How would Milt respond to the opening game? How about the freshman post man Ellison? Could he hang in there? These are the kinds of questions everyone was asking.

Put a win down for the Cards as they defeated Miami 81-65. By the time the game was over, everyone realized

COMPLETE LOUISVILLE-MIAMI BOX SCORE

LOUISVILLE

Player	FG	FGA	FT	FTA	REB	PF	TP	A	TO	BLK	S	MIN
Crook	5	7	5	6	6	1	15	1	3	1	0	24
Thompson	9	13	1	2	17	3	19	7	3	4	0	33
Ellison	5	8	1	2	7	4	11	2	1	4	1	33
Hall	4	8	0	0	1	3	8	3	1	0	0	30
Wagner	3	16	3	3	3	4	9	4	5	0	1	37
McSwain	0	1	0	2	3	1	0	0	2	1	0	6
Kimbro	4	8	0	0	4	4	8	2	0	0	1	18
Abram	0	0	0	0	0	0	0	0	0	0	0	4
Payne	2	3	0	0	0	0	4	0	3	0	0	7
West	0	0	1	2	0	0	1	0	0	0	0	1
Walls	1	1	4	4	2	2	6	0	1	0	0	6
Olliges	0	0	0	0	1	0	0	0	0	0	0	1
Team					2							
Deadball												
Rebounds					2							
Totals	33	65	15	21	46	22	81	19	19	10	3	200

FG%: 1st Half 51.6 2nd Half 50.0 Game 50.8
FT%: 1st Half 85.7 2nd Half 64.3 Game 71.4

MIAMI (OHIO)

Player	FG	FGA	FT	FTA	REB	PF	TP	A	TO	BLK	S	MIN
Harper	15	26	6	10	9	4	36	2	6	1	2	35
Hanna	0	2	3	4	13	3	3	1	0	1	3	28
Lampe	1	3	1	3	2	0	3	0	3	0	0	21
Newsome	3	13	6	7	4	3	12	5	1	0	1	32
Schilling	1	4	1	2	2	2	3	4	3	0	1	28
Hunter	0	3	0	0	0	2	0	0	1	0	0	8
Staker	0	4	0	0	3	3	0	1	0	0	0	17
Clayborne	3	4	2	4	6	3	8	0	2	0	2	23
Fuerst	0	0	0	0	0	0	0	0	0	0	0	2
Ronan	0	0	0	0	0	1	0	0	0	0	0	3
Newell	0	1	0	0	0	0	0	0	0	0	0	1
Doyle	0	0	0	0	0	0	0	0	0	0	0	1
Team					4							
Deadball												
Rebounds					4							
Totals	23	60	19	30	34	21	65	13	16	2	9	200

FG%: 1st Half 43.3 2nd Half 33.3 Game 38.3
FT%: 1st Half 77.8 2nd Half 57.1 Game 63.3

Halftime: Louisville 38, Miami 33
Attendance: 10,416

Harper's reputation was for real. He drilled the nets for 36 points but his supporting cast was not enough help to get the win.

That same night, Tulsa defeated Dayton and would be

U of L's next opponent. A win over the Hurricanes and Louisville would be headed for the Big Apple, New York City. A loss, however, and they wouldn't play another game until Dec. 7, 15 days later. That's an eternity in a basketball schedule.

Tulsa had a new coach, J.D. Barnett. He was a proven coach who was very successful at Virginia Commonwealth. I found him to be a little less cooperative than a guy in my position hopes for. I made a trip to Riverfront Coliseum and waited through a closed practice only to be given the runaround as far as my interview was concerned. Some of these guys think they are changing the shape of the world with their work, but you and I know that's not true.

Whatever, the Cards put Tulsa away 80-74 and won the right to play in their first Final Four of the season. Coach Barnett's interview didn't seem to matter anymore.

The freshmen did pretty well in the first two games. Ellison got 24 points, Kimbro had 12, Payne scored four and Walls added seven. We all found out that, even without showing

COMPLETE LOUISVILLE-TULSA BOX SCORE

LOUISVILLE

Player	FG	FGA	FT	FTA	REB	PF	TP	A	TO	BLK	S	MIN
Crook	2	4	2	2	1	4	6	2	1	0	2	18
Thompson	6	10	9	11	8	2	21	6	5	1	1	33
Ellison	4	7	5	6	10	3	13	1	2	2	0	23
Hall	6	11	3	3	3	2	15	1	1	1	1	32
Wagner	5	10	4	5	1	2	14	5	3	0	0	32
McSwain	2	3	2	2	3	2	6	0	2	0	0	16
Kimbro	2	4	0	0	0	3	4	0	1	0	2	23
Payne	0	2	0	0	1	2	0	0	0	0	0	8
West	0	0	0	0	1	0	0	0	1	1	0	6
Walls	0	0	1	3	0	1	1	0	1	0	1	7
Olliges	0	0	0	0	0	0	0	0	0	0	0	1
Team					1							
Deadball												
Rebounds					4							
Totals	**27**	**51**	**26**	**32**	**29**	**21**	**80**	**15**	**17**	**5**	**7**	**200**

FG%: 1st Half 50.0   2nd Half 57.1   Game 52.9
FT%: 1st Half 62.5   2nd Half 87.5   Game 81.3

TULSA

Player	FG	FGA	FT	FTA	REB	PF	TP	A	TO	BLK	S	MIN
B. Rahilly	0	3	2	4	0	3	2	4	3	0	1	25
Moss	6	12	2	2	4	4	14	0	3	0	0	36
Fobbs	3	4	4	4	4	5	10	0	2	1	0	27
Moore	6	11	6	7	1	5	18	0	2	0	0	31
Boudreaux	6	10	1	2	3	1	13	3	4	0	3	40
J. Rahilly	1	1	0	1	4	2	2	0	1	0	0	17
Suggs	5	6	3	5	3	5	13	3	3	0	5	23
Deckard	1	1	0	0	1	0	2	0	0	0	0	1
Team					2							
Deadball												
Rebounds					2							
Totals	**28**	**48**	**18**	**25**	**22**	**25**	**74**	**10**	**19**	**1**	**9**	**200**

FG%: 1st Half 65.0   2nd Half 53.6   Game 58.3
FT%: 1st Half 72.7   2nd Half 71.4   Game 72.0

Halftime: Louisville 35, Tulsa 34
Attendance: 6,720

a lot of excitement, they were able to function. Amazing.

Speaking of freshmen, there was now another mountain to conquer. Keep in mind these guys had heard of and dreamed about playing in Madison Square Garden all their lives. Now, here it was!

The first big charter flight for the year was ready to head east. That meant, besides the players and regular traveling party, there would be fans, lots and lots of them. All the red and black the eyeballs could stand, buttons everywhere, and constant Cardinal conversation and enthusiasm that bubbles over.

Katie Lacefield has got to be captain of the Cardinal Fans. She's always there, always enthusiastic and ready to yell, scream, sing, whistle or do whatever it takes to give the Cards a boost. There are lots and lots of Cardinal fans who are the same but Katie has always been there doing her thing, with a megaphone around her neck. In the five years I've been with the Cardinals — and we've been everywhere from Hawaii to New York — Katie has been with us. The freshmen on the team would get their first peek at what Louisville basketball is all about.

Traveling on a charter teaches anyone to be mentally tough. The first big problem is always getting the luggage from point A to point B, then back to its rightful owner. Next comes the problem of trying to move 200-plus people around, which naturally takes several vehicles. With that accomplished comes the awesome task of getting everyone checked into the rooms with satisfactory accomodations.

One Cardinal fan wound up with a room at the Penta Hotel in New York that had nothing but banquet tables in it. Another fan received a room with nothing in it! Incidentally, the telephone number at the Penta is Pennsylvania 6-5000. It would make a catchy little tune, wouldn't it?

Once the fans finally got settled in their rooms, next came the shock of the cost of eating in New York. Unless, of course, you wanted to do all your dining at the little cubbyhole restaurants or at the street-side vendors. As far as I was concerned, the only good thing about staying at the Penta was that Madison Square Garden was directly across the street. But that, I promise, was the only convenience anyone on the trip could find in New York.

The people were rude. I asked a guy on the elevator what time it was and he told me it was none of my business. But none of this really matters on this kind of trip. The main reason for being in New York was to watch the Cardinals play basketball.

One more thing about the Penta — the statue in the lobby. It sorta looked like someone had just awakened from a very obscene dream, jumped out of bed and put his thoughts in the form of a statue. The statue was of two women and one man. From what I could figure, the man seemed to be on the road to happiness. There were private parts exposed on all the figures, there for God's children to see. It was the type of art that you'd definitely not want your old-fashioned grandmother to see. Seriously, it was the pits, but it blended in very well with the city of New York.

Louisville's first opponent in the Garden was Kansas. Shouldn't have been a problem.

Wrong! Kansas was my choice all year as the toughest team I saw. To my surprise, however, the Cards played them right down to the wire. Denny went with his philosophy of exposing as many players as possible to game action. I still

Kansas' Calvin Thompson led the Jayhawk attack with 25 points in the win over the Cards at Madison Square Garden.

believe Louisville would have won that game had they stayed with the proven players. But the reason for being there was to get experience for the players before the conference schedule began.

Kansas won 83-78, but it was a struggle. In the other semifinal game, Duke beat a very good St. John's team to advance to the championship. Louisville was faced with meeting St. John's in the consolation game in the Redmen's own back yard.

During the post-game show with Denny after the loss to Kansas, I remember saying that Kansas was really a terrific team and should have a great season. Denny's answer to me was, "Whoever wins the national championship this year will have to beat this Duke team." So help me, that's what he said. I thought to myself, "What does he know. I like Kansas." Well, we all know who was right.

Following the Kansas game, Van Vance (my radio partner at WHAS) and I ran into Jack Savage as we were leaving the Garden. Jack is another terrific Cardinal fan who follows them wherever they go. It seemed like we were all thinking the same thing — where to eat?

The three of us wound up at the hotel restaurant. Naturally, it was rip-off city time. But it was all there was. As we ate we discussed the game, taking turns at what we thought. They did most of the talking about the game and I did most of the complaining about the price of the food. But I was listening and liked what I heard.

12

Van and Jack both seemed to be encouraged about what they had seen in the Louisville-Kansas game. It's always nice to hear people pick out the positive things and sorta let the negative ones slip away into the darkness. The conversation ended with Van asking me, "How's that BLT sandwich, Jock?"

COMPLETE LOUISVILLE-KANSAS BOX SCORE

LOUISVILLE

Player	FG	FGA	FT	FTA	REB	PF	TP	A	TO	BLK	S	MIN
Crook	6	10	2	3	4	1	14	1	2	0	3	24
Thompson	7	13	4	4	8	3	18	7	4	1	2	37
Ellison	8	12	2	2	5	4	18	2	0	2	1	35
Hall	2	4	0	0	0	5	4	1	0	0	2	15
Wagner	2	15	1	4	7	4	5	5	2	0	2	37
McSwain	1	1	3	4	2	1	5	1	1	0	1	8
Kimbro	2	7	2	4	3	2	6	1	1	0	0	17
Payne	4	7	0	0	1	0	8	0	3	0	1	22
West	0	0	0	0	0	0	0	1	1	0	0	2
Walls	0	1	0	0	0	0	0	0	0	0	0	3
Team					6							
Deadball												
Rebounds					3							
Totals	**32**	**70**	**14**	**21**	**36**	**20**	**78**	**18**	**14**	**3**	**12**	**200**

FG%: 1st Half 47.0   2nd Half 44.4   Game 45.7
FT%: 1st Half 66.7   2nd Half 66.7   Game 66.7

KANSAS

Player	FG	FGA	FT	FTA	REB	PF	TP	A	TO	BLK	S	MIN
Kellogg	6	11	8	9	3	4	20	1	2	0	1	27
Manning	4	11	0	0	4	3	8	6	4	0	1	27
Dreiling	6	9	0	1	11	2	12	3	3	1	1	31
Hunter	4	6	4	6	6	3	12	9	3	0	2	32
Thompson	9	13	7	8	4	2	25	1	5	0	3	35
Piper	0	1	0	0	0	0	0	0	0	0	0	12
Turgeon	1	2	0	0	0	2	2	1	2	0	0	9
Marshall	2	4	0	0	2	1	4	0	2	0	0	15
Johnson	0	0	0	0	0	1	0	1	0	1	0	5
Barry	0	0	0	0	0	0	0	0	0	0	0	1
Campbell	0	0	0	0	0	0	0	0	0	0	0	1
Team					5							
Deadball												
Rebounds					1							
Totals	**32**	**57**	**19**	**24**	**35**	**18**	**83**	**22**	**21**	**2**	**8**	**200**

FG%: 1st Half 62.5   2nd Half 48.0   Game 56.1
FT%: 1st Half 90.0   2nd Half 71.4   Game 79.2

Halftime: Kansas 49, Louisville 42
Attendance: 14,225

My answer was, "It would be good if it didn't cost $7.50." Good ol' Jack finally eased my pain by paying the tab for me. Thanks, Jack.

St. John's did the Cardinals in 86-79 and the Cards finished fourth in the NIT. That wasn't too shabby for a team with all the question marks Louisville had going in.

Looking back, I firmly believe the NIT experience set the stage for all the great things that would happen to Louisville by the end of March. Facing these great teams from the opening gun sorta silently said to the young players, "You are now at the University of Louisville and this is the way it is here. We play all the tough guys, anywhere they want to play, and we take no prisoners and make no excuses. We will get better every day until we can beat anyone, anyplace." At least that's the way it looked to me.

Following the NIT, Louisville would play a schedule that would be ranked as the nation's second-toughest overall and as the toughest against non-conference opponents. Duke had won the batttle in New York but it would be Louisville who would go on to win the war.

New York was history and it was time for the chore of getting all the exasperated fans back to the city of Louisville. There's no way you can hang around New York for four days and not be exasperated. We seemed to be on a tight schedule so we didn't get to see the championship game. We had to be at the airport at a certain time.

Just like the Army, it was hurry up and wait, and wait, and wait. As it turned out, the airplane had returned to Atlanta and was having some sort of problem getting back to New York to pick up all these great, understanding Louisville people. Now the reason they were understanding, myself included, was that no one seemed anxious to travel in a plane that was having a mechanical problem. I thought that made good sense.

Another thing that helped everyone's toughness was the fact that Donald Swain (el-Presidente of the University) and his lovely wife, Lavinnia, were in the party as were Coach Crum, his wife Joyce and their young son, Scott. We would all tough it out together.

Well, all the rumors started floating around about not being able to leave until morning, about possibly returning to the same hotel, about maybe just sleeping in the hangar we were in. Since it was a charter we weren't in the regular terminal.

By this time, the lines were forming at the telephones, soda and candy machines. Most people began to settle in and were good-natured about the predicament. The one-liners tossed out got some laughs. The women were at their best, being ladies, settling into comfortable sitting positions. But as the night got longer the laughs grew shorter and the women's attitudes changed to "the hell with the lady routine, it's time to get comfortable." Most people just laid down and conked out wherever they could find a spot. Everywhere you looked there would be a pair of high heels.

Brian Faison and Don Russell seemed to be the "guys in the know" because of their positions in the athletic depart-

Cardinal fan Ken Schikler didn't have much to cheer about in New York.

Pervis Ellison and Milt Wagner surrounded St. John's Mark Jackson, but the Redmen managed to hand U of L an 86-79 defeat in the consolation game.

ment. Finally, they put out the word, "Get ready folks, here it comes." Believe me, that trip home was the quietest I have ever known a Louisville traveling crowd to be. Everyone was catching some ZZZ s.

It was very close to daylight when the plane landed in Louisville. This bunch was all used up. There wasn't enough energy left in the whole bunch to muster even a hiccup. People literally dragged their suitcases. My suitcase had wheels on it and three bird lovers tried to buy it. It was a tough trip but, as time passed, it would prove to be worth all the troublesome inconveniences, expense, aches and pains that would follow in days to come.

Actually, the trip wasn't over for me. I struggled to my car, winded and almost ready to surrender but happy to be heading home. I put my foot on the accelerator in the

15

COMPLETE LOUISVILLE-ST. JOHN'S BOX SCORE

LOUISVILLE

Player	FG	FGA	FT	FTA	REB	PF	TP	A	TO	BLK	S	MIN
Crook	3	5	1	2	9	4	7	3	4	0	1	31
Thompson	6	12	3	3	7	4	15	6	6	1	0	32
Ellison	8	11	0	0	7	3	16	2	0	2	2	35
Hall	7	13	0	0	0	2	14	4	1	0	0	29
Wagner	6	13	4	4	4	1	16	5	0	0	0	37
McSwain	1	2	0	0	1	3	2	0	1	0	0	9
Kimbro	2	5	1	2	2	1	5	1	0	3	0	15
Payne	2	4	0	0	1	0	4	1	0	0	0	9
Team					1							
Deadball												
Rebounds					1							
Totals	**35**	**65**	**9**	**11**	**32**	**18**	**79**	**22**	**12**	**6**	**3**	**200**

FG%: 1st Half	58.6	**2nd Half**	50.0	**Game**	53.8		
FT%: 1st Half	75.0	**2nd Half**	85.7	**Game**	81.8		

ST. JOHN'S

Player	FG	FGA	FT	FTA	REB	PF	TP	A	TO	BLK	S	MIN
Glass	6	10	2	2	5	4	14	1	1	0	1	28
Jones	3	7	0	0	2	3	6	1	2	0	1	28
Berry	7	14	8	10	13	0	22	1	2	0	2	38
Jackson	7	15	3	4	1	0	17	11	1	0	1	40
Rowan	5	11	10	10	3	2	20	4	1	0	1	40
Bloss	2	3	0	0	5	3	4	0	0	0	1	17
Hempel	1	2	1	1	1	1	3	0	0	0	0	9
Team					2							
Deadball												
Rebounds					1							
Totals	**31**	**62**	**24**	**27**	**32**	**13**	**86**	**18**	**7**	**0**	**7**	**200**

FG%: 1st Half	54.5	**2nd Half**	44.8	**Game**	50.0		
FT%: 1st Half	90.9	**2nd Half**	87.5	**Game**	88.9		

Halftime: St. John's 46, Louisville 37
Attendance: 8,598

prescribed manner. Nothing happened. I mean zippity doo dah. My battery had already given up. After sobbing quietly for about 10 minutes, I drug myself to the cashier's stand where I poured out my story to the clerk.

His first question was, "Do you have any jumper cables?" I replied, "No, sir." He told me to go into a building and he'd call a wrecker.

I'm thinking to myself, "Have I paid my AAA?" I'm also thinking, "Probably not."

After about 30 minutes a big truck with a hook showed and I got my first good news of this long, long day. At this wonderful airport, Standiford Field, there is no charge for the wrecker service if you've been parked in the lot. Of course, my parking charge would strangle Godzilla, but I thought that was very, very nice.

I reached my home at 7:20 a.m., very tired. But deep down inside me I felt really encouraged by what I had seen from the Louisville Cardinals at Madison Square Garden. I thought to myself, "Who knows? This season may turn out to be something very special. I'm talking VERY SPECIAL."

OVERALL RECORD: 2-2

Game #5
Purdue
December 7

Freedom Hall, what a beautiful sight if you are a Cardinal fan, player or coach. It's the night of the home opener and it's against the Purdue Boilermakers. Wow, what a way to start! The NIT on the road and then a game against Coach Gene Keady and his Big Ten school.

Freedom Hall was loaded to the brim with excited Cardinal fans, all anxious to see their beloved Cards take the court. Only a few had been in New York so this was a big, big night for Louisville basketball.

Finally, it was time. The horn blew and public address announcer John Tong started with the introductions as no other person can do. When John introduces you, it'll be one time in your life that you'll feel proud. He just has a way and a style that's all his own. He can make a player feel as if he's about to enter the Pearly Gates.

The players came out and went through all the "gimme five" routines. The buzzer sounded and it was time to play. The Louisville starters, a lineup that wouldn't change the entire year, were Thompson and Crook at the forwards, Wagner and Hall at the guards and "Never Nervous" Pervis at center.

This is a good time to get Ellison's nickname straightened out. I'm taking credit for it and here's how it happened. While broadcasting, I said to my colleague, Van Vance, "This guy never gets nervous."

"Ellison?" he asked.

"Yeah, Never Nervous Pervis," I said, and that's how the name got started. We used it all during the season and it just sorta caught on. Enough said, so let's play ball.

Following the NIT, Denny had been very unhappy with defense, both the man-to-man and the press. That had been his point of emphasis in preparation for Purdue, which meant bad news for the Boilermakers.

The Cards came out tough. Tony Kimbro summed it up best, "If you mess up on defense, you're not going to play. That's the way it is. If you want to play, you can play the 'D', if not, you can sit beside Coach Crum."

Purdue entered the game with a 5-1 record, the only blemish coming from the highly regarded Tar Heels of North Carolina. Purdue, for sure, wasn't chopped liver.

COMPLETE LOUISVILLE-PURDUE BOX SCORE

LOUISVILLE

Player	FG	FGA	FT	FTA	REB	PF	TP	A	TO	BLK	S	MIN
Crook	4	8	0	0	5	2	8	2	2	0	2	18
Thompson	5	12	3	5	9	3	13	7	2	2	0	23
Ellison	3	8	0	0	5	4	6	1	1	2	1	20
Hall	4	9	0	0	2	2	8	0	0	1	0	25
Wagner	4	10	2	3	2	1	10	3	1	1	2	24
McSwain	0	1	2	2	3	4	2	1	0	0	0	15
Kimbro	5	6	0	1	4	2	10	1	3	1	5	21
Payne	4	8	0	0	7	0	8	0	1	0	1	17
Walls	2	3	3	3	0	0	7	2	1	0	1	17
Abram	1	3	1	2	3	3	3	2	1	0	0	7
West	0	0	0	2	0	2	0	0	0	0	0	3
Olliges	0	1	0	0	2	1	0	0	0	0	0	3
Valentine	1	3	0	0	0	2	2	0	1	0	0	4
Marshall	0	1	0	0	1	0	0	0	1	0	0	2
Robinson	0	0	0	0	1	0	0	0	0	1	0	1
Team					3							
Deadball												
Rebounds					2							
Totals	**33**	**73**	**11**	**18**	**47**	**27**	**77**	**19**	**14**	**8**	**12**	**200**

FG%: 1st Half	46.9	**2nd Half**	43.9	**Game**	45.2	
FT%: 1st Half	66.7	**2nd Half**	50.0	**Game**	61.1	

PURDUE

Player	FG	FGA	FT	FTA	REB	PF	TP	A	TO	BLK	S	MIN
Gadis	2	6	2	2	4	2	6	1	3	0	0	24
Lee	2	5	3	6	3	3	7	3	2	0	3	32
Lewis	7	13	3	4	5	0	17	3	6	0	1	35
Jones	0	4	3	6	8	3	3	2	1	0	1	23
Mitchell	3	12	3	4	8	4	9	0	5	0	0	36
Stephens	3	8	5	7	2	2	11	2	2	2	1	23
McCants	1	2	0	0	5	4	2	0	0	0	0	17
Robinson	1	4	1	2	2	1	3	1	0	0	1	10
Team					3							
Deadball												
Rebounds					4							
Totals	**19**	**54**	**20**	**31**	**40**	**19**	**58**	**12**	**19**	**2**	**7**	**200**

FG%: 1st Half	40.0	**2nd Half**	29.2	**Game**	35.2	
FT%: 1st Half	66.7	**2nd Half**	63.6	**Game**	64.5	

Halftime: Louisville 38, Purdue 30
Attendance: 19,265

The Cards were way too much for the outmanned Purdue team and easily won the home opener 77-58.

By the half, Louisville was in control of a 38-30 lead. It was a good first half for both teams. But the second half would spell doom for the Boilermakers, a pattern the Cards would establish later in the season. When the final horn sounded, Louisville was on the front end of a 77-58 score.

The 58 points registered by Purdue supported the defensive work done in preparation for this game. Keady's squad shot only 36.2 percent for the game and a miserable 29.2 percent in the second half. Now that's what you call putting the 'D' to them.

All eyes were on Wagner this game. He showed signs of his old self by hitting 4 of 10 field goals and both his free throws for 10 points. But there were no stars in this game, just good, solid play.

"We were a long way from being perfect," said Crum after the game, "but we were intense. We did get after them on defense. When you do that and hustle, good things will happen."

There were 19,265 fans who left Freedom Hall that night and most were reasonably happy. Little did they know that a time would come when they would all be TOTALLY fulfilled. It was a good beginning for a five-game homestand.

OVERALL RECORD: 3-2

Game # 6
Iona
December 10

When Iona came calling, Pervis Ellison seemed to make a statement to the U of L fans. "Hello, I'm Never Nervous Pervis, and I'm here in Louisville to get a college degree and do my part in making the Louisville Cardinals national champions.

"It's true, I am a freshman but you will never notice it

COMPLETE LOUISVILLE-IONA BOX SCORE

LOUISVILLE

Player	FG	FGA	FT	FTA	REB	PF	TP	A	TO	BLK	S	MIN
Crook	5	11	0	0	2	3	10	1	0	0	0	23
Thompson	7	8	0	6	7	4	14	6	3	1	3	34
Ellison	8	11	3	4	13	2	19	5	1	3	5	32
Hall	4	9	1	2	1	2	9	7	0	0	2	30
Wagner	6	11	2	2	4	5	14	4	3	0	1	28
McSwain	0	0	0	0	2	0	0	2	0	0	0	8
Kimbro	4	6	2	4	2	3	10	0	5	1	0	21
Payne	4	6	0	0	1	1	8	0	1	0	0	15
Walls	1	1	0	1	0	2	2	1	2	0	0	8
Olliges	0	0	2	2	0	0	2	0	0	0	1	1
Team					4							
Deadball												
Rebounds					0							
Totals	**39**	**63**	**10**	**21**	**36**	**22**	**88**	**26**	**15**	**5**	**12**	**200**

FG%: 1st Half 55.6   2nd Half 66.7   Game 61.9
FT%: 1st Half 50.0   2nd Half 47.1   Game 47.6

IONA

Player	FG	FGA	FT	FTA	REB	PF	TP	A	TO	BLK	S	MIN
Kijonek	3	8	4	5	5	2	10	5	7	0	2	37
Wilder	1	1	2	2	2	5	4	0	3	0	0	21
Coleman	11	15	1	6	8	3	23	0	4	2	0	40
Green	1	4	1	4	3	3	3	7	1	1	1	31
Simmonds	9	14	4	7	2	2	22	4	2	0	1	32
Grant	0	1	0	0	1	0	0	3	0	0	0	10
Harris	1	1	2	2	1	1	4	0	2	0	0	7
Zona	1	1	0	0	2	0	2	0	1	0	0	3
Langdon	0	0	0	0	0	0	0	0	0	0	0	3
Payne	2	3	3	3	1	4	7	0	1	1	0	16
Team					5							
Deadball												
Rebounds					0							
Totals	**29**	**48**	**17**	**29**	**30**	**20**	**75**	**19**	**21**	**4**	**4**	**200**

FG%: 1st Half 60.0   2nd Half 60.7   Game 60.4
FT%: 1st Half 75.0   2nd Half 52.4   Game 58.6

Halftime: Louisville 32, Iona 30
Attendance: 19,038

Freshman red-shirt Kevin Walls came off the bench to score a basket.

because I just don't play like one. To prove it to you, tonight I will score 19 points in 32 minutes of play, get 13 rebounds, dish out five assists, block three shots and make five steals. Ho hum, it's all in a day's work."

What's that you say? How many turnovers? Only one, and the ref probably missed that call.

The Gaels stayed close to the Cards in the first 20 minutes, and the teams went into the locker room with Louisville holding on to a slim 32-30 lead.

No problem, however, as the home team blitzed the Iona group 17-6 to open the second half, spurting to a 49-36 lead. The two teams played even after that and U of L hung on to win 88-75.

Five Cardinals scored in double figures. It was an especially good night for freshman Tony Kimbro in the scoring department with 10 in the first half, but the bad news is that he had five turnovers. Freshmen will be freshmen.

Thirty-nine of Louisville's points were scored by the yearlings, and four of the freshmen were in the lineup during the last five minutes of the game.

"U of L's freshmen were a concern to us," said Iona coach Pat Kennedy. "They're going to make the older kids better players. I think Ellison is going to be super. He's one of the finest freshmen in the country."

That's two consecutive wins for the Cardinals. How sweet it is!

OVERALL RECORD: 4-2

Game # 7
Western Kentucky
December 14

T he Battle of I-65. Western Kentucky was in town and Clem Haskins' team brought some very good credentials with it.

Haskins was under a lot of pressure to win 20 games this season, at least that was the word. His team was loaded with talent and Louisville hadn't faced a team to date that was as physical as the Hilltoppers. The school from Bowling Green took no prisoners and spared the rod for nobody.

I remember two seasons ago when Jeff Hall took a blow

U of L's Chris West scored three very important points in the 73-70 win over Western Kentucky.

from a player named Bryan Asberry (6-6, 240 pounds), a freshman at the time. It was a forearm across the chest that put Hall in a daze.

Any time you play another state school, there is added pressure to win. Western was not supposed to beat Louisville, so the Hilltoppers entered the game loose. As the

WKU's Bryan Asberry scored 15 points as the Hilltoppers gave the Cards all they could handle in Freedom Hall.

season wore on, the Hilltoppers would prove just how good they really were, but not on this particular night.

As usual, Coach Haskins was very gracious during the pre-game interview. "Louisville is a big game for us," he said. "Beating Louisville would tell everyone that Western is for real."

COMPLETE LOUISVILLE-WKU BOX SCORE

LOUISVILLE

Player	FG	FGA	FT	FTA	REB	PF	TP	A	TO	BLK	S	MIN
Crook	6	9	8	13	9	9	20	0	3	0	3	37
Thompson	5	14	0	1	10	3	10	3	0	1	2	30
Ellison	4	10	2	4	6	3	10	2	2	5	1	35
Hall	4	8	4	4	3	3	12	1	1	0	0	32
Wagner	3	14	8	9	4	2	14	4	3	0	3	35
McSwain	0	0	2	2	1	0	2	0	2	0	0	12
Kimbro	1	3	0	0	0	1	2	2	2	0	0	10
Payne	0	1	0	0	1	2	0	0	1	0	0	2
Walls	0	1	0	0	0	0	0	0	1	0	0	6
West	1	2	1	1	0	1	3	1	0	0	1	1
Team					1							
Deadball												
Rebounds					3							
Totals	**24**	**62**	**25**	**34**	**35**	**19**	**73**	**13**	**15**	**6**	**10**	**200**

FG%: 1st Half	50.0	2nd Half	30.6	Game	38.7
FT%: 1st Half	53.3	2nd Half	89.5	Game	73.5

WESTERN KENTUCKY

Player	FG	FGA	FT	FTA	REB	PF	TP	A	TO	BLK	S	MIN
Johnson	2	6	4	4	7	5	8	1	1	0	2	31
Frank	0	0	0	0	4	4	0	1	4	1	0	17
Martin	3	5	1	2	3	4	7	1	2	2	0	21
McNary	2	5	2	2	6	4	6	11	7	0	2	40
Gordon	13	18	2	2	1	4	28	2	2	0	2	34
Swogger	0	2	0	0	1	0	0	1	0	0	0	11
Miller	1	1	0	0	2	0	2	0	1	0	1	10
Tisdale	2	4	0	0	3	3	4	0	4	0	0	18
Asberry	4	8	7	10	3	1	15	0	1	0	0	18
Team					3							
Deadball												
Rebounds					5							
Totals	**27**	**49**	**16**	**20**	**33**	**25**	**70**	**17**	**22**	**3**	**7**	**200**

FG%: 1st Half	65.2	2nd Half	46.2	Game	55.1
FT%: 1st Half	83.3	2nd Half	50.0	Game	80.0

Halftime: Western Kentucky 45, Louisville 34
Attendance: 19,308

I also interviewed Dwayne Casey, an assistant coach at Western, which was a real pleasure. Both these guys are class people. Actually, I've gotten to know all the Western people real well. I was the moderator of their annual coaching clinic for two successive years. The school is loaded with people who have made their mark in the world of sports, including athletic director John Oldham and Jim Richards, the former WKU basketball coach and coach of the high school state champion Glasgow team.

With homecoming over, it was time to play. Keep in mind that this Hilltopper team brought a 7-0 record into Freedom Hall which included wins over Cincinnati and highly-ranked Auburn. Also, Western had a guard by the name of Billy Gordon, brother of former Cardinal great Lancaster. The word was out that this guy could shoot.

Boy, the word wasn't wrong. On this night Gordon burned the nets for 28 points. How could the Cards let him get away? Why wasn't he wearing the red and black of Louisville? It seems he didn't want to try and follow in Lancaster's shadow. Billy wanted to do his own thing, and he was doing it quite well.

Western had a great first half and had the Cards on the ropes with a 45-34 lead at intermission. Louisville, it seemed, wasn't doing anything right. Thompson had picked up three quick fouls while Wagner and Hall had two apiece. Haskins' team had blitzed the nets with 65 percent shooting. Not too bad for a bunch of country boys.

But the pattern had been established and the second half was a different story. Louisville outscored the Hilltoppers 21-9 in the first 10 minutes of the second period to take a 55-54 lead. The teams played even over the next five minutes and it was at the 4:57 mark that the Hilltoppers regained the advantage.

With 2:55 left, Louisville led 65-62 behind the offensive play of Pervis Ellison and Herbert Crook. But with under one minute left on the clock that lead was cut to 66-65 and it was anybody's contest. That set up some dramatic final moments.

The Cards had the ball and a 67-66 lead when Wagner fired up a desperation shot as the 45-second shot clock was about to expire. WKU rebounded and its splendid point guard, James McNary, romped full speed toward the go-ahead basket. But the "Rubber Man," Herbert Crook, reached around McNary and knocked the ball to Wagner.

Western had no choice but to foul Wagner, and we all know what happens when you put the "Ice Man" on the line in that type of situation. It's like hiding money under your grandmother's rocking chair. Forget it.

Put down two dead-center swishes for Milto and the Cards win a very tough 73-70 game. It wasn't a win for Western but it proved they were indeed a very good Division I basketball team. Great job, Clem Haskins.

"We came in here tonight and took a test," said the WKU coach, "and I feel like we got an 'A'."

Crook stole the win from the Hilltoppers and was rapidly showing everybody he wasn't just the "other forward." The sophomore led the Cards with 20 points, nine rebounds and three steals.

"Herb is a tough competitor," said Crum, "and he always seems to play good against the good teams."

Amen.

OVERALL RECORD: 5-2

Mark McSwain pulled down just one rebound against Clem Haskins' team.

Game #8
Indiana
December 18

Bobby Knight

Well now, what have we here? The man in the red sweater has brought his Hoosiers to town. This always adds to the excitement of a regular-season game.

My big problem was, "Should I go for the interview or play the chicken role?" Well, I walked around to the Indiana dressing room and there he was, talking with ex-Louisville and pro player Bud Olsen.

I immediately remembered my experience in the visit to Bloomington one season earlier. I got the interview that time but paid a very big price. Billy Packer of CBS-TV went in first and I was to follow. All the other media people were told to get lost.

"The Man" gobbled me up and I came out a nervous wreck. Remembering all this mental and emotional anguish, I decided to pass on the interview this time. Instead, I talked to one of Knight's assistants, a person I had played golf with while in Bloomington during the Olympic practices. During those practice sessions, Coach Knight was more than generous to me. But on game day it was a little tougher.

Coach Knight made his usual late entrance to the playing court. Not even a trace of a smile could be found. It was time for the business at hand.

IU's Steve Alford played up to his billing by hitting 11 of his 16 field-goal attempts for 27 points.

COMPLETE LOUISVILLE-INDIANA BOX SCORE

LOUISVILLE

Player	FG	FGA	FT	FTA	REB	PF	TP	A	TO	BLK	S	MIN
Crook	3	5	0	0	5	3	6	3	6	0	0	26
Thompson	3	9	1	3	7	4	7	2	2	2	1	31
Ellison	5	7	1	4	11	4	11	5	2	1	1	34
Hall	2	8	3	4	1	0	7	1	1	0	1	24
Wagner	7	2	8	10	3	2	22	1	2	0	0	35
McSwain	0	0	3	4	0	1	3	0	0	0	0	6
Kimbro	3	4	0	0	4	3	6	2	2	4	0	25
Walls	0	0	0	0	0	0	0	0	1	0	0	1
West	1	3	1	3	1	2	3	2	1	0	1	18
Team					1							
Deadball												
Rebounds					1							
Totals	**24**	**48**	**17**	**28**	**33**	**19**	**65**	**16**	**17**	**7**	**4**	**200**

FG%: 1st Half	48.1	2nd Half	52.4	Game	50.0	
FT%: 1st Half	42.9	2nd Half	78.6	Game	60.7	

INDIANA

Player	FG	FGA	FT	FTA	REB	PF	TP	A	TO	BLK	S	MIN
Harris	4	5	0	0	2	5	8	1	2	1	1	23
Calloway	2	7	1	3	3	4	5	2	4	0	0	23
Thomas	5	10	3	4	1	4	13	0	3	1	1	28
Morgan	0	1	0	0	3	2	0	1	2	0	0	18
Alford	11	16	5	6	4	3	27	5	3	0	2	40
Jadlow	1	4	3	4	4	3	5	0	2	0	1	14
Robinson	0	1	0	0	0	2	0	1	0	0	0	12
Brooks	0	0	0	0	1	1	0	1	0	0	0	14
Eyl	1	3	3	4	8	2	5	1	1	0	1	28
Team					1							
Deadball												
Rebounds					3							
Totals	**24**	**47**	**15**	**21**	**27**	**26**	**63**	**12**	**17**	**2**	**6**	**200**

FG%: 1st Half	59.1	2nd Half	44.0	Game	51.1	
FT%: 1st Half	72.7	2nd Half	70.0	Game	71.4	

Halftime: Indiana 34, Louisville 32
Attendance: 19,493

Hey, the Cards beat this outfit last year in Bloomington and did it easily. This should be no sweat. Wrong!

It was a very tough day. The best news before the game was that there were lots of professional scouts in attendance. And we all know how Wagner does his thing when the pro guys come to town. He didn't disappoint anyone.

The senior guard played like the old days, hitting 7 of 12 field goals and 8 of 10 free throws for 22 big ones. It was a good thing, though, because no other Card could get into double figures.

Both teams had 17 turnovers but the Cards won the board battle by six, 33-27. Louisville shot a poor percentage from the free-throw line, 60.7 percent, but did manage to make 17 to Indiana's 15. Each team had 24 field goals so I guess you can say the Cards won the game at the free-throw line.

The Never Nervous man led all rebounders with 11, and Louisville won the game 65-63 in a very close contest.

The game featured two of the nation's top guards, Louisville's Wagner and IU's Steve Alford. Milto was brilliant at the end and lived up to his nickname "Ice" by scoring 16

Andre Harris tipped in this shot but the Cards won the overall board battle and the game.

of the Cards' final 21 points. Alford had a terrific day with 27 points.

"Indiana didn't give us anything," said Crum later. "We had to earn everything we got tonight."

U of L reserve guard Chris West, who defensed Alford for 18 minutes and did a creditable job, talked about Alford's ability. "Getting to Alford a split-second late is too late," said West.

Knight was his usual talkative self afterward and supplied the media with two whole mimeographed quotes. "They really had a great last 10-minute effort out of Wagner," Knight supposedly said. "He made the difference in the ball game, scoring and hitting free throws down the stretch."

Indiana turned in a nice effort, but finishing second in a two-team game just isn't good enough. Another win for the Cardinals, their fourth straight.

OVERALL RECORD: 6-2

Exhibition Game
Athletes In Action
December 21

This is always a game that doesn't seem important until it gets underway. Most of the fans spend the day trying to find out just who or what is Athletes in Action. Well, it's a religious organization and the team is composed of ex-college players usually in their mid-20s, many of them stars during their days.

Make no mistake, AIA is always loaded with talent. Tracy Jackson, for example, was a very good player at Notre Dame. Lorenzo Romar did his thing at the University of Washington.

When AIA entered the game against Louisville, they had already recorded victories over the likes of Alabama-Birmingham, Pepperdine, Marquette and Nevada-Las Vegas. These guys were for real. They were already 19-5 and it was still December. AIA was a seasoned group of veterans.

AIA's Paul Renfro was held in check by Louisville's Mark McSwain.

It was a good solid effort by the Louisville starters but the bench, as had been the case for most of the early games, was very undependable. Tony Kimbro had been reasonably solid but that was about it as far as the reserves were concerned.

Louisville, for a change, led at the half, 45-41. They had shot the ball extremely well (62.1 percent) and held AIA to a mediocre 44.8 percent from the field.

The Cards mounted a good offensive run in the second half, their trademark, and outscored AIA 12-4 to go ahead 69-62. AIA pulled within 88-84 in the late going, but Louisville stretched out its lead. The final numbers were 91-84, Louisville's advantage.

"Momentum is important and winning keeps the momentum going," said Crum. "When you've got things going good, you don't want to blow one. Then you have doubts. At least now we have a positive approach about ourselves going into the Kentucky game. Maybe we'll play well there."

The 18,984 fans had seen their Cards win in a tuneup for the next game and now it was time to turn all attentions to the Wildcats of Kentucky, a team really playing well. Going into Rupp Arena to play the Cats in basketball is about like going into a haunted house and never knowing what will happen. It's not a very good place to visit with the hopes of coming out ahead. Maybe things would be different on this trip.

COMPLETE LOUISVILLE-AIA BOX SCORE

LOUISVILLE

Player	FG	FGA	FT	FTA	REB	PF	TP	A	TO	BLK	S	MIN
Crook	3	6	13	14	11	1	19	3	3	0	0	35
Thompson	7	10	5	9	8	1	19	4	4	2	0	28
Ellison	6	10	0	1	14	3	12	1	3	1	1	32
Hall	6	10	11	12	3	1	23	6	1	0	1	37
Wagner	2	7	2	2	2	4	6	5	2	1	0	24
McSwain	2	2	2	2	1	0	6	0	1	0	1	8
Kimbro	1	2	0	0	0	2	2	0	0	0	0	17
Payne	0	0	1	2	1	2	1	0	1	0	0	3
West	1	2	0	1	1	0	2	0	2	0	1	14
Abram	0	0	1	3	1	3	1	0	2	0	0	1
Marshall	0	0	0	0	0	1	0	0	0	0	0	1
Team					1							
Deadball												
Rebounds					5							
Totals	28	49	35	46	43	25	91	19	19	4	4	200

FG%: 1st Half 62.1   2nd Half 50.0   Game 57.4
FT%: 1st Half 64.3   2nd Half 81.3   Game 76.1

ATHLETES IN ACTION

Player	FG	FGA	FT	FTA	REB	PF	TP	A	TO	BLK	S	MIN
Jackson	6	15	5	7	7	5	17	0	1	0	1	36
Wiley	7	14	2	2	1	5	16	2	1	0	2	36
Renfro	1	2	1	2	5	5	3	3	4	0	3	22
Romar	7	16	8	8	4	4	22	9	2	0	4	40
Hinz	1	1	0	0	2	2	2	0	1	0	2	21
Cieplicki	6	14	0	0	1	5	12	0	1	0	3	22
Taylor	0	0	0	0	1	1	0	1	0	0	0	1
Duncan	5	7	2	4	2	4	12	0	1	0	1	20
Radford	0	0	0	0	0	0	0	0	0	0	0	0
Gettys	0	1	0	0	1	1	0	0	0	0	0	2
Team					2							
Deadball												
Rebounds					2							
Totals	33	70	18	23	26	32	84	15	11	1	16	200

FG%: 1st Half 44.8   2nd Half 48.8   Game 47.1
FT%: 1st Half 88.2   2nd Half 50.0   Game 78.3

Halftime: Louisville 45, A.I.A. 41
Attendance: 18,984

Game #10
Wyoming
January 4

The Cowboys had arrived for a shootout against the Cardinals. I didn't even know they had a team. I thought Laramie was just some land where they filmed all the western movies. You know the ones — the coyotes moan and talk coyote talk all night.

But it didn't matter what I thought. They did indeed show up in Freedom Hall, and by the end of the season they'd

Jeff Hall applied the pressure to Wyoming's Jon Sommers in the lopsided 32-point victory by U of L.

shoot their way all the way to the finals of the post-season NIT. Not only did they have a team but it was a very good team.

Actually, when I look back at the season, I think Wyoming executed their game plan and style just about as good as anyone the Cardinals played. Louisville was able to win in a blowout but even when the game had ended I had found a new respect for the Cowboys. Louisville received excellent play from everyone and Jim Brandenburg's team was just outmanned.

Billy Thompson had an outstanding game. After missing his first field-goal attempt, Thompson connected on 13 straight shots and finished with a career-high 30 points. He also added seven rebounds, three assists, two steals and one

COMPLETE LOUISVILLE-WYOMING BOX SCORE

LOUISVILLE

Player	FG	FGA	FT	FTA	REB	PF	TP	A	TO	BLK	S	MIN
Crook	6	11	1	1	8	3	13	3	0	0	2	24
Thompson	13	14	4	5	7	3	30	3	4	1	2	31
Ellison	2	5	3	4	4	2	7	4	2	3	2	24
Hall	3	7	0	0	3	2	6	6	0	0	1	27
Wagner	4	9	2	2	1	3	10	6	3	0	4	27
McSwain	1	2	0	0	1	1	2	1	2	1	0	7
Kimbro	1	1	0	0	0	4	2	0	2	0	0	11
Payne	5	9	2	3	6	1	12	1	1	0	2	21
West	0	0	0	1	2	0	0	0	0	0	0	1
Valentine	2	5	0	0	2	0	4	0	0	0	0	4
Abram	1	1	1	2	1	0	3	1	0	0	0	12
Walls	0	1	3	4	3	0	3	1	2	0	1	9
Robinson	1	3	0	0	3	0	2	0	0	0	0	2
Team					2							
Deadball Rebounds					2							
Totals	**39**	**68**	**16**	**22**	**43**	**19**	**94**	**26**	**16**	**5**	**14**	**200**

FG%: 1st Half 58.1 2nd Half 56.8 Game 57.4
FT%: 1st Half 83.3 2nd Half 60.0 Game 72.7

WYOMING

Player	FG	FGA	FT	FTA	REB	PF	TP	A	TO	BLK	S	MIN
Dent	0	2	0	0	1	3	0	5	5	1	3	32
Bolden	2	5	1	3	1	5	5	0	3	0	2	25
Dembo	9	16	5	7	5	4	23	3	8	1	2	40
Leckner	4	9	8	9	2	4	16	0	2	1	0	28
Sommers	4	7	0	0	3	3	8	3	1	0	0	33
Boyd	3	6	2	2	1	0	8	1	3	0	0	23
Hunt	0	0	0	0	1	0	0	0	0	0	0	1
Lodgins	1	1	0	0	2	0	2	0	1	0	0	16
Wirth	0	0	0	0	0	0	0	0	0	0	0	2
Team					1							
Deadball Rebounds					1							
Totals	**23**	**46**	**16**	**21**	**17**	**19**	**62**	**12**	**23**	**3**	**7**	**200**

FG%: 1st Half 52.4 2nd Half 48.0 Game 50.0
FT%: 1st Half 85.7 2nd Half 57.1 Game 76.2

Halftime: Louisville 46, Wyoming 34
Attendance: 19,037

blocked shot to the cause. Everything he did turned out good for Louisville.

Thompson had plenty of support help. Superb Herb picked up 11 points and eight rebounds, and freshman Kenny Payne came off the bench to chip in 12 points and six rebounds.

Louisville pulled out to a 46-34 lead by halftime and eventually went on to win 94-62. There really wasn't much to say after this one, but Brandenburg tried.

"I apologize for not being more competitive right now," he told the media, "but we are going to get better. I promise you it won't be a 30-point game next year when Louisville comes to Laramie."

The Cowboys' success in the NIT proved Coach Brandenburg to be correct about getting better, but at that point in time Louisville was just too much better than Wyoming.

OVERALL RECORD: 7-3

Game #11
Eastern Kentucky
January 6

Here we go again, another state school in Freedom Hall ready to take a shot at the Cardinals in hope of some instant recognition and fame. This time it was Eastern Kentucky's turn.

Coach Max Goode had a fine player in junior guard Antonio Parris, who entered the game with a 20.9-point scoring average. And by the end of the first half, the Colonels had outrebounded Louisville by a 20-14 margin. Still, U of L led 45-35.

The game really turned into a rout as the Cards turned it

on in the second half. The final score, 86-55, was indicative of the 40 minutes of action.

The senior duo of Thompson and Wagner led the Cardinal attack with 19 and 17 points respectively. Two freshmen,

COMPLETE LOUISVILLE-EASTERN BOX SCORE

LOUISVILLE

Player	FG	FGA	FT	FTA	REB	PF	TP	A	TO	BLK	S	MIN
Crook	5	11	0	0	8	1	10	2	2	1	4	27
Thompson	6	11	7	8	5	2	19	7	6	3	2	37
Ellison	0	3	1	2	1	0	1	1	0	1	0	9
Hall	4	7	0	0	1	3	8	2	3	1	1	27
Wagner	7	10	3	4	3	0	17	3	2	0	6	26
Kimbro	5	6	1	2	7	0	11	1	1	1	2	21
Payne	5	8	5	5	5	0	15	2	0	0	1	25
West	0	0	0	0	0	1	0	0	1	0	0	4
Valentine	0	1	1	2	0	1	1	0	1	0	0	6
Abram	2	3	0	1	2	0	4	0	1	0	2	11
Walls	0	0	0	0	0	0	0	1	0	0	1	7
Team					3							
Deadball												
Rebounds					2							
Totals	**34**	**60**	**18**	**24**	**35**	**8**	**86**	**19**	**17**	**7**	**19**	**200**

FG%: 1st Half 51.7   2nd Half 61.3   Game 56.7
FT%: 1st Half 78.9   2nd Half 60.0   Game 75.0

EASTERN KENTUCKY

Player	FG	FGA	FT	FTA	REB	PF	TP	A	TO	BLK	S	MIN
Parris	3	9	2	2	2	4	8	0	3	0	2	28
DeCamillis	4	5	0	0	1	4	8	7	6	0	2	22
Spence	10	16	1	1	4	2	21	1	6	1	0	32
Anderson	4	7	0	0	2	3	8	0	1	0	0	15
Taylor	3	8	2	2	6	1	8	0	1	0	1	30
McGill	1	5	0	0	3	2	2	4	5	1	1	22
Collins	0	1	0	0	2	3	0	0	2	0	0	7
Manning	0	0	0	0	0	0	0	0	0	0	0	1
Davie	0	0	0	0	2	2	0	0	0	0	2	8
Hughes	0	1	0	0	0	1	0	0	0	0	0	2
Herndon	0	0	0	0	0	0	0	0	0	0	0	1
Pearson	0	7	0	0	4	1	0	1	3	0	1	22
Team					3							
Deadball												
Rebounds					0							
Totals	**25**	**59**	**5**	**5**	**29**	**23**	**55**	**13**	**27**	**2**	**9**	**200**

FG%: 1st Half 48.4   2nd Half 35.7   Game 42.4
FT%: 1st Half 100.0   2nd Half 00.0   Game 100.0

Halftime: Lousiville 45, Eastern 35
Attendance: 19,235

Kenny Payne and Tony Kimbro, had good nights with 15 and 11 points. But the biggest scare of the evening came not from EKU but from Pervis Ellison when he had to leave the game just nine minutes after the start.

As it turned out, Ellison had aggravated a strained groin muscle when he was bumped out of bounds and his leg slipped out from under him while attempting a dunk. A trip to the hospital for X-rays, which proved to be negative, was made.

"We'll treat him a bunch of times before this season is over," said trainer Jerry May. "It'll get better but it could be aggravated again."

Coach Crum elected not to use junior Mark McSwain in

Reserve Mike Abram is about to slam down one of his two baskets in the 86-55 win over Eastern Kentucky.

Ellison's absence, and that's where the other bad news of the night came in. With the Cards holding a 66-51 lead at the 11:59 mark of the second half, McSwain was seen heading to the locker room. As it turned out, McSwain was told by Crum to go in for Ellison, but the reserve said he didn't want to play. According to Crum, he told him that he wasn't doing him any good on the bench and he should just go on back to the locker room. McSwain returned to the team the next day after apologizing to his teammates.

In retrospect, it was a little frustration attack by Mark because he hadn't played in the first half. The two parties met, talked it out and all was forgiven. Let it be said that from that point on, Mark became a better player for the Cardinals. He would go on to become a real asset in a lot of critical times as the season progressed.

Despite the absence of Ellison and McSwain in the lineup that night, Eastern was obviously no match for the superior Cards. "I'd be pretty foolish if I said Louisville didn't intimidate us," said EKU's Goode. "Louisville has a great basketball program."

Max, it looks like you were right on both accounts.

OVERALL RECORD: 8-3

Game #12
Memphis State
January 9

Metro Conference play was about to begin. Conference play is very important to a team because it's a way to get an automatic bid into the NCAA Tournament and a chance at the big show, the Final Four in Dallas, Texas. It makes me quiver just to think about the possibility of getting there.

Most of any team's pre-conference games are geared toward getting the players ready for conference games and winning on the road. That's the reason the Cards play such a tough schedule in December.

Unfortunately, dear ol' Memphis, home of the late Elvis Presley and then sixth-ranked Tigers of Dana Kirk, would be the first stop for Louisville. And that's always a tough stop for the Cards.

To make matters worse and a lot tougher, this game would be just the first stopping point of a marathon road trip that would keep the Cardinals traveling for nine days. Now that's a long time for any team to hit the road. Of course, playing Memphis first on the trip could be considered as good news. At least they wouldn't be travel weary.

The plans looked like this: play Memphis; head to New Orleans to practice at New Orleans University for a day and give the players a little R&R; travel on up to Hattiesburg for a conference game against Southern Mississippi; then run down to Tallahassee for another conference battle, this time against the Florida State Seminoles. It all sounds simple, but what you don't understand is that this trip takes you through the Atlanta airport five times as well as on two pretty good bus rides to Hattiesburg and back.

But back to the business at hand — Memphis State and our old buddy Dana Kirk.

Memphis had been ranked in the top five all season long and had plenty of good horses. Even at the end of the season, considering all the players on the teams the Cards played, it was MSU's Andre Turner who struck the most fear in my heart. This little guy could do it all and he had the heart of a lion. Add such names as William Bedford and Baskerville Holmes and I start shaking.

The game in Mid-South Coliseum was obviously played above the rim.

Mid-South Coliseum is no rose garden for any opponent. The Memphis folks can really make you feel like you're in another world a long, long way from home. They can boo

43

anyone with the best of them and they don't hesitate to let it fly. Denny Crum is one of their favorite targets and Louisville is the team they love to beat.

It's so bad at Mid-South that I waited for Denny for the pre-game interview, along with Van Vance, so I could lead him behind the bleachers to tape the segment and spare him from the rowdy greeting they had planned for him. It really doesn't bother Coach Crum, but it bothers me.

It was a terrific game and one that saw the Cardinals in control for most of the way. It was a very poor shooting night for Billy Thompson as the forward hit just 2 of 7 shots from

Tiger coach Dana Kirk gave Baskerville Holmes some instructions during the heated contest.

the field and 1 of 3 from the free-throw line. Five points just won't get it from a guy with the talent of Thompson. He did muster eight boards but recorded four turnovers.

It was a night when Pervis Ellison wasn't at full strength because of the groin pull, but the freshman gave it his best shot and scored 11 points in only 23 minutes of play while pulling down five rebounds.

The Tigers outrebounded Louisville 35-31, but the biggest factor of winning or losing came down to the Cardinals being their own worst enemy. It looked like they really hated themselves at the free-throw line, hitting just 17 of 31 for a very poor 52.9 percent. Louisville did score six more field goals, but back at the ranch Memphis was burying 23 of 27 from the charity stripe for a super 85.2 percent. Simply stated, Louisville did everything it had to do to win but shot themselves out of it at the freebie line.

MSU's "Little General" Andre Turner and U of L's Milt Wagner opposed each other for the first of three times in 1985-86.

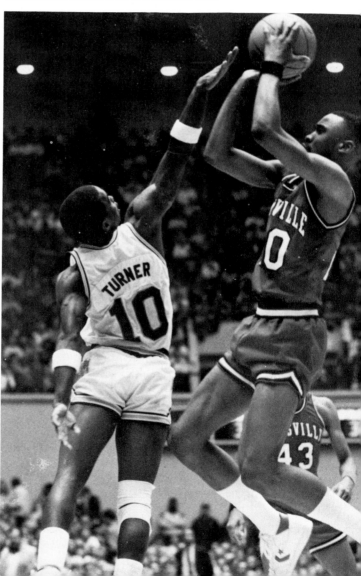

COMPLETE LOUISVILLE-MEMPHIS STATE BOX SCORE

LOUISVILLE

Player	FG	FGA	FT	FTA	REB	PF	TP	A	TO	BLK	S	MIN
Crook	7	11	0	2	1	5	14	2	1	0	2	28
Thompson	2	7	1	3	8	2	5	1	4	1	1	34
Ellison	4	6	3	4	5	4	11	3	1	1	1	23
Hall	3	6	2	2	1	1	8	2	1	0	0	33
Wagner	5	10	2	4	2	2	12	5	4	0	2	35
Kimbro	6	9	1	2	5	4	13	1	1	0	2	27
Payne	4	7	0	0	1	1	8	0	0	0	0	11
Abram	0	2	0	0	5	2	0	1	2	0	1	9
Team					3							
Deadball												
Rebounds					3							
Totals	**31**	**58**	**9**	**17**	**31**	**21**	**71**	**15**	**14**	**2**	**9**	**200**

FG%: 1st Half 56.3   2nd Half 50.0   Game 53.4
FT%: 1st Half 25.0   2nd Half 61.5   Game 52.9

MEMPHIS STATE

Player	FG	FGA	FT	FTA	REB	PF	TP	A	TO	BLK	S	MIN
Askew	2	5	10	10	11	1	14	5	3	1	2	40
Holmes	4	11	6	6	12	2	14	0	3	1	0	40
Bedford	9	18	2	4	7	5	20	1	1	2	0	33
Boyd	1	7	3	4	0	4	5	2	1	0	3	33
Turner	7	11	1	1	3	2	15	5	5	0	0	33
Wilfong	1	1	0	0	0	1	2	2	0	0	1	10
Bailey	0	0	0	0	0	1	0	0	0	0	0	1
Moody	0	2	0	0	0	0	0	0	0	0	0	3
Alexander	1	2	1	2	2	2	3	1	1	0	0	7
Team					0							
Deadball												
Rebounds					2							
Totals	**25**	**57**	**23**	**27**	**35**	**18**	**73**	**16**	**14**	**4**	**6**	**200**

FG%: 1st Half 46.7   2nd Half 40.7   Game 43.9
FT%: 1st Half 88.9   2nd Half 83.3   Game 85.2

Halftime: Louisville 37, Memphis State 36
Attendance: 11,200

The Tigers' defense, here by Marv Alexander, held Billy Thompson to just five points.

Crum's troops led 37-36 at the half and what was really needed for this team was a good win against a tough team on the road. This wouldn't be the night. When Jeff Hall's 23-footer at the buzzer bounced off the rim, Memphis had a 73-71 victory.

"If you expect to beat a top 10 team on the road," said Crum afterward, "you have to have all your people play well at the same time. We did a lot of things very well, except connect at the free-throw line."

The Cards suffered their fourth loss of the season, but on a good note the freshmen reserves played well for the Cards. Tony Kimbro poured in 17 points and Kenny Payne added eight.

The loss put Louisville at 0-1 in league play and the road ahead didn't look any easier. Could the Cards get it all together, and fast? We left Memphis with Coach Kirk sporting a big smile on his face, but maybe there would be another day when the Cardinals would have the last laugh.

OVERALL RECORD: 8-4
CONFERENCE RECORD: 0-1

Game #13
Southern Mississippi
January 13

Catfish country, that's what Mississippi is. I had chosen to drive to Memphis so that my wife, P.J., could go with me. We had made plans to go through Nashville on the drive back to watch Vanderbilt play Georgia. Vandy's coach, C.M. Newton, and his wife Evelyn, were our good friends.

My radio companion, Van Vance, needed to return to Louisville after the Memphis game to do some work, so neither one of us made the trip to Hattiesburg with the team.

On Sunday, Van and I were joined by Don Russell and Jack Tennant, who were going to do the television broadcast back to Louisville for WDRB-TV, and team doctor Rudy Ellis. Our destination — Hattiesburg.

Now, you just can't fly to Hattiesburg direct. You have to go through Atlanta (of course) and hitch another plane ride down to New Orleans. After grabbing some form of transportation, a van in this case, you're ready for the drive to catfish country.

In Hattiesburg, we always stay at the Ramada Inn. It's somewhat below par compared to the other places we usually stay, but it's OK.

The long trip is over and it's game day. It's a must-win situation for the Cards. Any chances of a conference title would be remote, at best, with an 0-2 league record. Everybody knew it wouldn't be easy. It had been one of Coach M.K. Turk's better years. Turk, who is from Bardwell, Ky., is a good coach and his Golden Eagles were playing well. It would be a tough game for Louisville but one that was needed very much. USM was smaller but was probably the quickest team U of L would face all year.

It's a fact that you have to get a few breaks as the year passes in order to reach your goals. Louisville got a break here just by winning. Southern Miss beat them to death statistically. As I was watching the game, I had a difficult time understanding just how the Cards were hanging in there.

Louisville had a slim one-point lead at the half, 27-26. And this was after the Cards had gotten off to a roaring start, getting a 22-9 lead. But as the game progressed, it hit me. Southern Miss was a team that couldn't shoot. They couldn't get anything to fall in. The Golden Eagles shot a miserable 34.5 percent in the first 20 minutes, burned the nets up for 31.3 percent in the second half, and finished the game at 32.8

percent. Believe me, you can't beat a little house on the prairie by shooting those kind of numbers.

Louisville, meanwhile, shot 53.3 percent for the game. Still, the outcome wasn't decided until the final minute. With 1:29 to go, the score was even at 54-54. But Jeff Hall swished a 17-footer, and Billy Thompson canned a couple of free throws. That was enough for the Cards as they won 59-54.

It was a fitting shot for Hall. Early in the game he had become the 33rd player to break the 1,000-point career scoring mark at the University of Louisville.

The Cards had added to their problems by being outre-bounded by the smaller USM team by a 44-30 margin. On top of that, Louisville hit only 11 of 22 free throws. Now if that isn't a recipe for losing, I'm not sure what is.

Following the game, when they were about ready to turn out the lights in Green Coliseum, a very depressed Turk emerged from his dressing room. I walked over to him, not sure about what I was going to say. But before I could open my mouth he said, "Jock, I've got 'em playing as good as they can play. What can I do to get something to go in?"

"Well," I told him, "a bigger hole or a smaller ball might help, but since that's impossible, you have to keep putting it up and hoping."

COMPLETE LOUISVILLE-SO. MISS BOX SCORE

LOUISVILLE

Player	FG	FGA	FT	FTA	REB	PF	TP	A	TO	BLK	S	MIN
Crook	5	8	1	6	6	1	11	4	1	1	3	26
Thompson	2	4	4	7	6	4	8	1	5	2	1	29
Ellison	7	14	4	7	9	2	18	0	2	1	1	37
Hall	3	7	0	0	1	2	6	1	2	0	1	36
Wagner	4	7	2	2	3	2	10	5	4	0	1	37
Kimbro	2	3	0	0	4	1	4	2	1	0	1	22
Payne	1	2	0	0	0	0	2	0	3	0	0	13
Team					1							
Deadball												
Rebounds					1							
Totals	24	45	11	22	30	12	59	13	18	4	8	200

FG%: 1st Half 48.1   2nd Half 61.1   Game 53.3
FT%: 1st Half 00.0   2nd Half 61.1   Game 50.0

SOUTHERN MISS

Player	FG	FGA	FT	FTA	REB	PF	TP	A	TO	BLK	S	MIN
White	2	4	1	2	0	1	5	0	0	0	0	8
Hamilton	2	12	0	0	9	2	4	3	6	0	1	35
Keys	7	17	0	0	10	4	14	1	2	0	2	36
Fisher	3	7	3	4	2	3	9	3	3	0	0	30
Siler	2	12	6	6	7	3	10	3	1	0	2	36
Brown	1	3	2	4	8	3	4	1	2	1	7	27
Jett	3	4	0	0	2	0	6	1	1	0	1	15
Hinton	0	1	0	0	3	1	0	0	0	0	0	9
Ginley	0	1	2	2	1	2	2	0	0	0	0	4
Team					2							
Deadball												
Rebounds					2							
Totals	20	61	14	18	44	19	54	12	15	1	13	200

FG%: 1st Half 34.5   2nd Half 31.3   Game 32.8
FT%: 1st Half 83.3   2nd Half 75.0   Game 77.8

Halftime: So. Miss. 27, Louisville 26
Attendance: 8,053

Assistant coach Bobby Dotson pointed out a play to Jeff Hall in U of L's conference win over Southern Miss.

Turk, who went on to be voted as the Metro's Coach of the Year, drives a pick-up truck given to him by the USM boosters. And that's the type of coach he is. He's really a gem of a person. The only thing I ever received from a booster was a parking ticket.

The Southern Miss roster has a touch of Louisville flavor in John White, a product of Ballard High School. He is a good player for them but on this night he had to leave the game because of an injury. Still, USM had played well.

"Every time we line up," said Denny Crum, "it's a crusade. Everybody comes to play against us."

Can you imagine what kind of crusade it'll be next season? Whew!

It's a fact the Cards were really fortunate to get out of the quaint little Mississippi town with a win. The only thing I wanted to remember about the visit was the great catfish at Catfish Cabin. Would you bring me another order, please? What do you mean you're closed?

Nothing worse than a poor loser.

OVERALL RECORD: 9-4
CONFERENCE RECORD: 1-1

Game #14
Florida State
January 15

First, it's a long ride back to New Orleans in the very dark of the night. Once in New Orleans, we all rose early to grab another plane to Atlanta, make connections, and then head to sunny Tallahassee, Fla., for a Metro game against Florida State. But not before hitting a little place late in the night for a little "toddy" for the old body.

As planned, we winged it to the Sunshine State and stayed at the Hilton, which is not bad but also isn't up to the normal standards of most Hiltons.

The Seminoles can normally give you fits but on this trip at this particular time, Florida State was really struggling. Coach Joe Williams was having his own troubles. "Joe must go" chants from the crowd were more the norm than the exception. And as it turned out, Joe did go after the Metro Conference Tournament.

Next season I'll be chasing Pat Kennedy around for a few words with my friendly microphone. With Joe it was usually, "Talk to Rex," so I nailed his chief assistant, Rex Morgan, for the interview. He always does a nice job.

The game was about like the rumors. FSU was having its troubles. And because they played so poorly that night, it was a "piece of cake" game for the Cards. Whew, it was about time!

The Ice Man, Wagner, broke loose and set the place on fire with 27 points by hitting 13 of 15 field goals. That's an incredible 86 percent! That's burning as only the Ice Man can do it. I had known someone would have to eventually pay after he'd missed all those shots early in the year. Florida State paid dearly!

Louisville's starting forwards, Crook and Thompson, grabbed 10 rebounds apiece. Wagner's running mate at guard, Jeff Hall, picked up 16 points. Give Pervis 13.

The halftime had Louisville ahead by 12 at 41-29. The Seminoles had shot a very poor 38.2 percent. They wouldn't beat many teams shooting at that rate.

When all the fireworks were over, the Cards had won by a surprisingly easy margin of 85-64. And after two games on the road trip where the Cards had combined for only 28 of 53 free throws (52.8 percent), Louisville canned 23 of 27 (85.2 percent) free throws against the Seminoles. It could only happen to Joe.

COMPLETE LOUISVILLE-FLORIDA STATE BOX SCORE

LOUISVILLE

Player	FG	FGA	FT	FTA	REB	PF	TP	A	TO	BLK	S	MIN
Crook	2	6	5	6	10	3	9	4	3	0	0	34
Thompson	3	9	6	6	10	4	12	3	6	0	0	30
Ellison	4	9	5	6	5	4	13	2	1	4	0	34
Hall	6	10	4	4	2	2	16	1	0	0	0	31
Wagner	13	15	1	2	4	3	27	3	2	0	1	38
Kimbro	0	5	2	2	1	0	2	0	0	1	0	16
Payne	2	4	0	0	2	0	4	0	0	0	0	4
McSwain	1	1	0	1	2	0	2	1	3	0	0	8
Walls	0	0	0	0	0	0	0	1	0	0	0	2
West	0	0	0	0	0	0	0	0	0	0	0	2
Robinson	0	0	0	0	0	0	0	0	0	0	0	1
Team					4							
Deadball												
Rebounds					5							
Totals	**31**	**59**	**23**	**27**	**40**	**16**	**85**	**15**	**15**	**5**	**1**	**200**

FG%: 1st Half	54.8	**2nd Half**	50.0	**Game**	52.5		
FT%: 1st Half	87.5	**2nd Half**	84.2	**Game**	85.2		

FLORIDA STATE

Player	FG	FGA	FT	FTA	REB	PF	TP	A	TO	BLK	S	MIN
Allen	5	16	5	5	2	5	15	1	3	4	2	37
Fitchett	5	11	0	0	7	3	10	1	1	0	4	39
Choice	5	8	2	4	5	2	12	0	1	2	0	32
Davis	5	6	2	2	2	5	12	3	2	0	1	20
Barber	5	15	3	4	3	4	13	8	5	0	3	36
Hunter	1	6	0	0	7	1	2	0	1	0	0	17
Mateer	0	2	0	0	0	3	0	0	1	0	0	9
McCloud	0	1	0	0	0	0	0	0	1	0	0	1
Mabry	0	3	0	1	4	0	0	1	0	0	0	9
Team					0							
Deadball												
Rebounds					3							
Totals	**26**	**68**	**12**	**16**	**30**	**23**	**64**	**14**	**15**	**6**	**10**	**200**

FG%: 1st Half	36.1	**2nd Half**	40.6	**Game**	38.2		
FT%: 1st Half	60.0	**2nd Half**	81.8	**Game**	75.0		

Halftime: Louisville 41, Florida State 29
Attendance: 7,198

FSU's Randy Allen, one of the best players in the league, was coming off an ankle injury. He did pick up 15 points that night but it was obvious he wasn't up to his old self.

The win put Louisville at 2-1 in the conference. Florida State would go on to help the Cardinals later in the year, but it wouldn't be by winning or losing. How? You'll have to wait and see.

But the important marathon trip was over and the Cards had won two of the three. It was time to ease on back to Louisville and rest on the laurels. Not so! The Pearl would be waiting in Freedom Hall just three days later.

OVERALL RECORD: 10-4
CONFERENCE RECORD: 2-1

Game #17
Kansas
January 25

T he Kansas Jayhawks — it seems to me we've seen these guys before. Yes, it must be them because over there is the biggest bear in the woods, Greg Dreiling, and one of the nicest and best coaches in the business, Larry Brown.

It was a beautiful day in Lawrence, Kansas. Van Vance and I walked over to the arena. We were about the first people there and immediately we ran into Doug Vance, the sports information director at Kansas. Nope, he's no kin to Van but he is a Kentucky product and does a super job in his capacity.

It didn't take me long to get pumped up. As I was doing my interview with Coach Brown, he told me he listened and enjoyed our weekly radio show called "Sound Off." He said he would pick up the show as he would be traveling to and from somewhere, and it made his trip shorter.

The Cards had practiced in Lawrence the night before and, believe it or not, the students had already lined up to get tickets out of the student allotment. They had spent the night outside in 30-degree weather. No problem. A little "internal" beer antifreeze and everything was OK.

I interviewed them as a group that night for the radio show. Believe me, it was wild. So, on game day, I made another trip outside to see how they were doing. They looked as fresh as a daisy. Unbelievable. But how could that be? Well, it seems they had gotten a little rowdy because of all the antifreeze they had consumed and were all sent home with a number. That number guaranteed them their same place in line if they returned by 11 a.m. the next morning. It was a smart move by the campus police.

The teams were on the floor for warm-ups when I looked over at Dreiling, a 7-1, 250-pound monster of a man. I found myself thinking if we could get this bear out of the lineup we just might sneak this thing out of Kansas. And I got my wish.

The game had barely gotten underway when bingo-bingo-bingo, Dreiling had three of the quickest fouls in the history of college basketball. I smiled and thought to myself that the Cardinals would zoom right past the awestruck Jayhawks. Kansas was just a mediocre team without Dreiling in the lineup.

Louisville did indeed zoom. The Cards held several

Kansas' Greg Dreiling
dwarfed Milt Wagner and
the rest of the Cards, finishing with 18 second-
half points.

double-digit leads over the nation's seventh-ranked team in
the first half, and with 50 seconds left before intermission
they maintained a 36-27 advantage. It was about then,
however, when the worm began to turn. Archie Marshall
tipped in a shot for the Jayhawks with six seconds showing
on the clock. Milt Wagner then tried a desperation shot that
found its mark, but the sound of bad news came by way of
a referee's whistle screaming through the roar of the crowd.
The official disallowed the basket and called a charge on the
offensive man, Wagner — his third of the game. Yuk, what
a repulsive announcement that was.

Oh well, a 7-point lead wasn't all that bad. But wait a
second, there was still one tick showing on the clock. No
problem, so we all thought. Ron Kellogg took the length-of-
the-floor pass down the right sideline and flung the ball at
the basket. As the horror story continued, the ball seemed
to say, "Open up net, I'm coming through." And it did.

The halftime buzzer sounded and Louisville's lead was cut
to 36-31. It was still a 5-point advantage for the Cards but
the last minute had taken something out of them. The game

would go down to the final wire before the outcome was decided, but I'll always believe it was really decided in that final minute of the first half.

It was a day that saw Milt turn in a fine performance by hitting 7 of 14 from the field and all nine of his free-throw attempts, ending with 23 solid points. But it was also a day in which his co-pilot, Jeff Hall, would be the only other Cardinal to score in double figures (11 points).

It was possibly the worst day that Billy Thompson had ever had as a Cardinal player. The senior made just 1 of 5 shots from the field and 6 of 8 from the free-throw line for eight points. He did pick up six rebounds but also recorded six big turnovers, a couple of them coming at very critical times.

The other Cardinals played adequately, but that's about it.

Dreiling returned in the second half and my worst fears came true. He totally controlled the final 20 minutes with 18 second-half points. The giant hit all seven of his field goals, not such a great feat when you consider five of them were dunks. Louisville just had no way to match him physically. That's the reason I would later pray for a Duke victory on March 29 in Dallas.

The Cards somehow managed to stay close. With Kansas

COMPLETE LOUISVILLE-KANSAS BOX SCORE

LOUISVILLE

Player	FG	FGA	FT	FTA	REB	PF	TP	A	TO	BLK	S	MIN
Crook	1	7	3	3	8	4	5	1	0	0	0	24
Thompson	1	5	6	8	6	4	8	1	6	1	2	34
Ellison	3	7	0	1	7	4	6	1	1	1	0	17
Hall	4	10	3	4	1	5	11	2	2	0	0	33
Wagner	7	14	9	9	5	4	23	3	4	1	2	40
Kimbro	3	5	0	0	2	0	6	1	1	1	0	23
Payne	1	3	0	0	2	0	2	2	0	0	0	8
McSwain	2	4	2	4	3	3	6	1	0	0	1	18
Abram	1	1	0	1	0	1	2	0	2	0	0	3
Team					3							
Deadball												
Rebounds					1							
Totals	23	56	23	30	37	25	69	12	16	4	5	200

FG%: 1st Half 39.4   2nd Half 43.5   Game 41.1
FT%: 1st Half 71.4   2nd Half 81.3   Game 76.7

KANSAS

Player	FG	FGA	FT	FTA	REB	PF	TP	A	TO	BLK	S	MIN
Manning	3	9	3	3	2	3	9	1	4	0	1	32
Kellogg	7	18	5	7	2	3	19	1	2	0	1	40
Dreiling	7	7	4	6	5	4	18	0	1	0	0	21
Hunter	3	6	2	3	5	2	8	5	5	1	2	33
Thompson	3	10	2	2	7	5	8	5	0	0	1	30
Turgeon	1	3	1	2	0	0	3	1	0	0	0	12
Marshall	3	3	0	0	7	5	6	0	1	0	0	11
Piper	0	0	0	0	3	3	0	0	2	0	1	21
Team					4							
Deadball												
Rebounds					2							
Totals	27	56	17	23	35	25	71	13	15	1	6	200

FG%: 1st Half 43.3   2nd Half 53.8   Game 48.2
FT%: 1st Half 62.5   2nd Half 80.0   Game 73.9

Halftime: Louisville 36, Kansas 31
Attendance: 15,000

leading 71-69 with :04 left in the game, Louisville had the ball with 94 feet to go. Sounds tough, but Denny is a magician in these situations.

Naturally, a timeout was used and Crum diagrammed the play. Thompson would inbound the ball. It was no secret that Milt would take the last shot, if possible. The official handed

Kenny Payne came off the bench to add two points and two assists in the losing effort.

the ball to Billy, Milt made his move and the pass was in the air. Surprise! The ball got there but Milt was gone. The game was over and Kansas had a 71-69 victory.

What happened could have happened to anybody. Both Thompson and Wagner read the defense and made their cuts accordingly. Unfortunately, there was a split-second difference in what they saw. The Ice Man had beeped when Billy thought he would bop. As Porky Pig says, "That's all, Folks."

It was another disappointing loss for Louisville, its second defeat in a row. Still, Crum managed to find a few bright spots. U of L held Danny Manning to nine points and Kansas to just 71, nine less than their average.

"We did a great job on Manning and most everybody other than Dreiling," said Crum. "Actually, we played pretty good. We kind of beat ourselves. It's no disgrace to lose to a team like that on the road, but let's face it, we could have won the game.

"These are the sort of situations that strengthen mental toughness, if there is enough character there to withstand the disappointment. Teams will either stay after it following this kind of a loss or wilt a little."

Well, we all know there would be no wilting.

OVERALL RECORD: 11-6
CONFERENCE RECORD: 2-2

Game #18
LaSalle
January 28

One of the nicest things about Freedom Hall is regardless of how bad things are going, being at home seems to motivate everyone to fight back. True, this building had been the scene of the crime the last time Cincinnati was in town but, for sure, it wasn't any fault of Freedom Hall. It just happened to be a fantastic performance by a Cincinnati player that did the damage.

Louisville was back home following two successive losses, unusual for the Cards. I wondered before the game how the fans would react but, as you might expect, they were all there with the same amount of enthusiasm.

There was an incident during the game, however, that was a little unusual. At one point there was some booing directed toward Billy Thompson. At least, that's what most of the

Leonard Robinson tried to get around Jeff Hall in the Cards' 12th victory of the season.

18,908 fans and media thought, but I sure didn't see it that way. Kenny Payne had been in the game and was playing well. Billy reported in at the scorer's table as Payne's replacement.

Yes, I heard the boos, but I thought it was because Kenny was being taken out, not because Billy T. was coming in. Personally, I think whoever had been at the scorer's table would have heard the same boos. Granted, Billy had been

Billy Thompson outre-bounded LaSalle's Eric Lee for this missed shot.

COMPLETE LOUISVILLE-LASALLE BOX SCORE

LOUISVILLE

Player	FG	FGA	FT	FTA	REB	PF	TP	A	TO	BLK	S	MIN
Crook	5	8	4	6	8	3	14	0	2	0	2	34
Thompson	4	10	4	4	10	5	12	4	3	2	0	32
Ellison	4	11	4	5	9	0	12	1	1	1	0	27
Hall	3	7	0	0	3	5	6	4	2	0	0	29
Wagner	6	10	1	1	2	1	13	3	3	0	0	31
Kimbro	0	4	1	2	3	2	1	0	1	1	0	13
Payne	4	6	0	0	3	2	8	0	5	0	0	11
McSwain	1	2	2	2	4	1	4	0	1	0	2	12
Abram	1	1	0	0	1	2	2	0	1	0	0	6
Valentine	0	0	0	0	0	0	0	1	1	0	0	1
West	0	0	0	0	0	0	0	2	0	0	0	4
Team					2							
Deadball												
Rebounds				4								
Totals	28	59	16	20	45	21	72	15	20	4	4	200

FG%: 1st Half	52.2	2nd Half	44.4	Game	47.5
FT%: 1st Half	75.0	2nd Half	83.3	Game	80.0

LASALLE

Player	FG	FGA	FT	FTA	REB	PF	TP	A	TO	BLK	S	MIN
Tarr	0	3	1	2	0	0	1	0	1	0	0	14
Greenburg	1	8	0	1	2	4	2	4	4	0	1	32
Robinson	1	4	2	2	4	1	4	2	4	0	0	32
Barnes	0	1	2	2	4	4	2	0	0	4	5	22
Legler	11	17	1	2	4	3	23	1	1	0	2	32
Koretz	4	13	4	4	4	4	12	0	1	0	0	31
Philson	0	0	0	0	0	0	0	0	0	0	0	1
Jones	0	0	1	2	0	0	1	1	1	0	1	8
Lee	4	5	1	3	2	2	9	0	1	0	0	9
Palczewski	0	0	0	0	0	0	0	0	0	0	0	1
Conlin	3	5	0	2	4	2	6	0	4	0	1	18
Team					1							
Deadball												
Rebounds					2							
Totals	24	56	12	20	25	20	60	8	17	4	10	200

FG%: 1st Half	30.8	2nd Half	53.3	Game	42.9
FT%: 1st Half	50.0	2nd Half	64.3	Game	60.0

Halftime: Louisville 30, LaSalle 19
Attendance: 18,908

having a tough time as of late. Good things weren't happening for him nor for the team. But I believe he was working at it. Denny Crum, afterward, wanted no part of the booing.

"That shows stupidity," said an angered Crum. "Billy is trying as hard as anybody I've ever coached. He's doing everything right but he just doesn't happen to be playing well right now."

If it really did happen that way, I would feel the same way as Coach Crum. But I don't believe it happened as most thought.

This was the night Crum would go for his 350th career win and get it. But a dark cloud hovered above. Kevin Walls was AWOL on this night and nobody seemed to know why. I spotted his absence early in the warm-ups. In fact, Van and I discussed it on the air during the radio broadcast.

I went down the bench and asked the people who should have known but never got a solid answer. On our return trip from Kansas, I'd sat with Kevin all the way back. He had seemed to be the same Kevin Walls — no signs of unhappiness as far as his situation was concerned. We had discussed the game and basketball in general. He knew his time would come and seemed willing to wait for it. Losing has a way of making all concerned discontented. I was surprised by his absence but, knowing Kevin, felt sure everything would work out.

It was game time. Louisville needed a win in the worst way, and they went after it. They outrebounded LaSalle by an astonishing 45-25 margin. That alone would beat about anybody. Billy and Pervis combined for 19 rebounds, with Billy getting 10. The pair also registered 12 points each.

Herb Crook led the balanced scoring with 14 while Milt Wagner pitched in 13.

It was a sloppy game with Louisville committing 20 turnovers while the Explorers added 17. The Cards led 30-19 at the half and were never seriously threatened.

Louisville could only get off 50 shots (they made 28), but a win is a win. Denny Crum had the answer, "Since we've played so many good games and still not won, it's nice to play an average game and win. We played hard, we just didn't get a whole lot done."

I agreed with Crum but I sure did moan and groan about the quality of play on the radio. I'm sure coach Dave "Lefty" Ervin's deliberate style of play had some affect on the Cards' performance.

Thompson probably said it best, "It was a little sloppy out there. The crowd wasn't into it, it was a slow first half and we were rushing. We've been taking some emotional rides, but that's something we have to work on."

Crum spent much of his post-game speech defending his team's record. "I don't know what people expect," said the coach. "I knew when the season started, with the schedule we were playing and where we were playing them, that we probably wouldn't end up with a great record. But we had the potential to be an outstanding team by the end of the year. We're as good as any of those teams when we play hard."

Perhaps we should have listened to Coach Crum. Regardless, a win is a win, especially if you've lost two in a row and UCLA is the next opponent. Coming out on top is the name of the game, no matter if you crawl on your belly like a reptile or get there with a back flip. We'll take the victory over LaSalle.

OVERALL RECORD: 12-6
CONFERENCE RECORD: 2-2

Game #19
UCLA
February 1

The network television people were in town so we all knew "you know who" would have a good game. The best news this Saturday, though, was that all the Cardinals played well. To say the least, it was a very unusual day in Freedom Hall.

Why? When the teams were set for the opening tipoff, "Cool Hand Luke" was still on his farm in eastern Jefferson County. In fact, Coach Crum would spend the day in bed. It seems the old flu bug had put the full-court press on him.

Just how do you play UCLA, Crum's alma mater, with the boss man on the farm? Simple. You turn to the well-trained staff, install a phone hookup to the bench and let the assistants turn the game into a clinic for the fans.

The Cards played super.

Jerry Jones took the coach's seat and directed the game from Crum's normal chair. He did one terrific job. The responsibility was shared with assistants Wade Houston and Bobby Dotson, who both contributed as much as Jones, but it was Jones who could be seen standing and directing as the game went on.

Denny spent the day talking on the phone to trainer Jerry May. May passed Crum's comments on to Jones, Houston and Dotson. But even if Denny had not been able to communicate, I'm convinced the Cardinals would have done about the same.

The most disappointed guy in the building was UCLA head coach Walt Hazzard. He had looked forward to matching wits with his very good friend, Cool Hand Luke. I'll tell you, those UCLA guys from the John Wooden days are thicker than chickweed. At the end of the game, Coach Hazzard said, "I don't like being beaten by a coach that isn't even here."

The TV cameras were lit and ready to go. It would be a quality performance turned in by U of L, one that would carry them all the way to Dallas. They were superb. All five starters were in double figures and the team registered 27 assists. That means everyone was looking for the open man.

Louisville shot 55.1 percent from the field and 71.5 from the charity stripe. They outrebounded UCLA 38-32 and, mark it down, they only committed 10 turnovers. It was a blue-ribbon performance.

It really didn't matter what the Bruins did. No one could

COMPLETE LOUISVILLE-UCLA BOX SCORE

LOUISVILLE

Player	FG	FGA	FT	FTA	REB	PF	TP	A	TO	BLK	S	MIN
Crook	4	11	3	5	7	2	11	2	3	0	1	28
Thompson	7	12	2	2	8	2	16	6	1	2	0	28
Ellison	8	15	1	3	10	1	17	2	1	1	2	29
Hall	6	9	0	0	0	2	12	4	0	0	0	34
Wagner	9	14	2	2	4	2	20	7	2	0	1	34
Kimbro	2	2	2	3	0	2	6	1	2	1	0	15
Payne	0	2	0	0	2	0	0	0	1	1	1	10
McSwain	0	1	4	5	5	0	4	1	0	2	0	11
Abram	2	2	1	1	1	0	5	3	0	0	0	9
Olliges	0	1	0	0	0	0	0	0	0	0	0	1
Abram	0	0	0	0	0	1	0	1	0	0	0	1
Team					1							
Deadball												
Rebounds					2							
Totals	38	69	15	21	38	12	91	27	10	7	5	200

FG%: 1st Half	52.9	2nd Half	57.1	Game	55.1
FT%: 1st Half	71.4	2nd Half	71.4	Game	71.4

UCLA

Player	FG	FGA	FT	FTA	REB	PF	TP	A	TO	BLK	S	MIN
Hatcher	2	9	2	2	5	2	6	0	2	1	1	23
Jones	2	4	1	2	3	3	5	0	2	0	1	18
Richardson	3	8	3	4	5	3	9	9	4	0	1	38
Miller	11	17	3	5	2	4	25	1	0	0	0	39
Jackson	6	10	1	2	7	1	13	0	4	0	2	33
Haley	5	8	0	0	5	5	10	0	1	0	0	24
Morris	0	1	0	1	1	0	0	0	0	0	0	1
Palmer	1	2	0	0	1	1	2	0	2	1	0	17
Dunlap	0	0	0	0	0	0	0	0	0	0	0	1
Rochelin	1	4	0	0	1	1	2	0	0	0	0	6
Team					2							
Deadball												
Rebounds					3							
Totals	31	63	10	16	32	20	72	10	15	2	5	200

FG%: 1st Half	54.5	2nd Half	43.3	Game	49.2
FT%: 1st Half	40.0	2nd Half	72.7	Game	62.5

Halftime: Louisville 41, UCLA 38
Attendance: 19,384

Assistant coach Jerry Jones did the directing while team trainer Jerry May communicated with Coach Crum by telephone. Crum was home in bed recovering from the flu.

have beaten the Cards that day. Sorry, Denny, but I don't know if they EVER played a more complete game than they did on that Saturday.

Louisville led 41-38 at the half and won easily, 91-72.

"We were beaten by a better basketball team," said Hazzard. "Louisville is a very powerful team. I'd compare their talent to the North Carolina team we played earlier in the year. I'd say Louisville is one of the finer teams I've seen all year. We were in the wrong place on the wrong date and were beaten by a very good team."

There was some more good news that day.

Kevin Walls was back in uniform after a five-day absence, even though he'd been unable to smooth things out with Coach Crum. Denny hadn't even been at practice since the game against LaSalle.

Overall, it was just a terrific day for Louisville. And, of course, "you know who" led the scoring with 20 points, seven assists and four rebounds. He was something. Milt was definitely one of a kind. Don't be surprised if someday you see him in the movies. He just loves those cameras.

Congratulations Jerry, Wade and Bobby. With 11 games ahead in the next 25 days, you supplied us with a "laugher" when one was needed the most. This day was the one that pulled the Cards together.

OVERALL RECORD: 13-6
CONFERENCE RECORD: 2-2

Game #20
South Carolina
February 3

Coach Bill Foster was in the Derby City with his South Carolina Gamecocks. They had a set of twins on the team, Terry and Perry Dozier. Rumor was that Terry, a starter and an excellent player, would be out of action because of an injury. If the rumor turned out to be true, things would be easier for the Cardinals.

Terry was indeed sidelined, so U of L had everything going for it. After all, the last time the Cards were in Freedom Hall

Gamecock coach Bill Foster gave Michael Foster some instructions.

Milt Wagner tried to get by South Carolina's Steve Holland in the Cardinal win.

they put on a clinic for the thousands in attendance and the millions watching on national TV. Surely they would pick up where they left off.

For awhile, it appeared that way. It hadn't been a good shooting night for either team (both teams shot under 50 percent in the first half) but Louisville led 36-31 after 20 minutes of action.

That lead went to 14 at the 9:13 mark of the second half but it was at this point momentum began to change. The Cards made several trips down the floor and came away with nothing. In the meantime, the Gamecocks were drilling the basket and scored 12 unanswered points. Louisville's lead had dwindled to 61-59. Nightmares of the Cincinnati game began popping into everyone's mind. It looked like another thief would return to the scene of the crime. Surely, not again.

Coach Crum had recovered from the flu some and was back on the sidelines. This is where he is at his best.

South Carolina had come back with four of the U of L starters on the bench for a rest. The four reserves who played didn't come through, combining to produce only three points. But the rested starters may have been the difference in the end, at least according to SC's head coach.

"We got a little tired at the end while Louisville seemed to be a little fresher," said Foster.

Linwood Moye of South Carolina carried the Metro school in the second half, posting 17 of his 19 points after intermission. Ironically, though, it was Moye who missed the final shot that would have tied the game in the closing moments.

LOUISVILLE

Player	FG	FGA	FT	FTA	REB	PF	TP	A	TO	BLK	S	MIN
Crook	6	15	2	5	6	3	14	3	2	0	2	31
Thompson	5	13	4	4	12	4	14	5	1	2	1	34
Ellison	3	7	5	5	5	3	11	2	1	6	2	33
Hall	8	12	0	0	2	3	16	5	2	0	1	36
Wagner	8	12	0	1	1	3	16	8	3	0	1	37
Kimbro	0	1	0	0	1	0	0	1	0	0	0	11
Payne	0	3	0	0	1	0	0	0	1	0	0	7
McSwain	1	1	1	1	0	2	3	0	1	0	0	9
Abram	0	0	0	0	0	0	0	0	1	0	0	2
Team					4							
Deadball												
Rebounds					1							
Totals	31	64	12	16	32	18	74	24	12	8	7	200

FG%: 1st Half 46.9	2nd Half 50.0	Game 48.4	
FT%: 1st Half 100.0	2nd Half 60.0	Game 75.0	

SOUTH CAROLINA

Player	FG	FGA	FT	FTA	REB	PF	TP	A	TO	BLK	S	MIN
Kendall	3	6	5	6	6	4	11	1	1	1	0	34
Foster	4	10	2	2	2	3	10	6	3	0	0	37
James	5	8	0	0	8	1	10	7	3	0	0	38
Moye	7	13	5	6	5	4	19	0	4	0	1	33
Martin	6	12	4	4	9	3	16	3	4	0	0	37
Holland	0	2	0	0	2	1	0	0	1	0	2	9
Dozier	3	7	0	0	3	1	6	0	0	0	0	12
Team					1							
Deadball												
Rebounds					0							
Totals	28	58	16	18	36	17	72	17	16	1	3	200

FG%: 1st Half 48.3	2nd Half 48.3	Game 48.3	
FT%: 1st Half 75.0	2nd Half 92.9	Game 88.9	

Halftime: Louisville 36, South Carolina 31
Attendance: 18,981

Senior co-captain Denise Zirnheld did her best to get the home crowd fired up.

The Ice Man, Wagner, came through again in the clutch. He canned a 17-footer from the right side with :24 left, giving Louisville a 74-71 lead. South Carolina added a free throw, but that's as close as they could get. Moye's 16-foot shot at the buzzer (over the outstretched arms of Pervis Ellison) missed its mark, and the Cards had a 74-72 victory.

The Gamecocks played well, as did the Cards. Only the poor shooting kept it from being a really good game. All five Cardinal starters scored in double figures, led by Wagner and Jeff Hall's 16 points. Crook and Thompson each tallied 14, while Never Nervous added 11.

Billy looked like the Billy everyone expected to see, pulling down a game-high 12 rebounds while committing only one turnover. It was an important game for him and an important conference win for the team. The big question mark now was the Cardinal bench help. Where, oh, where did it go?

It had to be found quickly if the Cards expected to mount a serious threat for the Metro regular-season championship, the conference tournament and the NCAA Tournament.

OVERALL RECORD: 14-6
CONFERENCE RECORD: 3-2

Game #21
Virginia Tech
February 8

When everyone entered Freedom Hall that night — players, coaches, media and fans — I'm sure they were all thinking the same thing. Virginia Tech was loaded with talent and experience, and they were on a roll. The Hokies had given Memphis State, the league's top dog, its only setback of the season and had just knocked off another top 20 team, Richmond. Tech was ranked No. 15 in the latest wire service poll, one notch ahead of Louisville.

The contest had all the ingredients of a quality event. VPI had one of the nation's premier guards, Dell Curry, who was later voted Player of the Year in the Metro Conference. And the awards kept coming as Curry was named as a second-team All-American by the Associated Press, the first ever in Hokie history, and picked to the first-team All-American squad by *Basketball News*. The outstanding guard averaged 19 points over his four-year career and the school honored him at the end of the season by retiring his jersey, No. 30.

Curry had a good supporting cast, including 6-9 senior Bobby Beecher. The forward had always been a thorn in the Cardinals' feathers.

I always enjoy my interviews with head coach Charlie Moir. He's a special man. When you talk with him it's as if you visit him everyday. Moir is a gentleman's gentleman. He has a way about him that immediately puts you at ease.

Virginia Tech head coach Charlie Moir.

The game didn't just start, it exploded. The Cards looked like they had been blown out of a cannon and roared to a 47-30 halftime lead. There's a saying among coaches that it's not how good you are, it's how good are you tonight? It really wouldn't have mattered what Virginia Tech had done in the 40 minutes that evening, nothing would have overcome the Cardinals.

On nights like this, the thought would flash through my mind: "If these guys could advance far enough, by hook or crook, to have a shot at Dallas and then put a couple of these games together, who knows what might happen." Well, I get carried away at times and dream these kinds of dreams. You never can tell when one of them just might come true.

Curry had a bad evening, hitting just 6 of 16 shots from the field and 1 of his 3 free throws. Beecher didn't fare much better, connecting on only 5 of 15 field-goal attempts. It was a lot of good "D" on the part of Louisville that led to those figures.

U of L turned in some awesome stats. They totally dominated a stunned VPI team on the boards, overwhelming them by a 54-25 margin. I'm still not sure I ever remember

COMPLETE LOUISVILLE-VPI BOX SCORE

LOUISVILLE

Player	FG	FGA	FT	FTA	REB	PF	TP	A	TO	BLK	S	MIN
Crook	6	11	7	10	6	3	19	0	4	0	1	31
Thompson	9	14	3	4	7	2	21	5	2	2	1	28
Ellison	3	5	2	2	11	2	8	6	2	4	2	27
Hall	7	11	0	0	2	3	14	5	1	0	0	27
Wagner	6	12	0	0	2	2	12	3	3	0	1	30
Kimbro	3	5	0	0	1	3	6	1	4	0	1	16
Payne	2	4	1	2	3	1	5	1	1	0	0	9
McSwain	3	6	0	0	10	0	6	6	1	1	1	16
Abram	2	2	0	2	1	0	4	1	0	0	0	4
West	1	1	0	0	2	1	2	0	0	0	0	3
Valentine	3	3	0	0	1	4	6	0	0	0	1	3
Walls	0	1	0	0	1	0	0	0	0	0	1	1
Olliges	0	0	0	0	1	0	0	0	0	0	0	4
Robinson	0	0	0	0	0	0	0	0	0	0	0	1
Team					6							
Deadball												
Rebounds					6							
Totals	**45**	**75**	**13**	**20**	**54**	**21**	**103**	**28**	**18**	**7**	**10**	**200**

FG%: 1st Half 60.0   2nd Half 60.0   Game 60.0
FT%: 1st Half 83.3   2nd Half 57.1   Game 65.0

VIRGINIA TECH

Player	FG	FGA	FT	FTA	REB	PF	TP	A	TO	BLK	S	MIN
Beecher	5	15	2	2	7	2	12	0	1	2	1	36
Colbert	5	15	3	4	4	4	13	0	1	0	1	24
Burgess	2	3	0	0	1	0	4	1	0	0	0	15
Fort	4	8	1	3	0	2	9	5	5	0	0	34
Curry	6	16	1	3	2	1	13	6	1	2	2	34
Ceasar	1	1	0	2	0	1	2	0	1	0	0	12
Anderson	1	4	6	7	6	4	8	0	2	1	1	20
Williams	0	0	0	0	4	0	0	0	1	0	0	11
Brow	3	4	1	1	0	4	7	0	3	0	0	14
Team					1							
Deadball												
Rebounds					2							
Totals	**27**	**66**	**14**	**22**	**25**	**18**	**68**	**12**	**15**	**5**	**5**	**200**

FG%: 1st Half 36.4   2nd Half 45.5   Game 40.9
FT%: 1st Half 60.0   2nd Half 66.7   Game 63.6

Halftime: Louisville 47, Virginia Tech 30
Attendance: 19,406

such a lopsided difference. Louisville shot a healthy 60 percent from the field (45 of 75) while Tech finished at 40.9 percent (27 of 66).

The final score was 103-68. That's a 35-point difference. Totally unbelievable Billy Thompson went on a rampage and had a terrific night with 21 points, seven rebounds, five assists, two blocks and one steal. When Billy plays tough, the Cardinals are really tough. And this night was vintage Thompson.

"It's the best I've ever seen Thompson play," said Tech's Moir, who hadn't had a team take such a beating since his seventh game as a head coach 10 years earlier when Elvin Hayes and the Houston Cougars whipped up on Tech 120-79.

The U of L bench, which vanished one game earlier against South Carolina, resurfaced led by Mark McSwain's six points and 10 rebounds. It was one of his better performances of the season and shades of things to come, hopefully.

Overall, it was an awesome performance and quite a night for Cardinal basketball. The 19,046 fans loved what they had seen and all left smiling, including me. It was time to enjoy, although everyone was a little apprehensive about going to Blacksburg just four short nights later. It wouldn't be that easy again, or would it?

OVERALL RECORD: 15-6
CONFERENCE RECORD: 4-2

Billy Thompson led all scorers with 21 points.

Game #24
Cincinnati
February 13

The Clarion Hotel is a nice place to stay in Cincinnati because it's connected to all sorts of retail stores and bumming-around opportunities. And you can travel underground via tunnels, not having to go out in the weather.

The bad news is this is the town where the "Boogie Man" resides and Louisville would have to face him once again. You remember him. He's the guy who kicked in all burners a couple of weeks earlier in Freedom Hall and sizzled the nets for 35 points, picking the Cardinal Birds out of the tree from long range. They won, Louisville lost. If he had done that in Louisville, what would he do to the Cards at his own place? It was time to find out.

Riverfront Coliseum had 12,663 fans in the stands, lots of them from Louisville. Denny Crum's troops would obviously be keeping a close eye on the Boogie Man, Roger McClendon. They'd have to work a little harder on the boards.

Well, they did all that and did it well. There were not any slip-ups this time. Louisville came out smoking and with the first-half clock showing 11:57, U of L was leading by 17 points, 26-9. With 2:12 left before the half, the score was 36-17. Now that's the way you take the wind out of any opponent's sails.

On this particular night, the mysterious Boogie Man became one of us normal people again. McClendon was able to get off only seven shots and make just one. And this is the same guy who was making them from the parking lot of Freedom Hall back on Jan. 20. I still believe there must have been some celestial being who slipped into McClendon's uniform in Louisville. Whatever, that night it was "Welcome back, Roger. We like you a lot better the way you are tonight."

Louisville had doubled Cincinnati's score by the half, 38-19. It was a blitz, the same treatment the Cards had handed out to Virginia Tech in their last two conference meetings.

Thompson, who had been on a surge, had another superb night. He hit all eight of his field-goal attempts and 7 of his 9 free throws for a game-high 23 points.

Not bad for a guy who supposedly had been booed by his own fans. At this stage of the season, Billy was rapidly becoming the baddest man in town, any town. Besides his scoring, he added eight rebounds and only one miscue. It was a great night in only 28 minutes of action.

The Bearcats had no chance for the simple reason Louisville was on a roll, a roll that was just going to gather momentum, keep rolling and rolling and rolling.

"I think Louisville played an excellent basketball game tonight," said UC coach Tony Yates in quite an understatement.

"We've been playing hard, shooting well and getting up on people early," said Thompson. That's for sure.

"The loss to Cincinnati at our place was on the players' minds," said Denny Crum. Right, Coach, it was on all our minds.

Billy Thompson swarmed UC's Kenneth Henry and the Cards swarmed the Bearcats.

COMPLETE LOUISVILLE-CINCINNATI BOX SCORE

LOUISVILLE

Player	FG	FGA	FT	FTA	REB	PF	TP	A	TO	BLK	S	MIN
Crook	4	9	2	3	5	4	10	3	2	0	0	28
Thompson	8	8	7	9	8	3	23	1	1	1	0	28
Ellison	4	8	3	6	9	3	11	2	2	0	3	32
Hall	4	7	0	0	3	3	8	2	1	0	0	29
Wagner	5	8	4	4	5	0	14	3	4	0	1	33
Kimbro	0	1	0	0	0	1	0	1	0	1	0	18
Payne	1	6	0	0	5	1	2	0	0	0	0	7
West	0	0	2	2	0	1	2	0	1	0	0	2
Valentine	1	1	0	0	2	0	2	0	1	0	0	3
Walls	0	1	0	0	1	1	0	0	1	0	0	8
Abram	0	1	0	1	0	0	0	0	1	0	0	8
Olliges	1	1	0	0	1	0	2	0	1	0	0	4
Team					2							
Deadball												
Rebounds					3							
Totals	**28**	**51**	**18**	**25**	**41**	**19**	**74**	**12**	**15**	**2**	**4**	**200**

FG%: 1st Half	51.8	2nd Half	58.3	Game 54.9
FT%: 1st Half	71.4	2nd Half	72.7	Game 72.0

CINCINNATI

Player	FG	FGA	FT	FTA	REB	PF	TP	A	TO	BLK	S	MIN
Henry	3	7	1	6	1	4	7	0	0	0	1	22
Hughes	1	9	1	2	5	4	3	1	3	0	1	22
Glover	3	8	0	0	8	3	6	1	1	0	0	17
McClendon	1	7	1	2	2	0	3	1	2	0	1	21
Wilson	4	7	0	0	9	1	8	2	3	0	1	32
Helm	0	3	1	2	1	3	1	0	1	0	0	19
Stiffend	5	10	3	5	3	2	13	0	0	0	0	28
Shorter	7	11	1	2	1	2	15	2	0	0	0	23
Jackson	0	1	1	2	2	0	1	0	0	0	0	4
Flynn	0	0	0	0	0	0	0	0	0	0	0	4
May	0	2	1	2	0	0	1	0	0	0	0	4
Ruehl	0	1	0	0	0	0	0	0	0	0	0	4
Team					3							
Deadball												
Rebounds					6							
Totals	**24**	**66**	**10**	**23**	**35**	**19**	**58**	**8**	**10**	**0**	**4**	**200**

FG%: 1st Half	28.1	2nd Half	44.1	Game 36.4
FT%: 1st Half	25.0	2nd Half	47.4	Game 43.5

Halftime: Louisville 38, Cincinnati 19
Attendance: 12,683

For the record, the final score was 74-58. It was time to head home and pack for the DePaul game in Chicago. Incidentally, on that night the Bearcats looked like teddy bear cats. That's the way it is when you don't have a Boogie Man on your team. I guess even Martians have to go home sometime.

OVERALL RECORD: 17-7
CONFERENCE RECORD: 6-2

Game #25
DePaul
February 15

The Windy City. That's where this big ol' airplane dropped us off. It was another charter trip, we were staying in the Hyatt, and a lot of the Cardinal followers were in the Windy City to see the sites. The site they really hoped to see, however, was a big win over DePaul.

For some reason, the Cardinals couldn't work out at the Rosemont Horizon, so practice was elsewhere. I remember walking into the gym and seeing Joey Meyer. He was the head coach at this independent school and seemed to be in a bit of trouble. A lot of people had been on him in a lot of different ways.

Kevin Walls was a suprise starter in the second half against DePaul.

In a local paper, Billy Packer of CBS-TV said, "If he is not having fun, he should quit." I asked Joey for the interview and before I turned the mike on we were just making social conversation and I asked him, "How's it going, Joey?" He replied, "It sure could be better," in a tone of voice that sort of made you think that Billy Packer was partially right. He wasn't having much fun at all.

Trying to follow America's favorite coach, Ray Meyer, is an awesome task. I would think it would take awhile before you could have any fun.

Still, the younger Meyer was extremely nice in granting the interview and even playfully took a few shots at the basket. He was laughing and playing around with different people but the pressure was still there — it was a forced smile.

Louisville's athletic director, Bill Olsen, had made the trip and had his young son David with him. The 9-year-old was

Dallas Comegys led the Blue Demon attack with 20 points.

shooting around a little, too. As a matter of fact, he was shooting better than his daddy.

Then another Louisville dignitary, Dr. Ed Hammond, was on the scene. He was wearing his jogging suit and decided he'd put up a few. It looked like Dr. Ed was in pretty good shape. Not bad for a University vice president.

My main man, Van, had deserted me. He was out rcaming the neighborhood looking for old friends. Van's mother, coincidentally, used to live in this very neighborhood and Van had spent a lot of time in Chicago. How he stayed out of the mob I'll never know!

It was an afternoon game so it was early to rise, get checked out, put the baggage in the lobby and get to the arena. The traveling party would return to Louisville following the game.

DePaul had a very talented group of athletes but, for some reason, were not playing very well. They just couldn't seem to win like they should. Looking at them in pre-game drills made you wonder how Louisville could beat this bunch. This team and the Auburn Tigers would probably have more athletes on their rosters than any of the teams Louisville would face all year. Southern Mississippi would be next in line, followed by Memphis State. At least, that's the way I saw it.

But back to the problem at hand, DePaul.

I thought about the last time Louisville had played here. It was Coach Ray Meyer's last season, and there were plenty of pre-game ceremonies. Bill Olsen and his wife, Sharon, made a presentation to the Meyers. I had a great interview with both of them. They were terrific. That's one of the reasons I get so aggravated with these jokers who are playing the "fat cat" role and put themselves on some kind of velvet cloud, acting like the rest of us are traveling on a cloud made out of burlap. The really big guys are the nicest people to deal with, as a rule.

Coach Meyer's wife died about a year after his retirement and, in the interview that I had with him this year, he said, "I gave up my two greatest loves — my job and my wife." His eyes got cloudy but he went on to say, "I really miss them both." To make it even worse, his son was struggling with the impossible task of replacing him. Coach Ray Meyer is a class man.

I took one last look at the awesome sight of Dallas Comegys, DePaul's 6-9 post man. The first time I saw him as a freshman, he just looked like he would be the best player who ever lived. So far, he has never fulfilled the expectancy that DePaul fans had for him, but a lot of players never reach that level.

As it turned out, DePaul would have the best of it in the first half, mainly because Louisville would commit 13 turnovers every conceivable way. That's even a little high for a full game. To add to their woes, the Cards shot a paltry 42.3 percent, not even good for a Pee Wee team.

The second half, however, was just like it had been in Cincinnati and Virginia Tech, a blowout was in the making. At the half, Louisville found itself trailing DePaul by five

LOUISVILLE

Player	FG	FGA	FT	FTA	REB	PF	TP	A	TO	BLK	S	MIN
Crook	9	13	10	11	9	4	28	3	3	0	0	35
Thompson	2	7	2	2	6	4	6	5	5	2	1	34
Ellison	5	12	2	4	9	5	12	0	3	3	0	30
Hall	3	7	4	4	3	1	10	2	1	0	1	31
Wagner	2	7	0	0	2	4	4	2	1	0	0	27
Kimbro	2	4	0	0	3	2	4	2	2	0	1	21
Payne	0	1	0	0	0	0	0	0	0	0	0	4
Walls	2	3	4	6	0	0	8	2	0	0	3	15
Olliges	0	0	0	0	1	0	0	0	0	0	1	1
Team					4							
Deadball												
Rebounds					2							
Totals	25	54	22	27	37	20	72	16	15	5	7	200

FG%: 1st Half 42.3   2nd Half 50.0   Game 46.3
FT%: 1st Half 80.0   2nd Half 81.8   Game 81.5

DEPAUL

Player	FG	FGA	FT	FTA	REB	PF	TP	A	TO	BLK	S	MIN
Comegys	7	10	6	8	2	4	20	1	1	0	0	36
Holmes	6	12	1	3	7	3	13	3	1	1	1	29
Lampley	1	9	2	2	6	2	4	0	2	1	1	24
Jackson	1	6	1	4	2	0	3	1	3	0	1	19
Strickland	2	5	0	1	4	5	4	4	4	0	2	35
Embry	1	1	2	4	4	1	4	0	2	1	0	22
Greene	1	4	3	3	1	5	5	2	4	0	1	23
Brundy	0	1	0	0	1	1	0	0	0	2	1	10
Laux	0	0	0	0	0	0	0	0	1	0	0	2
Team					3							
Deadball												
Rebounds					4							
Totals	19	48	15	25	30	21	53	11	18	5	7	200

FG%: 1st Half 39.3   2nd Half 40.0   Game 39.6
FT%: 1st Half 60.0   2nd Half 60.0   Game 60.0

Halftime: DePaul 31, Louisville 26
Attendance: 15,754

points, 31-26. This is about the time, however, that the "Crook" from Louisville would steal the game. He had 20 second-half points and finished as the game's leading scorer with 28. He also picked up nine rebounds and had three assists. Incidentally, the "Crook" I'm speaking of is the Louisville player who does the best job of moving without the ball, Herbert, a.k.a. the "Rubber Man."

Ellison scored 12 points and Jeff Hall added 10, and that was it for double-figure scorers. Louisville outrebounded the DePaul team, 37-30, which was quite a feat. The game was won with Milt and Billy combining for only 10 points. But that's what makes the Cardinals a fun team to watch. Every starter could burn you up on any given day. A team has to honor all of them, and that's difficult to do.

The final score was Louisville 72, DePaul 53.

In watching the DePaul team play, it seemed they over-executed. They looked as if they were over-coached, they didn't have the green light to use the abundance of talent that was just bursting to be turned loose. They ran the patterns over and over, waiting for the pattern to break someone loose, when any player on the court had the ability

DePaul's Kevin Holmes received plenty of attention from U of L's Pervis Ellison.

to make something happen if only the light would change and he could put the pedal to the metal. At least that's the way I saw it.

This had been a game that saw the Cardinals come out with a surprise starter in the second half, Kevin Walls. He performed admirably. DePaul was outscored 46-22 after intermission.

"Right now, after losing by 19 points, I feel a lot of pressure," said DePaul's Meyer.

Maybe Billy Packer was right. If you are not having fun, maybe it would be best to quit. But before the season would end Joey would have some fun as his team played some good games and made it to the NCAA Tourney. Nice going, Joey, and thank your dad for being just what he is — a heck of a nice man.

OVERALL RECORD: 18-7
CONFERENCE RECORD: 6-2

Game #26
Southern Mississippi
February 17

Four games was a long time to be on the road, so it was nice to return to the friendly confines of Freedom Hall. Southern Mississippi brought in a 14-9 record, but no one had forgotten how fortunate the Cardinals had been in defeating this same team in Hattiesburg back in January. And I mean REAL fortunate.

The Cards were on a three-game winning streak and playing well, but it would take a good effort to beat the Golden Eagles. This was a very quick team, quick with their hands, feet and jumping ability.

The fears proved to be accurate; Louisville was in a dogfight. Actually, Southern Miss outscored the Cardinals in field goals, 33-30, so it was at the foul line that the game was decided. The Cards made 23 of 29 attempts while the

Quickness was a key factor in the game against Southern Miss, demonstrated here by USM's Randolph Keys and the Cards' Milt Wagner.

LOUISVILLE

Player	FG	FGA	FT	FTA	REB	PF	TP	A	TO	BLK	S	MIN
Crook	6	9	2	3	8	4	14	1	2	0	1	30
Thompson	5	12	9	10	9	1	19	2	3	2	0	37
Ellison	6	13	5	7	13	1	17	4	1	2	3	37
Hall	5	9	5	6	3	3	15	1	3	0	0	32
Wagner	5	12	2	2	5	2	12	8	2	0	0	37
Kimbro	1	3	0	0	1	2	2	1	1	1	0	12
Payne	1	1	0	0	0	0	2	0	1	0	0	4
Walls	1	2	0	1	0	0	2	0	2	0	1	11
Team					2							
Deadball												
Rebounds					5							
Totals	30	61	23	29	41	13	83	17	15	5	5	200

FG%: 1st Half 56.7   2nd Half 41.9   Game 49.2
FT%: 1st Half 76.9   2nd Half 81.3   Game 79.3

SOUTHERN MISSISSIPPI

Player	FG	FGA	FT	FTA	REB	PF	TP	A	TO	BLK	S	MIN
White	2	7	0	0	5	4	4	1	4	0	0	26
Hamilton	13	17	1	1	7	4	27	0	1	1	1	39
Keys	2	8	2	4	4	4	6	3	0	1	2	31
Fisher	8	16	4	4	3	1	20	8	4	0	3	36
Siler	7	10	1	1	4	2	15	3	3	0	1	36
Jett	0	2	0	0	0	0	0	0	0	0	1	7
Brown	1	5	0	0	2	3	2	1	1	1	1	21
Hinton	0	0	0	0	0	1	0	0	1	0	0	4
Team					2							
Deadball												
Rebounds					2							
Totals	33	65	8	10	27	19	74	16	14	3	9	200

FG%: 1st Half 51.5   2nd Half 50.0   Game 50.8
FT%: 1st Half 100.0   2nd Half 75.0   Game 80.0

Halftime: Louisville 44, So. Miss 36
Attendance: 19,240

Golden Eagles were just 8 of 10. The Mississippi school outshot the Cards 50.8 percent to 49.2 percent, but the rebound totals were 41-27 in favor of the Cards.

Again, Southern Mississippi played well. But as happens a lot, smaller teams are very foul prone against larger teams and this night was a good example of that theory.

The game was close. At the 2:54 mark in the second half, Louisville led 75-72.

Again, all five Louisville starters were in double figures with Billy T. leading the way with 19. Pervis was close by with 17 and also won the rebounding contest with 13 big grabs. The Cards had been fortunate to get out with a win.

This Southern Miss team was a good team, one that will have to be dealt with next season. They had no senior starters.

"We're making progress," said Coach Turk, "and we are going to have to be contended with in the future."

As far as I was concerned, they had to be contended with this year.

But the Cards did just that.

OVERALL RECORD: 19-7
CONFERENCE RECORD: 7-2

Game #27
Florida State
February 19

During the month of February, the Cardinals had come up with a new twist. They would sorta slop it around in the first half and then surge in the second half. It was like the old fairy tale in reverse — the pumpkin would turn into a beautiful carriage.

DePaul was a perfect example. It happened again on this night.

Florida State had really been dealing with a lot of turmoil. By this time, head coach Joe Williams had already resigned, effective at the end of the season. He looked relaxed but gave me the same old answer when I asked for the interview, "See Rex." Rex Morgan was his right-hand assistant and he did it again.

Florida State helped the Cards a lot in the conference race. Not only did Louisville beat them twice but, out of the blue, the Seminoles would jump up and nail a defeat on poor ol' Dana Kirk three nights later. Now that's what I call a nice parting gesture as far as the Cards are concerned. For that, Joe, you are forgiven for not giving me the interviews. They would also help some more later on, but that's another story.

By the half of this game, Louisville led by a slim 34-31 margin. During the halftime break, however, they put on their "let's blow them out" face and returned to the court to do just that.

Bingo, it was over. Florida came out and went 2 for 16 from the field. The Cards were filling it up and by then it was over.

Pervis Ellison battled for a game-high 14 rebounds in the winning effort over the Seminoles.

Louisville got ahead by as many as 32 points and cruised in under the finish line with an 89-67 score.

It had been a night when Wagner was brilliant as he dumped 26 points upon the Seminoles in 31 minutes of action. That's close to a point per minute.

"I hit my first two shots and I started feeling my rhythm with the jumper," said Wagner.

Man, that must be some rhythm and it must feel real good. Pervis got all the rebounds (14), and the Cardinals cleaned the boards to the tune of 45 to FSU's 27. Again, Florida's fine player, Randy Allen was below par with just six points and six rebounds.

It was another conference win and a step closer to a chance to tie Memphis for the title. It seemed so remote after that earlier Cincinnati loss but "we ain't dead yet."

OVERALL RECORD: 20-7
CONFERENCE RECORD: 8-2

COMPLETE LOUISVILLE-FLORIDA STATE BOX SCORE

LOUISVILLE

Player	FG	FGA	FT	FTA	REB	PF	TP	A	TO	BLK	S	MIN
Crook	0	3	1	2	8	3	1	4	3	0	1	28
Thompson	4	9	5	7	5	1	13	1	5	1	1	29
Ellison	6	9	4	4	14	3	16	2	4	6	1	27
Hall	5	9	0	0	2	1	10	3	0	0	0	26
Wagner	12	16	2	2	4	1	26	4	4	0	6	31
Kimbro	4	4	0	0	2	2	8	4	1	0	0	19
Payne	2	7	2	2	5	2	6	1	0	0	0	16
Walls	1	2	3	4	2	0	5	2	1	0	0	7
Valentine	1	1	0	0	1	0	2	1	2	0	0	2
West	0	2	0	0	0	0	0	2	0	0	0	3
Olliges	1	2	0	0	1	1	2	1	0	0	0	6
Abram	0	2	0	0	0	1	0	0	2	0	0	6
Team					1							
Deadball												
Rebounds					1							
Totals	36	66	17	21	45	15	89	25	22	7	9	200

FG%: 1st Half	50.0	2nd Half 58.3	Game 54.5
FT%: 1st Half	100.0	2nd Half 76.5	Game 81.0

FLORIDA STATE

Player	FG	FGA	FT	FTA	REB	PF	TP	A	TO	BLK	S	MIN
Allen	2	9	2	6	6	2	6	1	4	0	2	28
Shaffer	6	13	3	4	12	4	15	3	6	1	4	29
Choice	1	6	0	2	2	1	2	0	4	0	0	27
Fitchett	3	5	0	0	1	1	6	0	1	0	3	22
Davis	2	3	1	2	1	4	5	0	1	0	2	31
Barber	9	12	0	0	0	0	18	3	3	0	0	33
McCloud	3	5	5	9	1	3	11	1	0	1	0	16
Mateer	0	1	0	0	0	0	0	0	1	0	0	1
Hunter	2	6	0	0	2	1	4	0	0	0	0	12
Carter	0	0	0	0	0	1	0	0	0	0	0	1
Team					2							
Deadball												
Rebounds					5							
Totals	28	60	11	23	27	17	67	8	20	2	13	200

FG%: 1st Half	55.6	2nd Half 39.4	Game 46.7
FT%: 1st Half	25.0	2nd Half 52.6	Game 47.8

Halftime: Louisville 34, Florida State 31
Attendance: 19,157

Game #28
Houston
February 22

More and more, every time the Cards entered a game, the opponent's coach had decided to throw in the towel. In this case it was a gaudy looking red towel that any legitimate basketball fan would recognize. Most had seen Coach Guy Lewis bury his head in it during previous NCAA tournaments.

Coach Lewis had been a good one all the way and had earned the right to "live a little." I asked him in the interview what he intended on doing with retirement , and he told me, "I intend to do whatever it takes to enjoy myself." I think he may have been thinking about a little fishing, a little traveling with his wife wherever he chose to go, and maybe a little golf, and for sure, a little peace of mind.

Tony Kimbro turned in a fine performance in the win with seven points, seven rebounds and three blocked shots.

Again, here was a big-timer, graciously agreeing to be interviewed. Like I said earlier, the really good ones are the people who are the easiest to deal with. I even took his and Coach Crum's picture together. How nice can you be?

Well, the team did its routine of stand around and goof off during the first 20 minutes, light the torch, and blast-o they went in the second half. I was having a hard time getting through those first-half blahs, so you can imagine how the coaches felt. Houston led 30-28 at the half. "Never Nervous Pervis" got it going after intermission and finished the game with 25 points, seven rebounds, five assists, four blocked shots and two steals. All this came after being named Player of the Week in the Metro Conference the week before. Billy T. came through with 17 points and 9 rebounds in another fine all-around performance.

It was really a super second half for the Cards and the final margin of victory was 76-59. Louisville outscored the Cougars 48-29 in the final 20 minutes of play.

You know, it would have been nice for all the Cardinal fans if U of L would get its 20-point leads in the first half and then goof around a little down the stretch, but the thrill of the finish would have been dull. Wouldn't that have been nice and relaxing? I imagine!

It was hard for me to believe the crowd that attended the game. They said 5,000, but I think it was more like 4,000. I guess I'm spoiled with the way fans are in the state of Kentucky. In this state, if Louisville or Kentucky were

COMPLETE LOUISVILLE-HOUSTON BOX SCORE
LOUISVILLE

Player	FG	FGA	FT	FTA	REB	PF	TP	A	TO	BLK	S	MIN
Crook	4	9	1	2	7	3	9	2	3	1	0	29
Thompson	7	12	3	5	9	4	17	3	2	0	1	25
Ellison	12	17	1	1	7	4	25	5	1	4	2	38
Hall	5	9	0	0	4	2	10	5	3	0	1	36
Wagner	3	11	2	2	2	2	8	6	4	0	1	37
Kimbro	3	6	1	1	7	0	7	3	1	3	0	25
Payne	0	1	0	0	0	0	0	1	0	0	0	6
Walls	0	1	0	0	0	0	0	0	0	0	0	4
Team					3							
Deadball												
Rebounds					2							
Totals	**34**	**66**	**8**	**11**	**39**	**15**	**76**	**25**	**14**	**8**	**5**	**200**

FG%: 1st Half 40.6   2nd Half 61.8   Game 51.5
FT%: 1st Half 50.0   2nd Half 85.7   Game 72.7

HOUSTON

Player	FG	FGA	FT	FTA	REB	PF	TP	A	TO	BLK	S	MIN
Belcher	4	8	1	2	6	5	9	0	3	0	0	26
Anderson	5	18	4	10	15	3	14	1	2	2	4	40
Jackson	0	3	1	2	5	1	1	7	5	0	1	28
McGee	4	7	1	1	2	1	9	1	2	0	0	23
Franklin	6	19	6	7	0	0	18	4	1	1	3	40
Rivera	2	4	0	0	3	0	4	0	2	0	0	14
Russell	0	1	0	0	2	3	0	0	2	0	0	13
Hobby	1	1	0	0	0	1	2	0	0	0	0	2
Smith	0	0	0	1	0	0	0	0	0	0	0	5
Small	1	2	0	0	3	0	2	0	1	0	0	9
Team					5							
Deadball												
Rebounds					3							
Totals	**23**	**63**	**13**	**23**	**41**	**14**	**59**	**13**	**18**	**3**	**8**	**200**

FG%: 1st Half 37.5   2nd Half 35.5   Game 36.5
FT%: 1st Half 54.6   2nd Half 58.3   Game 56.5

Halftime: Houston 30, Louisville 28
Attendance: 5,125

playing, Lady Godiva could drive by in a 1956 Chevrolet convertible, stark naked on a 90-degree day, throwing away $10 bills and kissing all the men, but nobody would see her, her money or her car. They would all be inside watching the game. Well, maybe Van Vance would be out there. After all, how long could it take her to drive by? He might sneak a peek, grab a couple of bills, taste her sweet lips and THEN run back inside. Am I exaggerating?

OVERALL RECORD: 21-7
CONFERENCE RECORD: 8-2

Game #29
South Alabama
February 24

The truth about this game was that the Cards needed the rest a lot more than they needed the game. But when the schedule was made, this was not a known fact.

Nevertheless, this was serious business time and I didn't think they needed a game just to be playing.

This game came between a national television game and a very important conference game, but it was there and had to be played. As you might expect, it was an opponent that played a slow tempo and that's always a tough style for the Louisville team to face.

The Cards were a pop music team, not a waltz team. That's about how a tempo team plays. It's a good style if you are a little short on talent, but it's not for the Cards.

It turned out OK, but I don't think anyone enjoyed it. Jeff Hall pretty well summed it up by saying, "It's frustrating to play like that." It's frustrating to watch them play like that, is what I said.

South Alabama's Darrell Faulkner finished with 14 points despite the defensive efforts of Milt Wagner.

This was an opponent that came into the game with an even 15-15 record and usually kept their opponent in the high 40s or low 50s. It was about like watching grass grow or paint dry. Only Wagner got as many as 10 shots. Boring, Boring.

"We're on a roll right now," said Wagner.

It was more of a crawl than a roll. If Louisville played that style of game, those 19,000-plus fans would disappear like ripe tomatoes in July. It would be amazing how the sport of bowling would grow in Louisville. I would probably order some shoes myself. I don't condemn anyone for that style, but it's just not for the folks in the Bluegrass State.

Louisville led 31-22 at the half and by the end of this affair it was Louisville 66, South Alabama 55. Neither team took 50 shots at the basket. That's like looking at a photo album with no photos in it. Yuk. On second thought, maybe the Cards got a chance to rest after all. Yes, that's what happened.

OVERALL RECORD: 22-7
CONFERENCE RECORD: 8-2

COMPLETE LOUISVILLE-SOUTH ALABAMA BOX SCORE
LOUISVILLE

Player	FG	FGA	FT	FTA	REB	PF	TP	A	TO	BLK	S	MIN
Crook	4	5	5	7	2	2	13	1	1	2	2	33
Thompson	4	9	3	4	5	4	11	2	4	1	0	24
Ellison	4	8	1	2	6	4	9	2	2	1	1	30
Hall	2	4	0	0	5	0	4	4	2	0	0	30
Wagner	6	10	0	0	5	1	12	2	2	0	2	36
Kimbro	4	6	1	1	2	4	9	3	3	1	0	28
Payne	3	3	0	0	1	0	6	0	1	0	0	4
Walls	1	2	0	0	0	0	2	2	1	0	0	13
Valentine	0	0	0	0	0	0	0	0	1	0	0	4
West	0	0	0	0	1	0	0	0	1	0	0	1
Team					2							
Deadball Rebounds					2							
Totals	28	47	10	14	27	15	66	16	18	5	5	200

FG%: 1st Half 48.0 2nd Half 72.7 Game 59.6
FT%: 1st Half 63.6 2nd Half 100.0 Game 71.4

SOUTH ALABAMA

Player	FG	FGA	FT	FTA	REB	PF	TP	A	TO	BLK	S	MIN
Brown	5	6	5	5	3	2	15	2	4	0	0	31
Butts	5	11	0	2	3	2	10	1	2	0	1	33
Waiteman	1	5	2	4	1	5	4	1	1	0	3	26
Faulkner	7	12	0	0	2	1	14	1	4	0	0	35
Hodge	1	4	0	0	2	1	2	4	1	0	3	38
Stanley	1	2	0	0	1	2	2	0	0	0	1	9
Osbourne	1	2	0	0	3	0	2	0	0	0	0	11
Kortokrax	3	6	0	0	2	4	6	1	2	0	0	17
Team					4							
Deadball Rebounds					3							
Totals	24	48	7	13	21	17	55	10	14	0	8	200

FG%: 1st Half 45.5 2nd Half 53.8 Game 50.0
FT%: 1st Half 33.3 2nd Half 71.4 Game 53.8

Halftime: Louisville 31, South Alabama 22
Attendance: 19,063

Game #30
South Carolina
February 26

Another ho-hum first half. Nothing to get serious about. But in this particular game, it almost spelled doom.

It was in this game the Cards would be alloted, by the man upstairs, two of the biggest breaks they would get in all of the regular-season games. Both would come with the clock showing under a minute to play.

The first break came when, with time becoming scarce, Herbert Crook got tied up. It just happened to be Louisville's ball out of bounds in the fairly new alternate ball possession rule. It could easily have been the other way, but that's the luck of the draw.

There was a timeout and, for sure, Louisville would try to keep the ball for the 45-second limit. The Gamecocks, obviously, would strive to make that difficult while at the same time prevent any and all easy shot opportunities.

The clock ran almost down to the limit. In desperation, Milt Wagner, who had the ball directly in front of the Cardinal bench, sorta ducked under the arms of two South Carolina players. He let it fly from about 20 feet. I saw Milt lean towards the basket and I heard the whistle. My immediate thought was "offensive charge." After all, we were on the road, and from where Van and I were sitting it could have been a charge. But the official signaled the foul on the defensive man, Terry Dozier. Only two seconds remained.

That was a monumental break. Even if it was a defensive foul, it was still a break to get it called that way.

"It was a foul, no question about it," said Denny Crum, who went on to give the official credit for calling it by saying, "It takes guts on an official's part to make that call."

The official, Dan Woolridge, was retiring at the end of the season. "I never came close to touching him," said Dozier. "He hit me on the arm," explained Ice, "and it threw my whole shot off."

"It was a charge in my way of thinking," said an angry Bill Foster.

The official was right on the play, almost in the play, so he had a perfect view of what happened. So that's the way it went. I'll always believe that the official's call on that single play was the best break the Cardinals received all year and, oh my, how important it was for the Louisville team! Mainly, it set up the showdown for the big game in Louisville against Memphis State that would determine the title.

It's just a fact that you have to get a break somewhere along the way to make things happen. That was two of them right there.

Naturally, Milt stepped to the line and automatically buried both shots. Louisville won 65-63.

The game itself was not that much. Tony Kimbro played

Gamecock coach Bill Foster was unhappy with a call that sent U of L's Milt Wagner to the free-throw line with two seconds left. Wagner made both, giving the Cards the win and setting up the match with Memphis State to determine the league title.

a magnificent role as a reserve and shot in 13 points. Kenny Payne hit four last-minute free throws in the first half to keep the Cards from going in the locker room down by a whopping 11 points. Being down by just five, 40-35, made it much easier to look forward to the final 20 minutes.

It was a game that pretty much saw the Cardinal seniors become almost invisible. There were foul problems and shot problems. Can you imagine Wagner, Thompson and Hall getting just 15 shots between them, hitting just six and still getting out of Columbia alive and kicking? Believe me, on that particular day there were times when I was about ready to put out the fire and load the dogs in the trunk because this hunt was over. For sure, on that day someone from way up in the sky was looking over the Cardinals' shoulders and

COMPLETE LOUISVILLE-SOUTH CAROLINA BOX SCORE

LOUISVILLE

Player	FG	FGA	FT	FTA	REB	PF	TP	A	TO	BLK	S	MIN
Crook	4	5	5	7	7	3	13	1	2	0	1	36
Thompson	2	4	3	4	2	4	7	3	4	1	0	18
Ellison	8	12	2	4	11	3	18	1	1	3	1	39
Hall	1	3	0	0	2	4	2	3	3	0	2	25
Wagner	3	8	2	2	4	3	8	4	2	2	2	37
Kimbro	6	9	1	2	3	3	13	1	3	1	1	31
Payne	0	3	4	4	1	1	4	0	2	0	1	13
Walls	0	1	0	0	0	0	0	0	2	0	0	1
Team					2							
Deadball												
Rebounds					3							
Totals	**24**	**55**	**17**	**23**	**32**	**21**	**65**	**13**	**19**	**7**	**8**	**200**

FG%: 1st Half 57.1 2nd Half 50.0 Game 53.8
FT%: 1st Half 73.3 2nd Half 75.0 Game 73.9

SOUTH CAROLINA

Player	FG	FGA	FT	FTA	REB	PF	TP	A	TO	BLK	S	MIN
Moye	5	11	1	4	7	4	11	3	2	0	2	33
T. Dozier	5	11	0	1	6	3	10	3	3	0	2	39
Martin	1	4	4	5	6	2	6	2	3	0	2	37
James	8	13	0	4	5	0	16	1	1	0	2	35
Foster	7	13	3	3	2	4	17	2	6	0	3	39
Kendall	0	1	1	2	1	3	1	0	1	0	1	9
Holland	1	2	0	0	2	0	2	0	1	1	0	6
P. Dozier	0	0	0	0	0	0	0	0	0	0	0	2
Team					0							
Deadball												
Rebounds					1							
Totals	**27**	**53**	**9**	**14**	**29**	**16**	**63**	**11**	**17**	**1**	**12**	**200**

FG%: 1st Half 54.5 2nd Half 40.9 Game 49.1
FT%: 1st Half 50.0 2nd Half 45.5 Game 47.4

Halftime: South Carolina 40, Louisville 35
Attendance: 6,071

giving them the push they needed when they needed it. I never took a deep breath until the Ice Man stood at the foul line. Then, I knew it was all over for the Gamecocks.

OVERALL RECORD: 23-7
CONFERENCE RECORD: 9-2

Game #31
Memphis State
March 2

Who'da thunk it! As late as the first week of February, Memphis was 5-1 in the conference and Virginia Tech was 4-2 while lowly Louisville was in third place at 2-2. Now, approximately three weeks later, the Cardinals would play for the undisputed league championship.

I think practically everyone had considered this to be a remote possibility. Some of the players had made comments following the Cincinnati loss that there was still hope, but most believed those remarks to be just optimistic hope.

Well, the Cardinals backed up their statements with wins, and Memphis helped the cause with a loss to Florida State. About all the Cardinal fans had to lean on was what they said about the fat lady, and so far, no one had heard a note.

This was the day it would happen. Memphis State and Louisville had identical records, 9 wins and 2 losses. A victory would bring no automatic NCAA bids, but it could influence a higher seed in the pairings of the NCAA Tournament. There was a lot of prestige at stake. Memphis had lived high in the polls all winter. Now it was time to find out who was the best team on this day.

Louisville's seniors were introduced to the 19,582 fans as their last official home game. They received the applause and all the goodies that go with the final game ceremony. It was nice and all enjoyed, except the Memphis State Tigers. Coach Dana Kirk paced the sidelines. He was so hoarse that he could hardly speak.

I had done my pre-game interview with one of the nicest assistants in the business, Coach Lee Fowler. Someday, I expect to pick up the paper and see where he has been hired as top dog by some good Division I school. He'll make a good one.

Game time approached and Freedom Hall was bubbling over with Cardinal fever. Most of the Cardinal fans were about to have a nervous breakdown.

Besides the score, the big stat on that day was rebounding. The Cards won that battle 36-29. This time, Pervis Ellison was healthy and Mr. William Bedford, the post man for Memphis State, discovered that Pervis played a little better when healthy. Pervis totaled 18 points and 8 rebounds on the afternoon. The bulk of those points came in the crucial second half.

MSU's Andre Turner fouls Milt Wagner from behind on this play as the game is about to end. "Ice" calmly sank both free throws, giving the Cards a 70-69 win and the regular-season championship.

Both teams shot right at the 50 percent mark and both teams had 14 personal fouls, but the 14th foul for Memphis spelled doom for the Tigers. It sent a guy to the line who had made his last 48 of 50 attempts, Milt Wagner. Can you imagine anyone hitting 48 of 50 free throws in real live games?

Louisville was behind one point at the time, 69-68. Heck, most of the Cardinal fans were getting ready to beat the crowd and had begun to pack up and leave.

With the Ice Man on the line, it was time to turn the lights out and go home. The chances of him missing were about the same as getting a full grown elephant into a Volkswagon. No chance, and that's the way it ended. Wag split the hoop, dead center, and it was back on I-65 South for the Tigers — losers on this day.

However, I left out about how Andre Turner, the dynamic

guard for Memphis, toed the free-throw line with a one-point lead and just eight seconds left on the clock. This guy was a great free-throw shooter. "I felt like I was holding blue-chip stock with Andre on the line," said Kirk later.

This was one of Louisville's top three breaks of the year. Turner missed the front end and Louisville received one of its top four breaks of the year. Turner slashed down the court at full speed, only to catch Milt in the deep corner of his offensive court, made possible by a heady outlet pass to Milt from Billy Thompson. Turner chose to foul him on what was a very difficult shot. It was only Milt's reputation as a crunch-time player that brought on the foul, a compliment for the Louisville player.

The rest is history. The regular-season championship belonged in Louisville at the University of Louisville, home of the Cardinals. It made you kind of proud when you heard those beautiful notes coming from the fat lady out yonder. It was over and it had been a quality basketball game.

How did it happen like that? Simple answer, there is only one real ICE MAN.

OVERALL RECORD: 24-7
CONFERENCE RECORD: 10-2

The game's two giants, Pervis Ellison and William Bedford, went head-to-head in a classic match-up.

COMPLETE LOUISVILLE-MEMPHIS STATE BOX SCORE
LOUISVILLE

Player	FG	FGA	FT	FTA	REB	PF	TP	A	TO	BLK	S	MIN
Crook	3	8	4	4	9	4	10	1	3	0	0	36
Thompson	8	10	0	2	6	2	16	3	4	2	1	36
Ellison	8	13	2	3	8	1	18	2	0	1	0	40
Hall	2	9	0	0	2	0	4	7	1	0	1	33
Wagner	8	19	2	2	4	2	18	4	5	0	0	39
Kimbro	2	3	0	0	3	5	4	3	0	0	0	14
McSwain	0	0	0	0	1	0	0	0	0	0	0	2
Team					3							
Deadball Rebounds					2							
Totals	31	62	8	11	36	14	70	20	13	3	2	200

FG%: 1st Half 50.0   2nd Half 50.0   Game 50.0
FT%: 1st Half 100.0   2nd Half 50.0   Game 72.7

MEMPHIS STATE

Player	FG	FGA	FT	FTA	REB	PF	TP	A	TO	BLK	S	MIN
Askew	2	7	0	0	6	1	4	2	2	1	3	38
Holmes	8	13	3	4	8	3	19	0	1	1	0	34
Bedford	6	11	3	4	4	3	15	1	1	2	0	40
Turner	8	14	2	3	3	2	18	5	4	1	2	40
Boyd	4	10	4	4	2	2	12	4	1	0	1	36
Alexander	0	2	1	2	2	3	1	1	0	0	0	12
Team					2							
Deadball Rebounds					2							
Totals	28	57	13	17	27	14	69	13	9	5	6	200

FG%: 1st Half 56.3   2nd Half 40.0   Game 49.1
FT%: 1st Half 83.3   2nd Half 72.7   Game 76.5

Halftime: Memphis State 41, Louisville 37
Attendance: 19,582

CHAPTER

3

Travel Tough via the Metro

The Metro Conference is a league where you meet a lot of very nice people. The Metro's commissioner, Steve Hatchell, is a prince of a person. When you talk to Steve it doesn't take you long to realize he's a first-class person. He's efficient, has a good sense of humor and mixes with everyone. There's never any telling when he'll pop up at a game.

His assistant, Craig Thompson, is the same way. Craig does a lot of the leg work for the conference and makes a good impression on those he deals with, especially the media.

Both of them showed up for Louisville's game in Columbia against South Carolina this past season, and I had a chance to visit with them. We met in the lounge of the Carolina Inn, the hotel where the team stayed, and we talked at length about the seven-team league as it currently stands. It was obvious that Commissioner Hatchell preferred an additional team in the league, something Denny Crum is opposed to. But we talked some about possible candidates and I mentioned that I thought the new basketball program at the University of Miami in Florida would be a good catch for the league, although he indicated that wasn't very probable. Actually, I was looking for a nice warm climate to visit in midwinter. I also mentioned West Virginia as a possibility and he indicated, at least to my recollection, that might be feasible at a later date. Overall, though, it was a nice visit. Heck, the gentleman even treated me to a nice "toddy" for my old and tired body.

I really like the cities and towns the conference schedule takes us to, but I never have understood why the league is called the Metropolitan Collegiate Athletic Conference. Metro sounds of big cities like Chicago or Philadelphia but, for sure, not Blacksburg, Virginia or Hattiesburg, Mississippi. Actually, Metro was apropos when the league was formed back on July 13, 1975. There were six charter members — Cincinnati, Georgia Tech, Louisville, Memphis State, St. Louis and Tulane — and all were located in very large metropolitan areas. That's since changed, but I prefer the smaller towns anyway.

The Metro Conference is pretty much the forgotten child

as far as all the "media experts" in the country are concerned. You always hear about the Big East, ACC, SEC and the Big Ten. There is usually something about the Metro Conference if you look long and hard enough, but I don't think the teams other than Louisville and Memphis State get enough respect. All Louisville fans know how tough it is to win at Virginia Tech and I've personally witnessed losses to Southern Miss in Hattiesburg, Florida State in Tallahassee and South Carolina in Columbia. All of this didn't happen in one season, but it happened. And don't forget how Cincinnati has come to Louisville and left with victories in each of the past two seasons!

Virginia Tech was ranked in the top 20 almost all of this past season, and Florida State upset Memphis State when the Tigers were ranked very high in the polls. Overall, the Metro Conference is a good, competitive league and underrated. The league posted a 7-2 record in NCAA Tournament play this past year. Louisville, obviously, had six of those victories, but that doesn't really matter because Louisville is in the Metro. Last year when Memphis State was in the Final Four, they were in the Metro Conference. As a matter of fact, Louisville's appearance in the 1986 Final Four marked the fifth time in the last seven years the Metro had been represented in the Final Four. Whatever these teams accomplish is also an accomplishment by the league.

Enough said.

Conference play is really the part of the season I like the best. It's more of an informal time. It's easier to visit with the players, but it's also a very competitive time. U of L's traveling party is small, normally about 24 people, but you are always in familiar surroundings and around familiar people when you travel within the league. The coaches are more laid back, but they probably would tell you they are always laid back. We all travel on the same bus and, in general, it's pretty much a family affair. Even the restaurants are convenient and reasonable in the cities that house Metro opponents.

Traveling is almost always done in casual clothes — not the coats and ties you see some teams wearing — which I think is great for the players. They still look nice and are comfortable without choking on ties. They are allowed to have their music, which is good for morale.

In other words, traveling with U of L is not a regimented affair and the players are always polite and nice to people.

Many of them carry textbooks along and do a little classwork on the plane or bus. The Cardinals always have nice buses to travel on and nice accomodations. Trainer Jerry May is the "trail boss" in these matters and he makes sure everything is A-OK.

Everybody knows the dos and don'ts of traveling. Coach Jerry Jones, for example, always rides in the front left seat and May sits in the front right seat. You might get away with sitting in Coach Jones' seat, but even Denny doesn't fool around with May's resting spot. Most of the time, Denny usually sits beside either Jones or May, but the head coach may just plop it down anywhere.

It never fails while traveling with the Cards, once everybody is on the bus the word "McDonald's" can be heard from the rear where all the players hang out. These Cardinals can smell a McDonald's from 25 miles away. There's no way to slip past one without it being pointed out.

A lot of the meals are eaten in airports. It's just a good policy to get there early, eliminating any problems of being late. Everybody always seems to carry the same things, trip after trip. For sure, you've gotta have a walkman, everyone has a walkman, unless you are a gin player like Denny, Bobby Dotson and Wade Houston. Sports information director Kenny Klein can always be found holding a little case that has just about everything in it imaginable. If you need it, Kenny has it. Doc Ellis and Jerry May always have their medical bags handy with, I'm sure, enough stuff in them to handle a train wreck. Denny has the cards and the players always have something to eat stuck in their pockets. Heck, traveling with this bunch, you could make it marooned on an island for at least a couple of weeks!

As a rule, Van Vance and I always sat together, usually close to the other media along on the trip. Russ Brown of *The Courier-Journal* was usually with us as was Jim Terhune of *The Louisville Times*. Terhune, however, had a bad stroke of luck at midseason and got asssigned to cover the University of Kentucky. I missed him, especially when he used to tell us all how to live on $10 a week and still be able to breathe.

Life in the motels is also very casual. We all pretty much live by the itinerary passed out by either May or Klein. The team usually eats in a separate dining room (prearranged by May) and it's always a well-planned meal. There are other times when the players are given money to eat on their own.

May is very particular about the arrangements for the players. He doesn't like it when things aren't exactly the way

Jack Bogaczyk, president of the MCSWBA, awarded Virginia Tech's Dell Curry the league's Most Outstanding Player award.

he ordered. During this past season while in South Carolina, Van and I went down to eat breakfast. May was already there with Dr. Ellis.

He was steaming. First, he had asked for a room where the players could look at video tapes of South Carolina, but was having a problem. Adding insult to injury, the previous night he was conducting a "bed check" and the house detective had given him a hard time. He thought Jerry had been disturbing the guests. Well, the trainer was very unhappy about the whole ordeal and it's my guess that those two events will mean a new home on next season's visit to Columbia. May, the man with the money sack, does a terrific job looking out for the athletes.

Play in the Metro Conference takes the Cards to Cincinnati (Ohio), Tallahassee (Florida), Memphis (Tennessee), Columbia (South Carolina), Hattiesburg (Mississippi) and Blacksburg (Virginia). Conference headquarters is located in Atlanta (Georgia), picked because of its central location — you can't get to any of the Metro schools without first stopping in Atlanta. Memphis is the largest of the seven towns with almost a million people. At the other end of the spectrum, Blacksburg is the smallest town with 30,000 people.

For some reason, it doesn't seem to matter which of the conference towns we visit because it's always cold and rainy. Of the accomodations, the best is the Hyatt Regency in Memphis while the worst is the Ramada Inn in Hattiesburg. Still, all are plenty good enough.

It's obvious Louisville is the biggest drawing card in the league. Everywhere the Cards go the opponent always expects its best crowd. I guess the fans in Memphis are the rowdiest, but everything always seems to be under control. For good measure, there are two Louisville policemen at these games to give Coach Crum some security and be of assistance to people in the Louisville traveling party. They drive to these games in a rental car and that takes dedication. But it's really nice having these people on the trips. It's reassuring, plus I just think it shows a little class. They were very pleasant people and, for sure, big Cardinal fans.

What really makes traveling so pleasant is that every member of the normal traveling party is a first-class person and a pleasure to be around. Traveling with the Cardinals is a terrific experience, one I love.

But it's fans, fans and more fans who make the Metro Conference work. The figures for home attendance in the league tell you something: Louisville (346, 782), Memphis State (179,200), Virginia Tech (109,836), Cincinnati (79,551), South Carolina (75,839), Florida State (57,232) and Hattiesburg (53,947). The Cardinals almost doubled the attendance of second-place Memphis.

Besides the automatic bid, the conference is important for another reason. It serves as a planning point of the season as well as a new incentive come January. As a league member, a team plays a pre-conference schedule where all the experimentation takes place. Pre-league games serve as a building period, a time to get ready for conference play and gain some valuable lessons of playing on the road.

Conference play puts a team in a lot of "must" situations. League wins are important and a conference win is more than just a win. It's a time when players can and must get tough. In Louisville's case, it's the conference travel which makes the Cards "travel tough." Some of the sites in the Metro are hard to get to, which teaches the players patience and mental toughness.

How important is playing in a conference? Just imagine what the two late-season wins over Memphis State this past year meant in preparing the Cardinals for NCAA play. There was no tougher game or opponent than the Tigers when the Cards met them for the regular-season crown. Louisville had no closer call than that game during late-season play. It was the conference and the important rewards of winning the conference that created all the pressures that these games were played under. The experience gained in these kinds of games is invaluable in developing the kind of toughness needed for the NCAA Tournament drive. The battle for the league crown was a toughness builder, a gut-checker and a man-maker.

Personally, I think the Metro Conference can hold its own with just about any other league. As long as you have to play at home and at their place, a lot of teams can be tough to beat. In retrospect, the Cardinals owe the conference members a "hats-off thanks" for forcing them to reach down and get that little extra that was hard to find. The other six teams in the league deserve a litle piece of U of L's championship because it took a lot of toughness on the part of Louisville to win it all. They got some of it at Hattiesburg, Columbia and Memphis.

As Herbert Crook said during an interview when asked about Pervis Ellison being so tough under pressure, "He's ice, just like all the rest of us." That's all that needs to be said.

The next time someone wants to put down the Metro Conference, remind them that in the last seven years, two of the national championship titles went to a Metro Conference member.

CHAPTER

Bye-bye Memphis, Hello NCAA

This was the week the Cardinals could win the automatic bid to the NCAA Tournament. It really didn't seem like a big deal at the time because Louisville was already a cinch to get an invitation to the big show anyway.

Wrong! It just so happened that it was a big deal to the Cards because getting there and getting there with a good seeding were two different things. Winning the Metro Tournament almost assured Louisville of getting a No. 2 seed. That meant they would be ranked in the second group of the four-best teams in the country and, thus, scattered around in the NCAA Tournament brackets.

The NCAA selection committee does the seedings to assure that they have the best teams divided among all the four regions. For example, had the Cardinals not won the league tourney and not received a No. 2 seed, they could very easily have been sent to Baton Rouge, Louisiana, where they would have had to face LSU on its home court. Coach Gene Keady of Purdue and Coach Dana Kirk of Memphis State got that kind of deal. Ask them about it and you'll get a real nasty answer, quickly. They both had the task of playing LSU in Baton Rouge and both came out with a one-way ticket home. Their "Destination Dallas" dreams were gone. Season completed. But with the No. 2 seed, U of L was sent to Ogden (Utah) to face Drexel.

With all this understood, it was time for the Cards to get on with the task of winning the Metro Conference Tournament. Since they had won the league's regular-season crown, Louisville received a bye in the first round which meant an added day's rest. They could "cool it" and sit back to watch the other six teams knock each other around. Wasn't it fun?

There are different opinions about which is better: play the extra game to get into the flow of the tournament or just enjoy and wait your turn. Assistant coach Jerry Jones likes the bye, "There is a distinct advantage to needing only two games to win the tournament while the other teams must win three." I like his answer and agree with him.

Louisville played the winner of the Cincinnati-Southern Mississippi contest. Before their opponent was known, however, the Louisville players and coaches would probably have said they really didn't care which of the two teams it would be, but my choice was to play Cincinnati. USM's speed and quickness seemed to be something to avoid, if possible. As it turned out, I got my wish because the Bearcats defeated Southern Miss 75-74.

By Saturday afternoon, I was ready for the Cards to take the court. I had seen all the first-round games (Memphis State easily defeated South Carolina and Florida State upset Virginia Tech) and was anxious to see Louisville in action. That morning I leaped out of bed, put my red and black on, positioned my lucky white hat and yelled at my wife, P.J., to hurry up and get ready. I had wanted to go to Methodist

U of L fan Randall Baron came dressed to win at the Metro Tournament.

Evangelical Hospital to see Gene and Betty Layman. Gene had suffered a stroke one week earlier during the Louisville-Memphis State game that decided the regular-season champion.

Since we live in Lexington, we'd spent the night in downtown Louisville at the Howard Johnson hotel. As always, we left for Freedom Hall so we'd get there two hours before game time. As we were casually driving along, I remarked to P.J. that Methodist seemed to be a really great hospital and if I ever had to go to a hospital in Louisville it would be my choice.

It was a beautiful day and a nice ride to Freedom Hall. I pulled over in the exit lane on I-65 South to get off on Crittenden Drive. There was a line of cars ahead of me so I made my stop and, by habit, glanced into the rear-view mirror. That's when I realized this was going to be a very, very bad day. There, in my mirror, was a 1970 4-door tank of some make just a mere 10 to 12 feet behind that was about to say "hello" to the rear end of my automobile. This car was really moving when "whamo!" All I could hear was the ugly sound of steel meeting steel. In the meantime, P.J. looked like a shake-and-bake pork chop in a cellophane bag as she bounced around inside the car. My head said "hello" to the windshield. Then, all of a sudden, it became very quiet.

By now, I was fully aware that I should have chosen another route. Next came an assessment of injuries and a

P.J. Sutherland enjoyed some dancing at the Metro Tournament reception at the Galt House.

COMPLETE LOUISVILLE-CINCINNATI BOX SCORE

LOUISVILLE

Player	FG	FGA	FT	FTA	REB	PF	TP	A	TO	BLK	S	MIN
Crook	3	3	13	15	4	3	19	4	3	0	2	28
Thompson	5	9	3	3	7	4	13	2	5	1	1	26
Ellison	2	5	3	6	7	3	7	4	2	3	1	27
Hall	5	7	6	6	2	0	16	1	1	0	0	25
Wagner	1	5	3	6	1	3	5	2	5	0	1	26
Kimbro	0	0	0	2	3	1	0	1	0	0	0	12
McSwain	1	2	3	4	5	1	5	1	2	0	0	11
Walls	2	3	2	2	0	1	6	0	1	0	1	11
Valentine	0	2	0	0	0	0	0	1	0	0	0	4
Payne	1	3	1	3	5	3	3	0	1	0	0	10
West	2	2	2	3	0	2	6	0	1	0	0	6
Olliges	0	0	0	0	0	0	0	0	0	0	0	4
Abram	2	3	2	3	1	1	6	1	2	0	2	9
Robinson	0	0	0	0	2	2	0	0	0	0	0	1
Team					3							
Deadball												
Rebounds					6							
Totals	**24**	**44**	**38**	**53**	**40**	**24**	**86**	**17**	**23**	**4**	**8**	**200**

FG%: 1st Half	70.6	2nd Half	44.4	Game 54.5
FT%: 1st Half	64.0	2nd Half	78.6	Game 71.7

CINCINNATI

Player	FG	FGA	FT	FTA	REB	PF	TP	A	TO	BLK	S	MIN
Henry	0	1	2	6	4	4	2	2	1	0	2	40
Hughes	5	13	2	3	5	5	12	3	3	1	0	23
Helm	3	8	0	0	4	3	6	0	2	0	0	19
Wilson	0	0	0	0	3	3	0	3	5	0	1	23
McClendon	6	11	1	2	2	3	13	1	1	0	2	27
Glover	1	2	0	0	2	5	2	0	2	0	0	9
Pfiffer	3	6	2	2	1	3	8	3	5	0	3	21
Shorter	2	2	0	0	0	4	4	1	1	0	1	5
Hodges	0	2	1	1	1	1	1	0	0	0	0	4
Ruehl	0	2	0	0	0	0	0	0	0	0	0	7
Stiffend	1	7	5	8	1	4	7	0	2	2	1	25
Jackson	2	3	1	1	1	1	5	0	1	0	0	7
Flynn	1	2	3	5	5	2	5	0	0	0	1	10
Team					3							
Deadball												
Rebounds					3							
Totals	**24**	**59**	**17**	**28**	**32**	**38**	**65**	**13**	**23**	**3**	**11**	**200**

FG%: 1st Half	29.6	2nd Half	50.0	Game 40.7
FT%: 1st Half	54.5	2nd Half	64.7	Game 60.7

Halftime: Louisville 40, Cincinnati 22
Attendance: 19,452

wait for the ambulance. I seemed to be OK, outside of a pretty good cut on my head that was emptying what little blood I had on everything and everyone in the car. I think it's the first time I've really been awake in a long time. P.J. was banged up pretty good.

The paramedics showed up and they were super in the way they handled everything. If that wasn't bad enough, it was then that I heard the worst news I would hear all day. The paramedic was on the remote phone to his headquarters when I heard him say, "Somebody had better call Freedom Hall and tell Van Vance of WHAS Radio that Jock won't be there today." I had already thought about that and it hurt me worse than any of the injuries I had suffered.

Plan No. 2 popped into my mind: find a TV somewhere. We were taken to Methodist, naturally, as my choice of a hospital came a little sooner than I had anticipated. As I expected, they were marvelous the way they cared for us. Dr. John Ellis came from Freedom Hall to check us over. My wife was admitted and once I was convinced there were no problems, I found a TV and watched the game against Cincinnati.

They had me lying in the emergency room on a stretcher, with a big, goofy neck brace on. I was totally helpless but they did it as a precaution. After it was known that I was OK, this little nurse came over to me with her University of Kentucky button on and drinking out of a big, blue cup. She smiled and asked, "Are you the Jock Sutherland that I hear on the talk show — Sound Off?" I nodded yes but then she asked, "When was the last time anyone poured Coke up your nose?"

That would have been worse than the wreck as far as I was concerned. Actually, she just wanted me to know that she

Cardinal Bird Beth Mattingly and a young friend got acquainted during the tournament.

was a Kentucky fan. She laughed and proceeded to give my wife and I the best of care, but, for a second there, she had me worried.

Since I had to miss one, the game against Cincinnati turned out to be a good one to miss. It turned out to be a fouling contest. Louisville jumped out to a 40-22 halftime lead and the game was just about history. This Bearcat unit, the same team that had downed the mighty Cards back on Jan. 20, was not anywhere close to being competitive. They shot a lousy 29.6 percent from the field in the first half while the Cards hit a blistering 70.6 percent. Wow!

The second half was about like a pick-up game in the park, no holds barred, except in this case there was a building full of officials. The whistles were humming. Louisville went to the foul line 53 times and hit 38. Now that's a bunch of free throws. It was obviously not a spectator's game, but the Cardinal fans remained patient.

It was on this Saturday that Florida State would help the Cardinals one last time. They gave Memphis State all they wanted before losing 73-71 in a game that took every ounce of energy that the Tigers could muster to squeeze out the win. Memphis was a spent team at the conclusion of that contest. But now it was settled — the championship game would be, as expected, between the league's two best teams, Louisville and Memphis State.

I spent that night at Methodist with my wife. While there, I had the chance to meet a really great Cardinal fan, Lavinnia Toole. She said she had been a big U of L fan for many years. She was something else! I'll let you in on a little secret about

Lavinnia — her undies are decorated and make mention of the Louisville Cardinals.

Sunday finally arrived and I watched it become daylight. You know, there's no way to sleep in a hospital. I knew a win over Memphis State would give the Cards a real good seeding in the NCAA Tournament, plus keep the old momentum going. Momentum is exactly what you need heading into post-season NCAA action.

It finally reached the time to head for Freedom Hall. Van Vance picked me up because he said he didn't trust my driving and he wanted to protect the citizens of Louisville. We arrived at Freedom Hall about two hours before tipoff. Fans were already in their seats, awaiting the big showdown. As we set up the broadcast equipment, the crowd grew larger and the buzzing got louder. The people were ready. As a rule, Louisville fans are always late. But on this day, they were there in plenty of time to hear the playing of the Star-Spangled Banner.

I didn't get a chance to interview Coach Kirk because his voice was gone, but assistant coach Lee Fowler bailed me out again. Off the microphone, he told me, "Jock, we (the team) are tired. I hope I'm wrong but I don't think I am."

When the home crowd needed a litle incentive, Cardinal rooter Sedat Akcakoca left his seat to join cheerleader James Speed for some gymnastics.

COMPLETE LOUISVILLE-MEMPHIS STATE BOX SCORE
LOUISVILLE

Player	FG	FGA	FT	FTA	REB	PF	TP	A	TO	BLK	S	MIN
Crook	1	6	4	4	8	3	6	2	1	0	1	32
Thompson	4	6	2	4	8	4	10	4	6	3	1	27
Ellison	9	15	3	3	13	4	21	3	6	3	2	37
Hall	3	7	2	2	0	2	8	4	2	0	0	32
Wagner	11	15	9	10	7	3	31	1	5	0	1	34
Kimbro	4	5	0	0	4	2	8	1	2	0	1	22
McSwain	0	0	2	2	2	2	2	0	0	1	0	6
Walls	0	1	2	2	1	2	2	2	1	0	0	9
Valentine	0	0	0	0	0	0	0	0	0	0	0	1
Team					1							
Deadball												
Rebounds						1						
Totals	32	55	24	27	44	22	88	17	23	7	6	200

FG%: 1st Half 60.7   2nd Half 55.6   Game 58.2
FT%: 1st Half 66.7   2nd Half 100.0   Game 88.9

MEMPHIS STATE

Player	FG	FGA	FT	FTA	REB	PF	TP	A	TO	BLK	S	MIN
Askew	4	10	2	2	5	3	10	4	1	0	1	33
Holmes	5	14	5	6	7	5	15	0	1	0	1	36
Bedford	7	13	5	7	8	0	19	1	0	0	0	39
Turner	5	20	6	7	4	3	16	8	4	0	5	40
Boyd	5	11	4	7	3	5	14	2	1	0	2	20
Alexander	0	3	1	2	2	3	1	0	3	0	0	14
Wilfong	0	1	0	0	0	1	0	0	0	0	0	5
Moody	2	3	0	0	1	2	4	0	1	0	1	8
Douglas	0	0	0	0	0	1	0	0	0	0	0	5
Team					1							
Deadball												
Rebounds					5							
Totals	28	75	23	31	31	23	79	15	11	0	10	200

FG%: 1st Half 41.7   2nd Half 33.3   Game 37.3
FT%: 1st Half 60.0   2nd Half 81.0   Game 74.2

Halftime: Louisville 40, Memphis State 36
Attendance: 19,611

The Cards dominated the Tigers on the boards, winning the battle 44-31.

He was right, as time would tell. It had only been a week ago when these two teams had put on a clinic titled "Everything You Would Want To See In A Basketball Game." It was a great show, with all the emotion and suspense anyone could handle. On this Sunday, most everyone in the building was expecting to see a repeat, complete with all the same spectacle.

It was game time and the crew at center table — John Tong at the P.A., Richard "Rozie" Rozel as the timer, Tom Curley at the 45-second clock, David Issacs as official scorer, and Kenny Young who, by his good nature, helps everyone out who needs help (he's the guy who you hope will never have to call your name) at the emergency phone — were ready.

The horn blew and the introductions began. It was the last time a lot of terrific athletes from these two teams would face each other in Freedom Hall, possibly forever. Over the past four years they had made a lot of memorable history for all their fans — players like Jeff Hall and Andre Turner, Billy Thompson and Baskerville Holmes, Milt Wagner and William

Bedford. I watched closely as the players met at midcourt and could see there was a lot of respect being exchanged, through eye contact, between the players.

The game got underway and the first half was a good match. Memphis got off to a quick start with an 8-2 lead and actually maintained a lead for over the first 16 minutes before Louisville crawled ahead 30-29. Louisville was having the better shooting in the first half with a hot 60.7 percent while Memphis could only manage 41.7 percent in the first 20 minutes. But even with the good shooting, the Cards took only a 4-point lead to the dressing room, 40-36. Memphis, at that point, looked a little tired as they left the court.

Still, it was a great half of basketball. Joe Rhodes of the Dallas *Morning News*, who set out in his van once the college season began and had covered hundreds of games throughout the season, said, "It was the best basketball game he had seen all year."

As it turned out, the second half was controlled by the Louisville team. Memphis State continued to fight like tigers, but they were, just as I had suspected, running out of gas. Memphis faltered some and the Cardinals ran the score up to 55-37. Half of Freedom Hall, the half loaded with Tiger

The U of L senior players showed off the hardware moments after playing their last game in Freedom Hall as Cardinals.

fans, were shocked and disappointed. What they didn't realize was that they were being pushed around pretty good by a determined group of Louisville players who would eventually be the last college team alive.

All the Memphis starters scored in double figures, led by William Bedford's 19 points. A very proud Andre Turner finished with 16. Now, as I look back over the season, Turner was the player among all the opponents Louisville faced who struck the most fear in my heart, including North Carolina's Brad Daugherty, Chuck Person of Auburn, Virginia Tech's Dell Curry, Kenny Walker of Kentucky, Duke's Johnny Dawkins and Pearl Washington of Syracuse. That's the best compliment Turner will probably ever get, even though he'll probably never know it.

U of L finished with Milt Wagner getting 31 big points, followed by Pervis Ellison's 21. To this day, I think Louisville would have beaten Memphis regardless of the circumstances, but I still believe Florida State helped a little by extending the Tigers only 24 hours earlier.

The final score was Louisville 88, Memphis State 79. The Cardinals were Metro Tourney Champs for 1985-86. Ellison was named Most Valuable Player of the tournament, and rightfully so. It had been a good event that went about the way most Cardinal fans expected.

The game was over and it was time for everyone to dash home, turn the TV on with anxious anticipation, and see exactly where it would be that the Cards would begin NCAA play. The question in the minds of Louisville fans was whether or not the win over Memphis would help the Metro champions get a No. 2 seed.

Can't talk now . . . gotta get on home and find out what's going on!

CHAPTER

5

'Who Dey?'

The pairings for the tournament were made on that late Sunday evening of March 31. All Cardinal fans gathered by the televisions, waiting to see who Louisville's first opponent would be. Hundreds of questions ran through the minds of everyone, questions that needed to be answered before the actual drawing took place.

One, for sure, was whether or not the NCAA would send Louisville and Kentucky to the same site. The Wildcats were a sure bet to get a No. 1 seed as one of the best four teams in the country. It was a possibility for the Cardinals, too, but most likely Louisville would get a No. 2 seed. Little did anyone think the NCAA would put the monkey on Western Kentucky's back as far as the state teams were concerned. After one win by both UK and WKU, they'd be looking eye to eye at each other.

As the bracket positions and sites began rolling off the lips of CBS-TV's Billy Packer and Gary Bender, it became obvious that for Kentucky or Louisville to win the national championship, they'd have to meet in the semifinals of the Final Four.

But at that point of the tournament, "Destination Dallas" would have been accomplished and Cardinal fans would have been happy to play anybody, even the Los Angeles Lakers.

Finally, there it was on the screen — Louisville would play . . . who? Drexel! Who were they? Where are they? What are they? Does anybody know anything about Drexel? Everybody was calling everybody with the same question — who is Drexel?

At the same time they announced Louisville would play Drexel, the site was announced — Ogden, Utah. Utah? Where in the world is Ogden, Utah? What kind of a tournament are the Cardinals in? They're going to play some team we've never heard of in some place we've never heard of! Man, what a revolting development this is!

Those were the type of remarks that were most assuredly being made by Louisville fans everywhere. But it didn't end there. Everyone headed for the cobwebbed attic to dig out the old globe from junior high school or scrounged around for the encyclopedias thinking, "I wish I had these things lined up alphabetically."

Finally, there it was — Ogden, Utah. The wife would repeat what she had heard her husband say, almost screaming in disbelief, "It's close to California? How many miles is it to Utah?"

"About 2,000 miles," replied the husband.

Her next remarks were censored, but that was the situation which faced hundreds of Cardinal fans who had planned to go wherever U of L would be playing. Many of them had built their vacations around the NCAA Tournament. But Ogden, Utah? Man, I don't know anymore.

Actually, Ogden is close to being in both Idaho and Wyoming. The city is tucked in the corner of Utah, not far from Nevada, so it looked real bad for the fans. There are those who can jump on the charters, but there are a lot of great U of L faithful who just couldn't. It would take a good hunk of money to make the trip. Ogden?

Well, once the disgusting site was known, everyone wanted the facts about Drexel. Common sense finally made everyone realize that this was a great draw for the Cards, as least as far as the opponent was concerned, so it was time to look past Drexel and the rest of the road to Dallas.

Denny Crum and Kenny Payne discussed some of the finer points while at practice in Ogden.

Once the whole picture was looked at, it became obvious that the teams to beat to get to the Final Four would be . . . ouch! There was Bradley, a top 10 team, and North Carolina would be waiting for us in Houston!

By now, though, everyone was convinced that a team you've never heard of, like Drexel, was going to beat the Cardinals. No way. Mercy, there was St. John's in the West Region and they'd probably be in the regional finals in Houston! So there it was in black and white, all figured out — it would take wins over Drexel, Bradley, North Carolina and St. John's to get to the Final Four in Dallas. Wow! That's going to take some doing.

With visions of disaster dancing through everyone's heads, it was time to take a big look at the other pairings in the tournament and see if the $5 plucked down in the jackpot was safe.

The Southeast Region bracket revealed a possible match-up between Kentucky and Western Kentucky. Lots of fans chuckled and crossed their fingers for the Hilltoppers. It looked like Kentucky would face Davidson, no problem, followed by WKU then probably Alabama, a team they'd already beaten three times. Then it would be either Memphis State or another SEC school, LSU. And Georgia Tech is in there, too. Well, most of the U of L fans didn't like it because Alabama and LSU were in there. That looked to most fans like a lot easier route than the likes of Bradley, North Carolina and St. John's.

By this time, there were plenty of obscene gestures made in respect to the NCAA Selection Committee, on top of the foul language here and there.

The bottom bracket showed probable meetings between Kansas and Michigan State, North Carolina State and Michigan, Duke and Oklahoma, and Indiana and Syracuse.

There was no way in a thousand-billion years that Cleveland State could beat Indiana. Boy, were we surprised. What you see is not always what you get.

Now it was back to the problem at hand — how to get to Utah. Was it too far to drive? Hell yes! Would the car make it? Hell no! Could we fly? Hell no! Did we have to stay at home? Hell yes!

Well, since that was settled, it was time to cry, kick the cat, pay the bills, burn the supper, leave the dishes, call your mother-in-law, go to bed early and probably sleep on the couch, at least for all those people who had all the "yes" and "no" answers in the wrong order.

The doldrums began again the next day when everyone arrived at work. Utah looked a million miles away, and it appeared that 95 percent of all the people who had made plans and saved their money would have to listen on the radio or watch on TV when the Cards played Drexel.

But how did Denny Crum feel about the pairings? Just one season ago, Louisville would have loved to have gotten the last bid given out. The NCAA could have sent the Cards to China and everyone would have been overjoyed. But as Crum has said so often, "You don't have any control over it so why worry about it?"

Looking back at the first and second-round pairings, Louisville's draw was perfect, except for the fans. It was exactly what the Cards needed — a chance to build upon their performances as they advanced. I'm sure Coach Crum liked the draw at the time it was announced. It was a way to start without too much hoopla.

I received a phone call from my radio partner, Van, and he told me we were leaving on Tuesday afternoon because Denny thought his team needed an extra day to get adjusted to the altitude. Louisville was scheduled to play on Thursday afternoon and again Saturday, if they won.

I arrived at the airport where the "usuals" were waiting. The first people I saw were Dr. Donald Swain and his wife, Lavinia. They are Louisville's No. 1 fans, not because they are the President and First Lady of the University but because they are just true rooters. Dr. Swain could become a plumber tomorrow and his feeling for the Cardinals would

Drexel was obviously no match for the superior Cardinals.

chose to follow the snow to Powder Mountain. It was a wise choice on their part because Michigan lost to Iowa State in the second round. Before I could blink they were off, zooming down the mountain, very proud of their correct decision.

My wife, P.J., is a good skier and I was wishing she could be enjoying this. But the little incident in Louisville had her in a prone position in Lexington at the moment.

The biggest problem up there was the fact it was cold, at least I was. Van had his "dancin' and romancin' pants" on. I think they were made from the hide of a shark. Garry was dressed a little better for the weather but none of us were properly attired, so it didn't take us long to head to the lodge for some hot coffee.

While sitting down at the table, some dude, all decked out in his million-dollar ski outfit, came over to me and said, "Just came up to look around, eh? Are those other tourists with you?" I asked him if he was related to Admiral Byrd and he told me, "You talk funny."

With that, I slithered away to pout in my own privacy. My two buddies were out in the blizzard acting like they were on assignment with National Geographic. But we had a real good time that day, as did most of the other U of L fans, before heading back to get our minds on the task at hand. I was ready for summertime again anyway. I like snow on Christmas cards, and that's about it.

That night Van and I went to dinner with Dr. Rudy and Ruth Anne Ellis at a place called the "Prairie Schooner." It was a unique place — the tables were all designed like the back of a covered wagon, canvas and all. In the center of the room was a camp fire, cactus and all the things you might see on the prairie, including a coyote or two. And the food was prairie good. We all had a real good time. Just being with Rudy and Ruth Anne is enough to make any evening nice.

When we got back to the hotel, a bunch of the players were just sitting around the lobby. Milt and Kevin were talking to anybody who'd listen, Kenny had claimed a big, plush chair as a resting spot and Herbert was just sort of hanging around. We got everyone huddled together for pictures for a couple of fans. It was a fun time but it was obvious to everyone that the next day was a step that had to be taken with sure-footing. At that point it was one down and five to go.

Bradley became Louisville's next opponent when the Braves escaped a tough battle with Texas-El Paso. It was a game that took a lot out of Dick Versace's team.

I hadn't been a Bradley fan the entire season. I even commented a couple of weeks earlier on the radio show and wrote the same in my column for SCORE**CARD** that Bradley was ranked 13th in the nation and had not played a single team in the top 20. I couldn't understand how a team could be rated that high without having played a nationally ranked opponent. Meanwhile, Louisville had played a bunch of top 20 folks.

Well, now I was going to get my wish. The Braves entered the game with a 32-2 record and it was time to find out if

Herbert Crook put up a shot over the outstretched arm of Bradley's Mike Williams.

they did indeed deserve their current ranking of No. 14. I didn't think they could beat Louisville because, if for no other reason, they had a weak schedule. They were well aware of Louisville and the type of competition they had faced. Bradley had some very good athletes but were about to face some great athletes.

Bradley had a very good point man, Jim Les, and he made a lot of things happen on the court. Against Louisville, however, he didn't do enough. Louisville clung to a 35-31 halftime lead and it was still close 12 minutes into the second half. With the score tied at 55-55 with 8:50 remaining, Milt Wagner made the play of the game as he dropped from the sky and blocked a seemingly wide-open shot by Les.

"Psychologically, that block and our impatience on offense the rest of the way in the game was our undoing," said the Bradley coach.

Louisville took the lead for good with 6:33 remaining on a 12-footer by Billy Thompson, and the Cards widened the gap to eventually win by an 82-68 margin. All the starters but

Billy Thompson stopped Bradley's Don Powell on this shot. The defense against the Braves was the deciding factor in the 82-68 U of L win.

COMPLETE LOUISVILLE-BRADLEY BOX SCORE

LOUISVILLE

Player	FG	FGA	FT	FTA	REB	PF	TP	A	TO	BLK	S	MIN
Crook	3	9	3	4	5	1	9	3	1	0	0	22
Thompson	5	8	4	4	7	4	14	6	2	1	0	31
Ellison	7	10	2	3	8	5	16	0	2	1	1	35
Hall	5	9	1	2	2	2	11	1	1	0	1	25
Wagner	6	13	4	6	3	1	16	1	3	1	2	35
Kimbro	3	5	2	2	1	2	8	4	0	0	0	23
McSwain	2	2	1	2	5	1	5	1	0	1	0	20
Walls	0	0	0	0	0	0	0	0	0	0	0	4
Valentine	1	1	1	2	2	0	3	0	0	0	0	1
Payne	0	0	0	0	0	1	0	0	0	0	0	1
West	0	0	0	0	0	0	0	0	0	0	0	1
Olliges	0	0	0	0	0	0	0	1	0	0	0	1
Abram	0	1	0	0	1	0	0	0	0	0	0	1
Team					0							
Deadball												
Rebounds					3							
Totals	32	58	18	25	34	17	82	17	9	4	4	200

FG%: 1st Half 51.5 2nd Half 60.0 Game 55.2
FT%: 1st Half 33.3 2nd Half 77.3 Game 72.0

BRADLEY

Player	FG	FGA	FT	FTA	REB	PF	TP	A	TO	BLK	S	MIN
Trimpe	2	5	0	0	4	3	4	7	3	0	0	39
Powell	3	4	2	6	8	1	8	1	5	0	0	23
Williams	7	15	3	5	8	4	17	1	0	0	0	38
Hopkins	11	22	0	1	7	3	22	3	2	0	0	40
Les	6	12	3	4	4	4	15	6	3	0	2	40
Manuel	0	0	0	0	0	0	0	1	0	0	0	2
Thomas	1	4	0	1	5	3	2	1	0	0	0	18
Team					0							
Deadball												
Rebounds					3							
Totals	30	64	8	17	35	18	68	20	13	0	2	200

FG%: 1st Half 46.6 2nd Half 47.1 Game 46.9
FT%: 1st Half 37.5 2nd Half 55.5 Game 47.1

Halftime: Louisville 35, Bradley 31
Attendance: 10,061

Crook scored in double figures, led by Wagner's and Ellison's 16. Bradley's Les was held to 15 points and hit just half of his 12 field-goal attempts.

I think the altitude of Ogden hurt the Braves some. Coach Crum used a lot of players while Versace used only one substitute for any length of time. The Braves were spent by the end of the game. Ex-UCLA great and current Weber State coach Larry Farmer had told me in an interview before the game that the players' "wouldn't notice a difference in the altitude." But I think they did.

Another step was completed and Louisville's next obstacle for "Destination Dallas" meant a stop in Houston for a game

Jeff Hall faked Bradley's Mike Williams off his feet before dropping the ball off to teammate Robbie Valentine (not pictured). Valentine scored on the play.

against the Tar Heels of big, bad ol' North Carolina, the team coached by Dean Smith — the ex-Olympic coach who invented the "four-corner offense."

North Carolina had been ranked No. 1 in the polls for 13 straight weeks but had tailed off a little as of late because of a couple of midseason injuries. They had been seeded No. 3 in the West Region of the NCAA Tourney but had regained a lot of their early season form and looked really tough to me. Could they be beaten in this tournament? Maybe, just maybe, the Cards could pull it off.

Before I left Ogden, I had a chance to visit with Denny's mother and stepfather, Mike and June Turner. Their plans were to drift on down toward Houston, taking their time and enjoying a few things along the way. They'd be in Houston by the time the Cards would arrive the following week. Now that's the way I would have loved to have gone to the NCAA. They had driven from California. They were super folks, my kind of folks. I told them they really knew how to live and even told them a semi-dirty joke. June really busted a gut laughing.

The plane trip home was relatively quiet. We had been in the air for a long time and most people were dozing. That's about all you can do in a plane seat. Suddenly, the ZZZ s were interrupted by a voice blasting out from the rear of the plane. "WHO DEY? WHO DEY? Who dey think they can beat my Cardinals?"

Before I could think, the chant started again, except this time it was two or three voices. Before long, most everybody was hollering the new cheer. Finally, it dawned on me that the first voices I heard had belonged to my good friends Alex Browne and Tom Moser, two of the hardiest of Cardinal fans. Alex had made the trip three years ago to Anchorage, Alaska

U of L trustee George Fischer was ready with his "victory cigar" in the late stages of the game against Bradley.

The Cardinal cheerleaders yelled for the CBS cameras after the win.

when the Cards were in the Great Alaska Shootout. He had been the scourge of The Whale's Tail, the lounge of Captain Jack's Hotel. Yes, I had made it there a time or two myself and that's where we became friends.

The chant started by Alex and Tom was now being encouraged by senior forward Robbie Valentine. "Who dey" became the unofficial password used between Cardinal fans all the way to the last tick of the clock on March 31 in Dallas' Reunion Arena. No matter where you were — in a mall, a plane, the lobby or on the street in the dark of the night — if you listened closely you could hear "Who Dey? Who Dey?" I remember saying it to myself several times when the Cardinals were in a tight spot, and it seemed to make something good happen in a matter of seconds. Alex and Tom gave the Cardinals something to hang on to, something to loosen everyone up in the tight and tense moments over the next few days. Those boys had done good.

It was late when we arrived at Standiford Field, but all those people who had been disappointed because they couldn't make the trip to Ogden, at least 5,000 of them, came out to say "hello" and "thanks for giving us a chance to go to Houston because we'll definitely be there."

Ogden had been a great place for the Cardinals to begin. They had accomplished what they set out to do — win two games.

CHAPTER

6

Destination Dallas

When I rolled out of bed it was early Sunday afternoon. I had gotten back to Lexington from Utah about 2:45 a.m., but it was about 4 a.m. before I made it to bed. Upon awakening, I ran to the front porch to get the newspaper so I could read about the NCAA games around the country. Naturally, it was the Louisville-Bradley game I wanted to read about the most. That was kind of stupid, I guess, because I had sat there and watched, even describing the action on the radio. What could I read that I didn't already see? But I enjoy reading about the games again.

It quickly hit me that it was time to start the ol' wheels turning about what was ahead for the Cards in Houston, U of L's next stop for "Destination Dallas." The big name of North Carolina with players like Michael Jordan and James Worthy jumped up in front of me. That's the kind of program North Carolina has, one which attracts the great athletes. Coach Dean Smith is probably the most visible name in college basketball today. That doesn't mean he's the best in the business, it just means his name is probably mentioned more often than any other collegiate coach in America. Coach Bob Knight of Indiana runs a close second. Who knows? With two national titles in the '80s, perhaps Denny Crum might start getting a little more national attention.

During the first part of the 1985-86 basketball season, it seemed the Tar Heels were going to totally dominate the picture the entire year. But injuries hit them and it sorta geared them back down to a level on par with a lot of other teams. After two games in the NCAA Tournament, though, it looked like they were getting back to their old form. Their injuries were healing and all the players were back in uniform. Steve Hale, the guard who made it all happen for Carolina, was playing well again after a collapsed lung had sidelined him for a few games. It just seemed that the Tar Heels were going to be the biggest obstacle of all in Louisville's drive to Dallas. They were scary, at least to me.

On the positive side, I realized that Louisville also had the kind of program that attracted the super athletes. I knew Denny and his staff would waste little time delving into the video tapes to come up with a solid game plan. Basically, U of L's biggest problem seemed to be how to keep the ball out of the inside as much as possible on defense and get it inside against the larger Carolina team on offense.

Playing the Tar Heels first in Houston was somewhat of a break for Louisville.

If the teams didn't meet until the regional final, there would have been just one day to work out.

Since it was just Sunday afternoon and the game wasn't until Thursday, I decided to give myself a break and think about something else. I had just about enough time to empty my suitcase and get everything ready to go again.

Ogden was a far cry from Houston, so I knew lots and lots of Cardinal fans would find a way to get there, by hook or crook. And they did, by just about any means available.

Some traveled by big recreational vehicles, people like Bob and Jean Ernst with their party of Gene and Edna Montgomery, Bill and Sally Hoback, Joe and Shirley McCullom. Others went by car. There were some who drove from Louisville to places like St. Louis, and flew from there to Houston, cheaper.

One couple, Steve and Vicki Orr, had just gotten married and spent their honeymoon watching the Cardinals fight for the right to move on to Dallas. They went by van and stopped in Hot Springs National Park, located in Arkansas, on the way. The Orrs told me enough about the hot baths in the springs, followed by a rub down and a cooling-down procedure, that convinced me to put it on my list of "things that I must do." All for $18.50 a head. Wow, what a honeymoon!

The travel plans were set. The team plane would leave on Tuesday and the Cards would practice in The Summit, home of the Houston Rockets, on Wednesday.

Just as I had anticipated, there were a lot more fans at the airport for the trip to Houston than there were for Ogden. We boarded an L-1011, which is a great big devil that seats nine people across — two aisles with two seats at each

Those who made the trip were all smiles after landing in Houston.

window and five seats across the middle. It doesn't seem like a plane ride on an aircraft like that, it sort of feels like getting on a big elevator which takes you to where you're supposed to be going. A team charter usually has all the old standbys on board — players, coaches school administrators, cheerleaders and media — and this time was no exception. I think it's a fact that the charter which carries the team is a little

There was no question as to who was super rooter Elaine Whelan's favorite team.

more expensive for the fans, but I guess there's a certain privilege to ride right along with the fellows who are going to do the work.

And it was going to take a whole lot of good work in Houston if the Cards were going to complete their destination.

There had already been one big surprise in the West Region. St. John's, the region's No. 1 seed, had been knocked off by Auburn. That was a good sign for Louisville because the Redmen were better, at least in my opinion, than the rest of the remaining teams in the upper portion of the bracket.

You could just sense the feeling that was present with the traveling party. There was sort of an urgency in the air. Not a hurry-up feeling, but the feeling you have when there is a big task to be done and the time is getting closer. In my bones, I felt there were two things that needed to happen for the Cardinals to go all the way. First, they had to get past North Carolina, which I had my doubts about. Second, Kansas needed to be eliminated. It broke my heart when Michigan State got rooked out of a win against Kansas due to that goofy clock situation. Because of it, the Jayhawks were still alive. Kansas was a team I feared since big Greg Dreiling had ruled the second half in KU's win over the Cards in Lawrence.

Although most Cardinal fans were still thinking "Destination Dallas," I heard very few say, "We're going all the way." For most, me included, the goal was just to make it to the Final Four. Anything after that would be a bonus. What I didn't know was how Milt Wagner and his teammates were thinking.

Wagner, on just the day before the national semifinals, told a writer for the Dallas *Times-Herald*, "I'm on a mission. I've already been to the Final Four twice. Just getting there isn't enough for me. This time I want to go out in style. I want to win it all."

I could identify with Milt's feelings. While coaching in high school, I remember just being satisfied getting to the state tournament the first couple of times. After that, though, anything less than winning it all was a drag. Milt's statement came after Louisville had already won the regional in Houston, but I'll bet his answer would have been the same if the question had been asked before the first NCAA game against Drexel. I'm sure all the other seniors felt pretty much the same way.

The flight to Houston was pleasant, Texas was bubbling with spring, and it was just a happy time for the Cardinals and their fans.

The NCAA housed us at the Westin Galleria. It was gorgeous but, for the average traveler, it was very expensive. The one drawback was that the hotel was surrounded by "Concrete City." There was nothing within walking distance so we were pretty much at the mercy of the merchants in the Galleria. Even so, it was extremely nice for the traveling fans to have a place to browse. It was an enormous shopping center with beautiful stores, but unless your Aunt Tillie had just left you a fortune in stocks, it was a lousy place to shop. Prices were out of sight. However, there were those shoppers who accepted the challenge of finding a bargain. Paying $8 for breakfast in those places is routine but $3 for a small glass of juice still bothers me, even if I am on an expense account. I just don't do it.

Actually, these NCAA games where you have hundreds of followers along are really just big lobby parties. The Westin was no exception. The lobby of the hotel was a constant sea of red at about any reasonable hour you happened to pass through. It was probably that way even at the unreasonable hours but, truthfully, I was never there at those times. It's a working affair for me and I make every effort to be ready to do a good job each day (even though I did slip off the track following the North Carolina game).

The day before the game arrived, and everyone looked eager and ready to see what made Houston tick. P.J. and

I ate breakfast to the tune of $16.40. The goose that lays the golden eggs must have worked there, at least that's what I told the waiter. He was Mexican, I think, and answered me in a language I never understood, and I think that's the way he wanted it. Somehow, though, I knew what he said wasn't nice.

I located the man with the "dancin' and romancin' pants," Van Vance, and we headed for the Summit for the practices and press conferences. Coach Smith had brought Brad Daugherty and Warren Martin, both dressed in coats and ties, with him. It was on this occasion when I heard with my own ears Daugherty say again, "I don't know much about Ellison. I've heard the name but that's about all." He also added, "They (Louisville) are supposed to be quicker, but we have been able to handle that problem all year."

North Carolina coach Dean Smith thought he had his team back in the groove.

Daugherty did most of the talking for the Carolina players. I quickly discovered that Coach Smith had a way of answering questions without really answering them. For example, one person asked him what he thought about Billy

Thompson. He answered, "A program like Louisville's is going to have good athletes. I'm sure Billy meets those qualifications." He went on to say he expected his team to be able to execute as they had all year.

I sorta got the feeling that Coach Smith felt like it would be a good game, but his team would win. I got the impression he and his players felt they had played well against a good UAB team in Utah and their overall game had returned. After watching them against UAB, they had me convinced. Against UAB, it had seemed like they were able to get it inside just about any time they wanted to. By doing that, they looked almost impossible to stop. After all, Brad Daugherty was the biggest bear in the woods!

The Cards looked impressive that day with their enthusiasm and attitude, but that didn't make Daugherty look any smaller to me.

We headed back to the hotel and set up for the live call-in show for WHAS. Our location in the lobby was very close to the same place U of L was having a reception, which made for a lively show. It was there that I got in bad graces with the Louisville followers. When pinned down for a winner, I said it would be tough to beat Carolina. My friend, or so I thought, Van wouldn't let it rest. He told me I wasn't answering and wanted me to pick a winner. I told him and everyone listening on the 50,000-watt station, "OK. My heart says Louisville but my head says North Carolina." That statement forced me into a bad hangover on Friday.

Thursday, game day, finally came. As usual, there was a pep rally. The charter package always includes a pep rally ticket, which otherwise costs $10. In this case, the price included a nice brunch buffet. This rally, which was really something, set the tone for the next three rallies.

The U of L pep band was on hand, as were Louisville's national championship (two years running) cheerleaders and their sponsor, Sherrill Travis. These groups are real eye openers. They were loud and you got a sincere feeling that you were with people who you care about and who care about you.

Royce Cook cheered on her team against the Tar Heels.

Athletic director Bill Olsen addressed the fans at the pep rally (in the Westin Galleria) before the game.

The Cardinal fans were well-prepared for North Carolina.

Van and I took an early exit from the pep rally and headed for the Summit. I wore my white shirt, short-sleeve red sweater and, most important of all, my white hat. The hat had gotten to be a big thing among Cardinal fans. Louisville never lost when I wore it and, for that reason, it had become a good-luck charm.

Everybody seemed to have their own superstitions. Coach Crum told about how his old boss, John Wooden, found a coin and put it in his shoe. Denny, being a non-believer, sorta chuckled. As the story goes, however, Denny found a coin in the elevator on this same trip and put it — you guessed it — right in the old shoe.

As for others, Gene Montgomery, a huge fan, wore a pair of red undershorts to every game. They, too, were undefeated. Unfortunately, Gene had to leave Houston because of a death in his family, but he left the shorts at the tournament site with his wife to be passed around at the game for good luck. There were at least 100 more stories about lucky items but I, like Denny, don't believe in superstitions. Still, it couldn't hurt, so why not give it a try?

The Cards played in the afternoon, following the UNLV-Auburn game. After Van and I finished setting up the radio equipment, I watched the first game to decide which team would be the best opponent for Louisville to play in the regional final. There was a small chore — North Carolina — to settle before it would really matter, but just for the sake of looking ahead, I decided Auburn would be better for the Cards. Nevada-Las Vegas had an awful lot of athletes, whereas I thought Auburn pretty much lived and died with what Chuck Person was able to do. And that's the way it went because UNLV blew a good lead and Person shot Auburn to the victory.

Denny came over to do his pre-game show with Van and seemed to be very collected. It was obvious the plan was there but that's not the big thing with Louisville. It's the changes that are made as the game progresses and the way the back-up people perform while the regulars are getting a break that was important to this team.

Coach Crum said they needed to do a great job inside and that it would take one of their better performances for them to win. When there is an unusually tough opponent to be played, Denny normally ends his pre-game show by saying, "We've done all we can do so let's just throw it up and see what happens." And that's exactly what they did.

The first half saw the score tied six times. Louisville's biggest lead was four points (43-39 with the clock showing :59 left in the period) and the biggest Carolina advantage was six (four times). Being behind by six points to any team is enough, much less to a team like North Carolina that can really protect a lead. At that point of a game, a couple of trips downcourt without scoring and "bingo," the next thing you know is you're behind by 10. Being behind by double figures is strictly a no-no.

But that never happened to the Cards and the guy who did the work for U of L during those crucial moments was Billy Thompson. The senior cut NC's lead back to four points three times and Milt Wagner did it once. The half ended with the score tied at 43-43.

A tie at the half was encouraging after being behind by six. The Cards had shot well (16 of 30 for 53.3 percent) but Carolina was right with them (18 of 35 for 51.4 percent). Daugherty had been the force expected with 11 points and five boards, but Jeff Lebo's 13 points were a surprise. I knew Denny would make adjustments for Lebo in the locker room, but the other stat that concerned me was on the boards, Carolina had 20 rebounds to U of L's 14. Pervis Ellison had a quiet half with six points and four rebounds.

The beginning of the second half, however, was when the Cards took control. Louisville blitzed the Tar Heels in the first 4:30 of the period, outscoring them 16-4. With 15:19 left on the clock, Carolina took a timeout, trailing 59-47.

They weren't ready to concede. Forward Joe Wolf brought his team back and Carolina tied the game at 71-71 with 6:23 remaining. Losing a 12-point lead against a great team like North Carolina can be a spirit breaker, for sure. But that wasn't the case with Louisville.

The Cards were down by a basket at the 4:31 mark, and, I'll have to admit, my spirit was about to break. But I looked at Carolina's players and it looked as if their comeback had just about wiped them out physically. They were tired, real tired.

The Cardinals looked good, showing no signs of fatigue, and had that look of the "eye of the tiger." From that point on, there was no monkey business.

Crum's troops pecked 'em right off the court. It was no contest. They mashed 'em, thrashed 'em and trashed 'em right into the dumpster, outscoring them 21-6. How had this happened?

I asked Denny after the game about the timeout he'd called after Carolina had cut the 12-point lead down to nothing. He said, "I didn't make any changes on the court. I just told them they had taken the lead by taking good shots and they had

Billy Thompson scores two of his 24 points despite the defensive efforts of North Carolina's Joe Wolf.

lost the lead by taking bad shots. If they wanted the lead back, they had to take good shots again."

Was this the key to the win? Actually, it took more than one thing for the Cards to win. One key was the preparation Denny and his staff had made before they ever got to Houston. These plans were made from studying tapes of Carolina and thoroughly understanding the capabilities of the Cardinals. Another key to the game was the use of the bench. Coach Crum also applied a 1-1-3 zone at exactly the right time.

Yes, those were all important to Louisville's win, but perhaps the biggest key to the game was the tough schedule Louisville had played over the season and the ground they had covered. They were not intimidated by anyone. They had survived a murderous schedule and now they feared no one.

Actually, as the game progressed, I got the feeling that North Carolina became a little intimidated themselves. Louisville never retreated a step. They said very little and there weren't any smiles or high-fives. U of L just performed with cold, icy execution, under the toughest of conditions and against the best. I knew right then "Destination Dallas" would not be my password anymore. It was national championship-time for these Cardinals. The Cards had beaten North Carolina and when Kansas got beat by Duke in the Final Four, my doubts were put to rest.

It had been a great basketball game against North Carolina, the type of game that had superior athletes and two of the best, if not the best, coaches in the world going head to head.

"Make no mistake about it," said Dean Smith afterward, "Louisville is a great basketball team."

Denny Crum, who called it a "team win," had made all the right moves against the Tar Heels. The 1-1-3 zone was again effective in the later stages of the game. All five starters scored in double figures and Billy Thompson had a great day

with 24 points, nine rebounds and only one turnover. Herbert Crook contributed 20 points to the cause, eight in the final stretch, and pulled down nine boards.

Pervis Ellison, Milt Wagner and Jeff Hall scored 15, 14 and 12 points, respectively. As a team, the Cards shot 50.8 percent while North Carolina finished at 49.3. Lebo, after 13 first-half points, finished the game with just 19. The big statistical difference in the game was at the free-throw line where U of L hit 28 of 33 compared to Carolina's 11 of 18. But that's what happens when you're able to work the ball inside for good shots.

It was on this afternoon that basketball fans all over the country thought, "Oh, oh, look out, it's national championship-time for Louisville again." Sure, there were still thoughts in a lot of minds that Kansas, a team that had already beaten the Cards twice, was still alive, but they didn't know that this was not the same Louisville team. It had the

Defense was a key to the Cards' success as Tony Kimbro and Jeff Hall try to contain Joe Wolf.

COMPLETE LOUISVILLE-NORTH CAROLINA BOX SCORE

LOUISVILLE

Player	FG	FGA	FT	FTA	REB	PF	TP	A	TO	BLK	S	MIN
Crook	5	9	10	10	9	4	20	2	3	0	1	34
Thompson	10	16	4	5	9	4	24	5	1	2	1	33
Ellison	6	12	3	4	6	3	15	3	3	3	2	37
Hall	5	11	2	2	3	1	12	5	1	0	1	37
Wagner	5	12	4	4	1	2	14	5	2	0	1	36
Kimbro	0	1	1	2	1	2	1	0	0	0	0	6
McSwain	1	3	2	4	1	1	4	1	2	0	0	9
Walls	1	1	2	2	0	0	4	0	0	0	0	5
Valentine	0	0	0	0	0	0	0	0	0	0	0	1
Payne	0	0	0	0	0	0	0	0	0	0	0	1
Abram	0	0	0	0	1	1	0	0	0	0	0	1
Team					2							
Deadball Rebounds					3							
Totals	33	65	28	33	33	17	94	22	12	5	6	200

FG%: 1st Half 53.3   2nd Half 48.6   Game 50.8
FT%: 1st Half 84.6   2nd Half 85.0   Game 84.8

NORTH CAROLINA

Player	FG	FGA	FT	FTA	REB	PF	TP	A	TO	BLK	S	MIN
Wolf	9	15	2	3	4	4	20	2	2	0	0	34
Daugherty	8	14	3	7	15	4	19	6	2	1	0	39
Lebo	8	13	2	4	4	2	18	4	1	0	1	35
Hale	2	10	0	0	6	5	4	5	4	0	0	31
K. Smith	4	12	4	4	4	5	12	8	5	0	1	37
Daye	0	0	0	0	0	0	0	0	0	0	0	1
Bucknall	0	0	0	0	0	0	0	0	0	0	0	1
Madden	0	0	0	0	0	0	0	0	0	0	0	1
R. Smith	0	2	0	0	0	1	0	0	0	0	0	4
Popson	0	0	0	0	1	0	0	0	2	0	0	7
Hunter	2	2	0	0	1	2	4	0	2	0	0	7
Martin	1	1	0	0	3	3	2	0	0	0	0	6
Team					2							
Deadball Rebounds					3							
Totals	34	69	11	18	40	26	79	25	18	1	2	200

FG%: 1st Half 51.4   2nd Half 47.1   Game 49.3
FT%: 1st Half 77.8   2nd Half 44.4   Game 61.1

Halftime: Louisville 43, No. Carolina 43
Attendance: 10,936

same faces but with a different mental attitude. These Cardinals were "road tough" and "game tested."

The possibility of meeting Kentucky in the Final Four was beginning to cross the minds of the fans. The Cats had beaten Alabama and had only another SEC school, LSU, in their way to Dallas. Louisville would have to beat Auburn but, as I look back on it, it really didn't matter who U of L would play in Dallas because they were the team that no one was going to beat.

Everybody headed back to the Westin for a little celebration party. The word quickly filtered down that there was a big bash going on up on the 24th floor. Should we go up and join them? Why Not?

Well, it seemed every Cardinal fan in the world was there and none of them let me forget that I had picked the Tar Heels to win. Boy, was I stupid to do that!

It also just so happened that there was a little indulging of the alcoholic nature going on. It was very hot so I decided to have a little toddy for the body. They were still pouring it on me about the game so I thought since I couldn't beat them, I'd join them. In fact, I joined them until about 3 a.m. before they threw us all out.

It was time to celebrate back at the hotel so the Cardinal Bird joined Terri and Sandy (once a cheerleader herself) Talbott for some cheer.

154

It was when I got off on the wrong floor and tried to put the key in the wrong door that it occurred to me that I may have over-indulged a little. The next day confirmed my fears because when I tried to exit my bed, all the parts of my body sent out rejection signals. Friday was a long day, but I survived.

P.J. went with me to the Summit for the press conferences. I made her go so she could help me cross the street. It was important that I got the interviews Van and I needed for the game broadcast between the Cardinals and the Tigers.

I interviewed Chuck Person and Coach Sonny Smith of Auburn. Chuck put down the importance of basketball in the Alabama state when he answered one reporter with, "It's the third-leading activity at Auburn. First is football, next is spring football and then comes basketball."

I asked Sonny if he had second-guessed his return to Auburn after resigning (after his team had gotten off to a

Jeff Hall, guarded by Mike Jones, had little trouble with Auburn's pressure defense.

slow start) and then accepting his job back. He answered, "After my wife had her stroke and recovered, I knew then I didn't need to worry about anything."

It was a terrific answer from a classy person and a fine coach. Even now, I'll use a joke on Denny that I heard Sonny tell once at a clinic: "You know, Denny fashions himself as a farmer. I say he is an excellent coach but not much of a farmer. He bought these 17 cows and soon figured that without a bull he was only going to have 17 cows. He soon discovered a farmer who had a bull that could service all 17 cows for $50 apiece. It sounded good to him so Denny loaded them up in his truck and took off for the bull. The owner told him to look out the window in the morning and any cow that was laying down was impregnated.

"The next day Denny looked out and all 17 cows were standing. He loaded them up another time and away he went, $50 apiece again. But the next morning it was the same thing again. All 17 were standing up. He loaded them up once more for another $50 rendezvous.

"The next morning Denny didn't have the heart to look out the window, so he told his wife, Joyce, to look out and tell him what she saw. Joyce looked and said, 'I don't understand it but there are 16 cows in the back of your truck and the other one is blowing the horn.' "

I finished my interviews so it was time to get back to the hotel and lie down.

Oh, what a day! A lot of the fans had made a day of it doing different things. One group went to Gilley's, a Texas-type saloon in Pasadena. Gilley's had been the site of a movie or two, so everyone was excited. Most of them came back disappointed, though, because they actually got there too soon and left too early. Those Texans don't start two-steppin' until the moon comes out.

Other fans made a trip to the Houston Space Center and seemed pretty happy with their choice. Me? I had been to the Summit.

That night a very nice thing happened to P.J. and me. We were invited out to dinner by Dr. Les and Jolene Lovett, a couple who lives in Bowling Green (Kentucky) and makes the round-trip for every Cardinal home game, and Rita and Milt Hughes of Louisville. We went to eat at the San Jacinto Inn, located in a state park about 30 minutes from downtown Houston. It was really a unique and nice evening. The restaurant sits at the site of the "Battle of San Jacinto" where General Sam Houston defeated Santa Anna's army in 1836. Santa Anna had approximately 1,600 men in his army while General Houston had a mere 780 men. In the battle General Houston lost only two men while his troops killed 630 of Santa Anna's army. This is also where the battleship, Texas, is anchored.

The inn was founded in 1917 and there is a register you sign. Pictures of dignitaries who have dined there adorn the walls. The menu was unique — no frills, just good food. First they brought us huge bowls of peeled shrimp on crushed ice, huge platters of oysters on the half-shell and huge plates of onion rings. It was an all-you-could-eat deal. The last course was fried fish and chicken with all the trimmings, including homemade rolls about the size of a hockey puck. Man, it was some good eating and a great way to spend the evening. In fact, it was so good it made me forget just how bad I felt.

Saturday arrived and just 40 minutes of playing time stood between the Cardinals and "Destination Dallas." Auburn had a lot of athletes — runners, jumpers and shooters. They were a scary bunch who had beaten Arizona, St. John's and UNLV — two big-time wins — so the Cards had better not take them lightly.

There was another pep rally, of course. I honestly leave these pep rallies with a better feeling than I go into them with. I'm always a little nervous because I have to get up and tell a story or two, but there is no better audience. The fans are usually dying to laugh, probably to keep from crying and worrying, and they sure do make a great audience. The rallies are a lot of fun.

The time had come to get on over to the Summit for a

Cardinal cheerleaders Karen Smith, Missy Perkins and Jennifer Haddaway showed some concern early in the game against Auburn.

showdown with Auburn. I had been at the last Cardinal practice session and watched the Cards go through some strategy, as Coach Jerry Jones talked with coaches Wade Houston and Bobby Dotson. Now, minutes before the game, I was standing at the same place where Coach Crum had stood that day in practice and said, "Let Person shoot from here. Let him show us that he can score from here. But don't," as he moved in some, "give him anything from here."

I was certain that if Auburn beat U of L, it would be Person who would do it. But I also knew Denny wouldn't let him do enough to beat them. That gave me a good feeling about the game. The other thing I liked in the Cards' favor was even though Person shot a lot and was dangerous, as long as he was out there firing them up he couldn't be inside rebounding. He couldn't be in two places at once.

The first half turned out to be close. Auburn twice built up leads of five points, while the best Louisville could do was 40-36 with 3:09 showing on the clock.

When the half ended with the Cards clinging to a 44-43 lead, I remembered what Chuck Person had said, "If we can rebound with them in the first half and be close, we can win in the second half." U of L had killed the Tigers on the boards,

Billy Thompson out-muscled Auburn's Frank Ford for one of his seven rebounds.

19-11, but Auburn was still right there in the game. Why? They had shot the lights out at a sizzling 62.5 percent. Louisville's 56.4 percent was keeping them in the game. Person had done his thing, hitting 6 of 10 from long range for 12 points, but Herbert Crook topped that for the Cards by hitting 7 of 10 for 14.

I felt real good about the way things had gone because I knew Auburn couldn't continue to burn the nets like that.

The teams exchanged baskets for a lot of the second half when Denny, with his team trailing 65-64, made a change which spelled doom for Auburn and Chuck Person. Crum went to his surprise 1-1-3 zone which finished off Chuck Person for the day. The All-American made just one field goal in the final 9:38 of the contest. He put up a couple of shots, outside of the imaginary line Denny had cautioned his team about, and hit iron.

The score was close until the final three minutes when Louisville outscored the Tigers 14-6. The final margin of victory was 84-76. It took a big play at the 1:53 mark, however, to seal the win. Auburn's Jeff Moore, launched a 12-footer when Pervis Ellison came out of nowhere to block the shot. The ball carried back to midcourt where Jeff Hall picked it up and took in for a layup.

"The big fellow (Ellison) turned it up about three notches for that block," said Auburn's Sonny Smith, "and Hall's layup was the clincher."

"Louisville played defense about as good as it can be played," said Person, who was voted the region's MVP. Coming from a great player like Chuck Person, that's about the ultimate compliment.

This Cardinal team had become a unit that was almost flawless down the stretch. There were no errors, the big plays were made and the big baskets went in. That was the way it was the rest of the way. This was the "Crunch Bunch."

Again, all five starters were in double figures. Herb Crook led the way with 20 points and a game-high 11 rebounds. Milt finished with 16 points, followed by Pervis' 15, Jeff's 14 and Billy's 13. The Cards shot 54 percent for the game and Auburn, as expected, returned to the real world and hit 43.3 percent in the second half and 53.2 in the game.

Coach Smith had done a terrific job with his team and Person turned in a good performance with 23 points. It was a good show by a great player but Louisville had once again finished off an opponent with team play. Any one of the Cardinals was capable of hurting the other team.

The key to the game was Louisville's ability to shut Person down going into the final minutes of action with the 1-1-3 zone. He was the man for the Tigers who could make it happen, but not on this day.

For the Cardinals, it had been Herbert Crook's tournament. He was sensational. In fact, the entire frontline trio of Louisville was honored on the all-regional team along with Person and North Carolina's Brad Daugherty. Person was voted the MVP even though Van's and my ballots had Crook at the top. I've never understood how an MVP can be on a losing team. Regardless, when a team places all its baseline players on the All-Tournament squad, it sends a message to any and all future opponents.

"Destination Dallas" was now a reality. There had been talk about it as far back as the Big Apple NIT and, now, here it was — time for the Final Four. My mind flashed back to the loss at home to Cincinnati, the loss at Kansas, the terrific wins in the Metro's final regular-season game and the Metro Tournament wins that had made the No. 2 seed possible.

I also thought back to the many times when Denny Crum had come to the post-game show, usually preoccupied with what he planned to say. That was always his toughest time of the day — the job had been completed and it was late. He's usually spent by this time but still manages to do the show and do it well. He had kept saying all year that his team was getting better. He was always positive and could usually see the good in any performance, always finding something good to say about his team and the game.

It was obvious after the win over Auburn that he was very, very proud of his Cards. I felt that even winning the championship wouldn't make him any prouder than he was at the time. He knew his team had reached a plateau where they could beat anyone. The fact they had reached that point meant he had done his job, the players had done their job and he felt proud. So did I, and I hadn't done anything! All Cardinal fans were proud. There had been a goal set and reached. It was now time to set a new goal but, regardless of what happened, the Cardinals had made it to the Promised Land of success — the Final Four.

The buses were loaded for the airport and a happy trip home. Someone had a small TV and the Kentucky-LSU game was on. The Cards would play the winner. It was a close game even though LSU had already lost three previous games to the Wildcats of Kentucky. Now that a game against

Approximately 5,000 people greeted the team at the airport upon its arrival back in Louisville.

Jennifer Haddaway was all smiles after a trip to the Final Four was certain.

COMPLETE LOUISVILLE-AUBURN BOX SCORE

LOUISVILLE

Player	FG	FGA	FT	FTA	REB	PF	TP	A	TO	BLK	S	MIN
Crook	8	12	4	5	11	3	20	3	1	0	1	39
Thompson	5	10	3	4	7	4	13	4	4	0	1	26
Ellison	7	14	1	3	10	2	15	0	2	2	3	35
Hall	7	12	0	0	0	1	14	2	1	0	0	36
Wagner	4	9	8	8	2	2	16	9	2	0	0	40
Kimbro	0	1	0	0	1	0	0	0	1	0	0	5
McSwain	2	3	0	0	4	2	4	2	1	0	0	15
Walls	1	2	0	0	0	1	2	0	0	0	0	4
Team					2							
Deadball Rebounds					0							
Totals	34	63	16	20	37	15	84	20	12	2	5	200

FG%: 1st Half 56.4   2nd Half 50.0   Game 54.0
FT%: 1st Half 00.0   2nd Half 80.0   Game 80.0

AUBURN

Player	FG	FGA	FT	FTA	REB	PF	TP	A	TO	BLK	S	MIN
Morris	7	10	3	3	9	4	17	1	4	1	4	34
Person	11	24	1	2	4	3	23	1	2	0	0	38
Moore	4	8	3	5	6	2	11	2	0	0	0	31
White	3	6	2	2	2	2	8	9	4	0	1	34
Ford	6	10	1	2	3	4	13	5	0	0	1	34
Howard	1	1	0	0	0	3	2	2	0	0	0	12
Jones	1	3	0	0	1	3	2	0	0	1	0	17
Team					2							
Deadball Rebounds					2							
Totals	33	62	10	14	27	21	76	20	10	2	6	200

FG%: 1st Half 62.5   2nd Half 43.3   Game 53.2
FT%: 1st Half 60.0   2nd Half 77.8   Game 71.4

Halftime: Louisville 44, Auburn 43
Attendance: 9,650

Kentucky was very possible, people on the trip weren't sure that's what they wanted anymore. Playing in a Final Four was tough enough and the Cards sure didn't need all the extra hoopla and added pressure that would be present with a matchup against Kentucky. It would have been great for the state but, at this point in time, my concern was for the Louisville Cardinals. Louisville could and would have beaten Kentucky but, for the sake of sanity and peace of mind, I wanted LSU to win.

It would make life in Dallas a lot more enjoyable.

LSU did come through and upset the Cats. Dallas was going to be fun.

We arrived back in Louisville at about 10:30 p.m. and were greeted by 5,000 excited Cardinal fans. All were extremely happy and anxious to get a glimpse of their rolling Cardinals in person. Getting out of the airport wasn't easy, but it was fun.

It had been a great trip with two super wins. The dream had come true and another giant step taken. Louisville was in the Final Four and those "Destination Dallas" T-shirts that had been around for awhile had taken on a new and serious meaning. No longer was it just words on a shirt. It was real. "Destination Dallas" was just four days away. How sweet it was!

7

The Final Four

The most important thing a Cardinal fan could say at this time was "I'm going to Dallas." The worst was "I can't go, but I'll be watching and listening," and even a lot of them ended up in Dallas.

As the week progressed, the anxiety began to build. Cardinal fans are prone to throw caution into the wind when their favorite team is in the Final Four. Then it hits them, "What the hell, this doesn't happen every day." It makes it easier to do something really wild, like taking the kid's money for a spring vacation to Florida out of the cookie jar, or selling the dog, or taking out a second mortgage on the house, or borrowing money from the in-laws, or maybe even giving blood everyday for a week and possibly even donating some body organs for a price, or selling the stamp or gun collection that's taken 27 years to accumulate because all they do anyway is just sit there.

Hey, this was the NCAA Final Four and the Cards would be there! The words of the week quickly became "I'm going." People staggering down the street were babbling "I'm going. I'm going. To heck with having no tickets, I'm going." And they went.

It'd be a conservative estimate to say 2,500 Cardinal fans went to Dallas without tickets. In all my traveling days of chasing athletic contests around, this was the toughest ticket of all to get. Take a look. Freedom Hall is sold out every game at 19,000-plus. For the Final Four, U of L's allotment was just 1,600 tickets.

Louisville's ticket manager, Betty Jackson, is the best there is at what she does, but her job that week was impossible. There was once a carpenter's son, who we all studied about in Bible School, who was able to take two fish and five loaves of bread and feed 5,000 worshippers and still have 12 full baskets of food left over. This was not the case with Betty and the 1,600 tickets.

She is a mere mortal, just like the rest of us, and the tickets could accommodate only 1,600 fans. Betty did a marvelous job with what she had, but I'm sure there were a lot of disgruntled folks who felt like they'd gone through rain, sleet and snow to be with their Cards and now, in the most important games of all, couldn't get a ticket. I'm sure there were some very unhappy people, but I never came across a single fan who had a bad attitude about the situation. Most of them were great about it and seemed to be real happy just being close to the games, still hoping for the miracle of a ticket to appear in their hands.

Nobody, me included, escaped the requests. I must have had 40 calls at home from fans wanting to talk about the Cards and their chances in Dallas, the possibility of tickets and a place to stay. I have several out-of-state buddies who call regularly, just to talk. Anytime something good or bad happens, I hear from all of them.

Dallas was something good to talk about so my phone was jumping. The talk now was about a national championship and, I'll admit, those were my thoughts, too. I guess when you can see the end of the tunnel it's just natural to make that the goal. Besides, Cardinal fans are eternal optimists when it comes to the U of L basketball team.

Before leaving for Dallas, I had my own questions. How did LSU beat Kentucky? Could they sneak up on the Cardinals?

I had taped a previous game between Kentucky and LSU so I quickly popped it into my VCR and got out the LSU media guide. My immediate thoughts were about what Denny and the gang were working on. There were four practice days before they left at 5 p.m. on Thursday. On Friday, the Cards could work out in Reunion Arena.

Those four good practice days in Crawford Gym were important to the Cards. Tony Kimbro and the rest of the players who were slightly banged up would have time to heal. As for practicing, everything is done by this time of the season. It was just a matter of keeping sharp and physically fit.

Part of the reason for Louisville's success was their ability to adjust to whatever was thrown at them. What was once a weakness during the early part of the season had now

become a strength. The communications between the players and Coach Crum had been tried and tested back in January, but now it was a complete and finished product.

I was happy when I found out Louisville would play the first game in Dallas. This would let the coaches, providing they beat LSU (and I felt really good about the Cards' chances of doing just that), scout the Duke-Kansas game. For sure, that game would be the toughest semifinal contest but that's one of the breaks that helps in a drive for a championship. It could have turned out differently but, on paper, that's the way it looked.

Standiford Field was packed for the departure to Dallas on Thursday. The team charter was again going on an L-1011, a big plane that seats over 300 people. Four of these planes full of Cardinal rooters would eventually leave from Louisville. Most everyone arrived at least 90 minutes early and the place was jammed with people wearing red. People were laughing and yelling, and it was obviously a different attitude than the trip to Houston, not nearly as tense. They all thought U of L would roll into Dallas, blow out LSU, jockey around with the Duke-Kansas winner, bring the hardware on home, have the celebration and then ask the same ol' question of "how do they look for next year?" As for myself, I was still concerned about Kansas.

Before the NCAA Tournament began, I received a clipping in the mail from an unknown person. It was an article written by Wayne Lockwood of the *San Diego Union* newspaper in California. In his article, Lockwood talked about Louisville losing to Kansas twice along with some other facts, but he went out on a limb and wrote, "I've got the horse right here and it comes from the same place where they run for the roses every May. The sun shines bright on my old Kentucky Homeboys. I like Louisville to win the whole thing. No real reasons, just a good team, good coach, good tournament history, good schedule and a good head of steam." That was pretty nifty to pick the winner before the 64 teams even began play.

It's easy to say to a group of friends that you think so-and-so will win it all, but to put it into print for thousands of readers to see takes either guts, being blurry eyed or temporarily out of your gourd, or having a crystal ball. I'd like to talk to Lockwood about the stock market someday so I wrote him back and thanked him for his confidence in the Cards.

Plane A included the team, coaches, dignitaries, athletic and academic administrators, media, politicians, judges, doctors, dentists, engineers and people like me. Right across the aisle and down a couple of rows from me sat Kay Morrissey, spokesperson for Weight Watchers. She gave my waistline a glance or two and sort of smiled. What could I say?

As the wheels of the plane touched ground at Dallas-Fort Worth Airport, I thought to myself that this was it. This was center stage of the best of 64 teams, teams that had advanced on their merits of battle to become one of the honored teams — the Final Four. I screamed aloud, "Destination Dallas," much to the pleasure of those sitting around me.

The Final Four had become an event that ranked up there with the Kentucky Derby, Indianapolis 500, Super Bowl, World Series and maybe even the 4th of July. It was something very big now although it wasn't always like that.

The first tournament was put on by the National Association of Basketball Coaches (NABC) back in 1939. There were eight teams and it was played on the campus of Northwestern University. Oregon defeated Ohio State 46-33

The team's arrival in Dallas was without much hoopla.

in the championship game. But the amazing thing about that first tournament was it took in a grand total of $42 while the expenses were $2,573. That was a pretty good loss and was the last time the coaches ever thought about sponsoring a tourney.

The NCAA took over in 1940. Twenty-four teams participated from 1954-73 and since that time the tourney has been

Immediately after stepping off the plane, Coach Crum and his son, Scott, were met by a television crew.

restructured to accommodate 32 teams, then 40, 48, 52, 53 and finally 64 in 1985.

The revenues have also increased dramatically. In 1983 in the New Orleans' Superdome, four teams — North Carolina, Georgetown, Houston and Louisville — played before 60,000 fans. In the 1984-85 Final Four, the teams were awarded checks of $708,000. Television commercial time was sold at $214,900 per 30 seconds. This past season, Louisville's championship year, each of the Final Four teams would receive in the neighborhood of $835,000. All of this happened in a span of 46 years!

The plane taxied to the terminal where 19 buses had been waiting patiently. You have to be patient on these trips because it's hard to move 1,200 or so people around without a few inconveniences. We left for the Fairmont Hotel without our luggage because, for some reason, the airline people couldn't get the cargo door open. About 20 of them stood around, scratching their heads as if to say, "I don't know what to do, do you?"

The 30-minute ride to the hotel gave everyone a chance to study Dallas. It's always exciting getting that first view of what you'll call home for the next few days. It was dark in Texas but the Fairmont looked beautiful on the Dallas skyline. Many tried to find the landmarks seen on CBS-TV's hit series "Dallas." The most prominent figure found was a big globe, lit up in the sky, that sat between the Hyatt Regency and Reunion Arena, the place where it would all happen. Our driver quickly told us that there was a restaurant in the globe and, believe it or not, a free elevator that would take you to the top for a beautiful peek at Dallas.

The lobby of the hotel was quiet when we walked in, something it wouldn't be again until four days later when the Louisville contingent left. The lobby served as the place to hang out, although it was tough on the pocketbook. A glass (not a bottle) of beer cost $3.50 in the lobby, a soft drink was $2 and a mixed drink was $4.50. It was a great place to give up drinking but the U of L fans, who like challenges, could be seen with Styrofoam coolers marching through the lobby after that first night.

Getting checked in can be a traumatic experience but, in this case, the Woodside Travel Agency had arranged these big tables alphabetically in this big ballroom. All you had to do was walk to your table and pick up your key. It was simple, providing your key was there. With a lot of people, you could expect a few problems.

One of the not-so-lucky guests was my comrade, Van Vance. He stood there with all the radio equipment and no place to go. All these people with no rooms began crowding around the tables in a panic, but Van, being the cool one he is, just sorta laid back away from the crowd like a cat in the night and waited for his opportunity to pounce upon a key. It happened just like that. In just a matter of moments, he was dangling a key around with a smile on his face. Where it came from is still a mystery.

Next came the task of getting the luggage. Somebody figured out how to get the cargo hatch open on the plane because everyone's luggage had been delivered to the hotel. Three hundred people looking for luggage at the same time can be hazardous to your health.

I saw Royce Cook holding a little bag, but she was smiling. I asked her if she had found her luggage and she answered, holding up her little bag, "This is the main one, this is my face! As long as I have this, I can make it." The bag turned out to be the one with her make-up in it that her husband, Dr. Clinton Cook, had managed to recapture. Royce was happy, to say the least, and added, "It was made possible by the skillful hands of a surgeon." That was the kind of spirit it takes to make it all work on a trip like this. Eventually, everyone got settled for the long day that awaited.

It was pre-game day on Friday and time to start worrying about LSU. Coach Dale Brown had done a magnificent job getting his team to the Final Four. They were the Cinderella of this year's ball. The Tigers had finished fifth in the SEC, so how could they be in the Final Four? I sincerely believe that half of the battle is getting the players to believe in themselves and in their coach. Dale Brown had done a masterful job of that. He had talked as if they were all like sons to him, they all loved each other and would fight to the finish because they did believe.

My duties were the same in the Final Four as they were before any game — get the interviews. My goal was Dale Brown.

When P.J. got down to the lobby, the usual adventure of

trying to find somewhere to eat began. The Fairmont was a beautiful place but, like in Houston, it was located in "Concrete City." Once again we were victims of the system. Breakfast cost about $17 for the bare necessities. Ever since I had been in Texas, I had a new admiration for egg-laying hens. It was only in Texas that I learned an egg is a treasured item and should be treated with respect. In Kentucky you could get a steak dinner for $17 but in Texas it would only get you an egg breakfast, if you were lucky. When the waitress asked you "how many" when she was seating you, what she really meant with her Texas NCAA accent was "Come on in, sucker. You're next." After that first morning, I told myself I was going to beat this game, but I never did.

Friday was a long, busy day for me. Most everybody else had big plans, including P.J. She had lived in Dallas for awhile and set out to visit some friends. Some folks went to

Scalping is legal in Dallas and tickets were at a premium.

"Southfork," some played golf and many went to the open practices at Reunion. That's where John Crawley, the editor of SCORE**CARD**, Van and I headed.

It looked like a short walk. Wrong! Van has that Park City Kentucky-lean when he walks. You've all heard the stories about how your parents used to walk 10 miles a day, one way, to the one-room school house. Well, it takes that certain lean that Van had to make it every day. Personally, I rode a school bus.

I was quickly losing ground with Van and John but managed to keep them in sight.

Along the way I ran into one of my ex-players from Lafayette High School, Irvin Stewart. He was with his new bride. Irvin was a fine player in his day and was also a good Louisville fan who just happens to live in Lexington. Actually, there are a lot of U of L fans in the Lexington area and it seemed like they were all in Dallas.

We approached a beautifully mirrored building with several different levels. It was stunning. Fortunately for my tired legs, it was the Hyatt Regency. The Hyatt was the media headquarters for the Final Four and the place where we needed to pick up our credentials. You had to identify yourself and sign for the passes. I felt like I was checking out of prison and they had to make sure they were letting the right guy go. These credentials were very, very valuable. All the members of the media received a big packet with information and a beautiful blanket that had the words "1986 NCAA Final Four" at the top. In the middle was a picture of a goal with a ball passing through, and at the bottom of the blanket were the words "Reunion Arena, Dallas Texas." The blanket was gray with red trim around the border. There was also an official tournament pin and a shaving kit with all the necessary ingredients. That was the good news. The bad news was that we had to carry it around with us all day. For sure, we didn't want to leave it lying around because it would be gone, pronto (that's Texas talk for fast). Van, John and I took turns guarding the packets the rest of the day.

Reunion Arena was decorated in a striking but unusual green and blue color combination. Between 6,000 and 8,000 spectators showed up for the practice sessions. You really got the feeling that something important was going to happen there. The atmosphere was exciting, but there was more to it than that. I felt privileged to be on the U of L radio broadcast team.

We found our broadcast position and, I have to admit, at that moment I felt a little important. There was my seat, and I had a pass to prove it. It was a special feeling for me so I could imagine how it must have felt to the players and coaches. I realized that my seat at the press table was a position earned for me by the Cardinals; but I began thinking about the other people who had made this possible and ran through the list in my mind, thanking each and every one of them. That's one of the things you do when you begin to get a little older and can appreciate the good things that have happened to you.

I watched LSU go through their paces. Dale Brown wore an all-white running outfit with white shoes. He was glowing and obviously proud of his team. Brown had his share of critics, but this was his time in the sun. You could tell he was loving it.

His players were zipping around the court but, as I looked at them, I knew in my mind that in no way could that bunch beat the Cards. Then reality struck. All the teams LSU had eliminated — Purdue, Memphis State, Georgia Tech and Kentucky — had probably felt the same way. Truthfully, the list of opponents they had faced in the tourney, overall, was a little better than Louisville's list, or at least as good. North Carolina was better than any of LSU's tourney opponents, but the Tigers had played the better four teams in my opinion. That thought got my attention again.

LSU's practice ended and it was time to head to the press conference to watch Dale Brown captivate the media. No one is better with the media when he's on a roll than Dale. I was looking forward to it.

The gathering became a lecture more than a question-and-answer period, though.

Dale had everybody in the room in the palm of his hand. He was truly on a natural high and you could just tell that he felt like his group of players had done something extra special. They had succeeded against all odds and had faced a solid string of adversities during the season. He told the media that being in the Final Four was "meant to be" for his group. They had been driven to this point by "determination within themselves."

It was a fact that LSU had succeeded beyond all the opinions of the experts. It was true they were fortunate to face Purdue and Memphis State at home and they had succeeded beyond the friendly confines of Baton Rouge. Personally, I gave the team and Dale Brown a lot of credit

LSU head coach Dale Brown talked about everything imaginable at the press conferences.

for getting to the Final Four. The bottom line usually is measured by how far a team got in the NCAA Tournament. LSU was there so what else needed to be said?

Coach Brown finally answered some questions from the press. He commented that he knew his team would be facing a team that was on a roll, just as his team was. Then he talked about his "freak defense," smiling in the process. Actually, the "freak" was just a blend of constantly changing combinations of different defenses, more a psychological ploy than anything else. Teams at this level are going to run what they know how to run best. There are very few secrets or tricks.

Dale is not recognized as a great tactician. Sam King, who covered LSU all season long, said in an article in the Dallas *Times-Herald*, "It is not with the X's and O's where Brown is outstanding, his forte is motivation, making one believe that anything can be accomplished."

It was easy to see that Brown was as King described. Dale has a treasure chest full of phrases and words. Dale said, "The impossible is what nobody can do until somebody does it." Now that's a statement we all need to dwell on.

I think he had a point. This LSU team had beaten Georgia Tech with its superstar, John Williams, scoring a mere four points. It sounded impossible, but it had happened.

Coach Brown rambled on some more about climbing mountains and conquering rivers, meeting and mastering challenges. His team had lost nine conference games, but Dale liked to think about it as his team had won nine conference games. They had faced chicken pox, ineligibility, discipline problems, transfers (Tito Horford) and just about everything else imaginable throughout the season. Now they were playing with four guards as starters with just one true inside player (Williams). Their center, Ricky Blanton, started out the season as a guard.

The LSU Tigers were mentally tough and tested, in a different way than the Cardinals. They had faced hard times and survived. They were in Dallas. Louisville had faced different kinds of hard times, but they, too, had survived. Both teams were mentally ready. Denny Crum had more heavy artillery to put on the court, but you knew Dale Brown had the Tigers believing no team had more to put anywhere than the LSU Tigers. After all, they had gotten to this point on belief.

I left the press conference feeling better about myself. It had been refreshing to listen to Dale and I really enjoyed it.

My goal for the day had been to get a one-on-one interview with LSU's head man. Thanks to two former U of L athletic department employees now at LSU, Joe Yates and Ed Atlas, I got my interview. Dale was extremely nice and cooperative.

After Dale, I interviewed the man who picked the Cardinals to win the national championship before the season even began, Larry Donald of *Basketball Times*. That was some kind of picking by the editor.

Denny's answers at his press conference were as expected, with no fancy phrases, just the facts and plain truth. He told the media he respected LSU and realized what they had accomplished. He's always talking about respecting the opponent and realized that LSU could put the Cardinals back on a plane if his players weren't ready.

Denny usually says whatever is necessary, and that's what he did after his practice. One of the Dallas writers had said in the Dallas *Morning News* that, "After Denny wins the national championship, he'll take it on back to Louisville and he won't be heard from until next year's Final Four news conference in New Orleans. Then he will walk quietly into the room and say, 'Good morning, gentleman, it's nice to be here.' " This same writer called Denny the "People's Express of college basketball coaching — no frills. Denny just gets you there."

Well, that's true in one sense, but if you are a Cardinal player or fan, there are lots of frills, including playing the best schedule in the country and still winning. That's a frill that tops anything a coach can do for his people.

The day was over and I was all tuckered out, but Van and I still had to get back to the hotel to set up for a three-hour talk show.

The lobby was packed, as usual, and the players were mixing in with the crowd.

But that's the way it should have been. There are some coaches, like North Carolina's Dean Smith who, while in Ogden, shielded the players away from everyone. Maybe that works for him, but the Cardinals need to be with their

Souvenir items were a priority with fans at the Fairmont.

fans. It's something they learn to deal with early in their careers at U of L and it becomes a normal part of their routine while on the road. It's great that Denny lets his players be involved in the total experience of college basketball, not just on the court. If a player of Denny's chooses to be alone, that's his privilege and he can plan his free time that way.

The radio show got underway and it worked out real well. A lot of WHAS people were on the trip, including Wayne Perkey, the very popular morning man for the station. He did his show earlier that day from the Fairmont and joined us on the call-in show that night. I listened to his and Van's great voices, and then there was mine! I was obviously outclassed. We took lots of calls and there were about 100 people hanging around us, all wanting to say hello to somebody back in Louisville.

All the activity in the lobby sorta reminded me of the way it used to be back at the corner drugstore when I was growing up. A lot of good times were being had by all. Everyone talked with everyone, there were no strangers. We were all operating under the same pressures for the same reason. It was just a group of people that had become close, and I really liked the atmosphere. Most of the talk centered around the game the next day.

Charles Jones, who had been a super player for the Cards and was now playing in the NBA with Phoenix, was getting so much attention that you'd have thought he was playing against LSU the next day. Another ex-Cardinal and a member of the 1980 championship team, Tony Branch, stopped by. People were reliving the shot he hit against Kansas State that kept the Cards' drive alive to the championship. Bill Darragh, a member of Louisville's 1956 NIT championship team, came by, just as he had done in all the post-season games. In fact, he was even with the Cards at the beginning of the season in New York.

Lee Murphy, Jim Coffey and Allen Sparr, all from Liberty, Ky., stopped by with William Hazlewood, a fan from Campbellsville. They told us that Tony York usually travels with them, but his wife had just made him a proud papa. For that reason he was excused. He had to spend some time raising the young one up to be a Cardinal fan.

Everyone who came by wanted to touch my lucky white cap. I play in a lot of golf tournaments over the year, and everyone tries to get my cap from me. I used to give a lot of them away, but it got a tad too expensive.

While doing the radio show, I talked about my day at the arena when I had climbed the rail and gone up into the stands. I talked to about 40 or 50 strangers that afternoon, representing 17 different states, including Alaska and Hawaii. It was amazing to me that people had come from everywhere to watch the Final Four even though their team wasn't playing. One young man I had talked to had ridden a motorcycle all the way from the state of Washington. Another family had come from Ft. Myers, Florida. They were all just basketball fans.

It had been a long day for everybody, but it had been fun. Van, P.J. and I joined the other WHAS people for a late

Former Card Charles Jones, now with the Phoenix Suns of the NBA, could be found wandering around in the hotel lobby.

supper in the Pyramid Restaurant, located in the hotel. It was a real nice place but a little expensive. Thanks to a nice boss, however, I was relieved of the pain and suffering of paying the bill.

Those who attended the pep rally before the LSU game were treated to a buffet.

Just a few hours later and it would be the day of the game. I thought to myself that Louisville should win and, if they did, this edition of the 1985-86 Louisville basketball team would be in the national championship game! Yes, it was possible that this same team that had lost to Cincinnati in Freedom Hall back on Jan. 20 could win it all. Who'da thunk it?

When I opened my eyes on Saturday morning to start what would hopefully be an exciting and rewarding day, all I could think about was "game day." I didn't just jump out of bed, I thought about the fact that Louisville's opponent, LSU, had defeated a No. 1 seed (Kentucky) and a No. 2 seed (Georgia Tech) on supposedly neutral floors. That meant, according to the way the NCAA seeds teams, that LSU's two latest victims were among the top eight teams in the country. That, by itself, was impressive, but I wasn't quite sure just how in the world they did it. When I saw LSU on the court they just didn't look very impressive.

Then I remembered that I needed to get some thoughts together for the pep rally, a rally that would be attended by Kentucky Governor Martha Layne Collins, ex-Governor John Y. Brown and his wife Phyllis George Brown, Jefferson County Judge Harvey Sloane, Louisville Mayor Jerry Abramson and anybody else who could get in.

This was the most excited I'd ever seen the Louisville fans during the five years I'd been associated with the Cardinals.

That morning, P.J. and I actually beat the "breakfast Trap" because there was a buffet served at the pep rally. When we arrived, it was all you could do to hear anybody's conversation above the noise. In all my experience with crowds, this room had the most electrifying atmosphere I've ever been a part of. The fans were ready to let it all hang out. The pep band knocked out some notes and the cheerleaders did their thing.

We sat down at the WHAS table with Bob Scherer, Lisa Von Kannel and Mary Jeffries. Van was in the ballroom, but I wasn't sure where. The breakfast was nice but, with all the things happening in the place, who could eat?

As usual, Van and I took the stage together. Van made a few comments and then introduced me. I got up and put Van down a little and then told my story for the day. I told everybody about the line I saw going into a room on the 14th floor.

I happened by the line and remarked that I didn't realize there was a public rest room on this floor. A young lady in line answered back, "Oh, this isn't a rest room, this is Van Vance's room."

Well, that warmed the crowd up some, not that they needed it, and I went on to tell another story. I told the crowd about this flat-chested young lady who was walking down the beach, seemingly very depressed because she was being completely ignored. All the other ladies on the beach who had been blessed with big chests had all the men chasing around after them. This bottle floated up and had a cork in it. She picked up the bottle and removed the cork. To her surprise out came a Genie who said, "You have freed me and I will grant you any one wish that you desire." The girl thought for a minute and said, "I would like to have the two biggest boobs in the world." Then, all of a sudden, before her very eyes appeared Dana Kirk and Dale Brown.

When I finished, I heard the loudest, most deafening outburst since I've been speaking to groups, and I've been speaking a long time. There was a huge explosion of laughter. As it turned out, it was just what the people needed. I'll always remember that outburst and the totally deafening roar the crowd made. The joke was not meant to cast any reflection on Dana or Dale, it just happened to be the names the fans wanted to hear.

Van and I left for the arena two hours before the 2:30 tipoff time and when we arrived the place was already swarming with people. Reports began circulating that there were people running up and grabbing tickets out of other peoples' hands and dashing off. That's when a good load of buckshot would have come in handy, cutting the thieves' dash time down a little. It was actually hard to get to the press entrance. Every spoken sentence was, "Do you have any tickets?" One guy who wasn't wearing a shirt had it written on his chest and back with a magic marker. Tickets were selling for $400 and $500 a throw. It was plain insane. Paying that much for a ticket to anything other than the pearly gates meant the brain was on the blink. I had my pass tucked inside my shirt to be safe and it sure was nice to get inside, even though it was a beautiful day. I was convinced that some of those folks would have killed just to get in the door.

They always have food and drink in the media room, along with the latest statistics. We needed the stats for our broadcast, so the press room was our first stop. While there, we ran into ex-*Courier-Journal* writer Dave Kinred, who was with the *Washington Post*. Dave is the Dr. J. in the world

of sportswriters. Mark Bradley, an ex-Lexington *Herald* reporter who was now with the *Atlanta Constitution*, also chatted with us, along with some others.

Jock Sutherland and Van Vance got ready for their pre-game radio show.

Everyone we talked to picked Louisville to win, no question about it. I brought up what LSU had done but the whole group of media folks standing around just said, "No way, not against Louisville. Pervis Ellison would eat Ricky Blanton's lunch." I asked one of them about John Williams and some guy snapped, "What about him?" as if to say he wasn't going to do anything.

Well, now that I was reassured, Van and I headed out to the floor so he could get us on the air. That's one thing Van will always do. He'd get us on the air from a cardboard box down in an elevator shaft if he had to. Unlike most play-by-play announcers, Van does his own engineering. We carry our own equipment and Van pieces it all together. That's the way he wants it and that's the way it is. In my opinion, he's the best there is at what he does. This day there weren't any problems, but that wasn't true at all our stops.

Reunion Arena filled up quickly for the double header. Across the floor from us was a sea of red. I spotted my friends from Vanderbilt, head coach C.M. Newton and his wife Evelyn, and assistant coach John Bostick and his wife Betty. Sitting next to them was the guy from Indiana, Bob Knight, who was wearing a Duke button. The ex-Olympic coach and bad boy of the college coaching world hates to be called

Bobby. I would have loved to have had a tape of the conversation they were having. Since C.M. and Bob were Olympic coaches together, they had become thicker than sorghum molasses in the wintertime.

But John and C.M. had already assured me that Louisville would win it all, and they made it sound so simple. Later, Coach Lake Kelly of Austin Peay and Coach Lee Rose of South Florida agreed. It seems that on this day the only LSU backers were from Baton Rouge. They had seen the miracle work.

Before I could look up at the scoreboard, LSU, a team seeded No. 11 by the NCAA, was ahead 11-4. Louisville tied it at about the 14-minute mark, but bingo, LSU started rolling again with some great shooting (20 of 35). Six straight points at the end sent LSU into the locker room with a 44-36 lead.

Turnovers by the Cards had done most of the damage. Turnovers are bad news for any team, but somehow the Cards had managed to win all season long in spite of them. Trailing by eight points at the half puts enormous pressure on the trailing team to get off to a quick second-half start. It doesn't take long for an 8-point lead to suddenly go to 12 and then to 14. Then you're in real trouble.

But the Cards had been a super second-half team during the latter half of the season, and this day it would have to be that way. Just as the second half was about to begin, Van said, "They have to do it now, right now." That should have been my line, but I was still grumbling about the nine first-half turnovers. Louisville was in its tightest spot since the beginning of the NCAA Tournament games.

In the first 20 minutes there were six ties, the last one coming at 33-33 with 7:01 on the clock. For the remainder of the half, though, the Cards were outscored 11-3 and they had had some type of mix-up on the last shot before the buzzer. It wasn't a very reassuring way to go in at the half but that's when having a strong personality and a man who you believe in becomes so important. No team goes out after halftime and timeouts better than the Louisville Cardinals.

Jeff Hall popped in 14 points and was one of five Cards in double figures.

The fact that the players realized they were a second-half team and LSU's shooting would eventually cool down was in U of L's favor. And that's exactly what happened. After hitting 57.1 percent of its field-goal attempts in the first half, LSU could do no better than 14 of 40 (35 percent) after intermission. On the other hand, Louisville sizzled the nets for 63.9 percent in the second period after shooting just 46.9 percent in the first half.

The second half was all Louisville. Billy and Milt scored quick field goals to pull the Cards within 44-40. At the 15:13 mark and still trailing 54-48, the lights went out in Baton Rouge. Two straight misses by LSU's Don Redden followed by baskets by Thompson and Wagner, a three-point play by Mark McSwain, and two more long-range bombs by Wagner put the Cards ahead 65-55. Redden ended U of L's run with a basket at the 10:06 mark, but the damage had been done as Louisville outscored LSU 17-1 during the five-minute stretch.

Playing while behind for some teams is not as easy as

playing while holding the lead, but you have to give the Tigers credit because they fought back. Redden, who reminded me of Tennessee's past great player Ernie Grunfeld, played tough and finished with 22 points. Big John Williams had a strong first half with 12 points, but Billy T. shut him down to only one field goal in the final period.

"I knew he [Williams] could hurt us," said Billy, "so I watched him to the very end."

Louisville went on to win 88-77, but LSU gained the respect of many when they battled back to within 82-77 with 56 seconds left. They were forced to foul after that and some clutch free-throw shooting by the Cards, which had become a trademark of U of L's in the NCAA Tournament, stretched the lead. Dr. Stan Frager, a U of L faculty member, had worked with the players on concentration after the team had shot poorly from the line during the beginning of the season, and it had paid off.

The miracles for LSU had run out. They had traveled all the miles they could go with what they had to roll on. Still, they showed a lot of toughness which only comes from being subjected to adversity and fighting your way against the odds. The Tigers committed only eight turnovers against the tough defensive pressure applied by Louisville. I went away from that game with a lot more respect for Dale Brown. It was easy to understand why he was so proud of his group.

Louisville was led by Billy (who tied Jerry Lucas' 25-year-old record for shooting accuracy in a semifinal game by hitting 10 of 11 field goals) and Milt with 22 points apiece. Milt had a bad first half but responded to a few choice words presented to him at the half by Denny Crum. Pervis led the rebounders with 13 big ones.

It was a good show by Louisville and all five starters had once again scored in double figures, another trademark of

Pervis Ellison stretched to block a shot by LSU's Don Redden.

the Cardinals. The fact they finished with 26 assists didn't hurt.

"We played with everything we had," said LSU's Brown, "as hard as we could possibly play. We gave it our best effort."

What had become "Destination Monday Night Final Game" had now become "Destination National Champions." Just thinking about the Cards playing in the championship game blew me away.

I'm normally a real fan of Kansas coach Larry Brown but, after the Cards had won, I pulled hard for the Duke Blue Devils. I knew U of L could beat Duke but, as I had said before, Kansas really scared me. It would make my Easter Sunday a lot nicer if the fellows from Lawrence were heading on back to the wheat fields to catch up on all that homework they had missed.

Following the win over LSU, Denny seemed remarkably relaxed and confident during his post-game show. He sorta reminded me of someone who knew he had the winning hand in a high-stakes poker game. He knew the other card players had strong hands and felt like they had the winning hand, but Denny knew that in his hand were the Cards that would win the pot. They were playing 5-card stud and Denny had three aces and a king showing, with another ace in the hole. The opponent had a possible ace-high straight showing, with the ace missing and a smile on his face.

Denny's confidence had come from knowing he could make the changes which needed to be made and get the performance and execution from his players he asked for. The only thing he was having a hard time controlling were

Pervis Ellison, Herbert Crook and LSU's John Williams battled for this rebound.

the turnovers. His team had improved so much in all phases of the game except in that category. He had the disease controlled at times, but the rash was subject to break out again at any moment.

The Cards had cut down on their turnovers in the second half against LSU, committing just five to finish with 14. Now that wasn't too bad. We found out in the championship game that this team could turn the ball over more than expected

COMPLETE LOUISVILLE-LSU BOX SCORE

LOUISVILLE

Player	FG	FGA	FT	FTA	REB	PF	TP	A	TO	BLK	S	MIN
Crook	8	13	0	1	9	3	16	3	2	0	0	32
Thompson	10	11	2	5	10	4	22	4	3	1	1	36
Ellison	5	11	1	2	13	3	11	1	1	1	0	34
Hall	6	11	2	2	1	1	14	2	2	0	0	32
Wagner	8	16	6	6	4	1	22	11	4	0	1	36
Kimbro	0	2	0	0	0	1	0	1	2	0	1	8
McSwain	1	2	1	1	4	2	3	0	0	1	0	14
Walls	0	2	0	0	0	0	0	4	0	0	0	8
Team					3							
Deadball Rebounds					1							
Totals	**38**	**68**	**12**	**17**	**44**	**15**	**88**	**26**	**14**	**3**	**3**	**200**

FG%: 1st Half	46.9	2nd Half	63.9	Game	55.9		
FT%: 1st Half	75.0	2nd Half	66.7	Game	70.6		

LSU

Player	FG	FGA	FT	FTA	REB	PF	TP	A	TO	BLK	S	MIN
Williams	7	17	0	1	9	4	14	6	4	0	0	35
Redden	10	20	2	3	6	3	22	1	2	0	0	28
Blanton	3	5	3	6	12	4	9	2	0	1	1	38
Taylor	7	17	2	2	1	2	16	4	1	0	3	38
A. Wilson	7	15	1	1	3	3	15	0	0	0	1	38
Woodside	0	0	0	0	0	0	0	0	0	0	0	2
Brown	0	1	1	2	3	0	1	0	1	0	0	13
Vargas	0	0	0	0	0	0	0	0	0	0	0	6
E. Wilson	0	0	0	0	0	0	0	0	0	0	0	1
Conley	0	0	0	0	0	0	0	0	0	0	0	1
Team					1							
Deadball Rebounds					2							
Totals	**34**	**75**	**9**	**15**	**35**	**16**	**77**	**13**	**8**	**1**	**5**	**200**

FG%: 1st Half	57.1	2nd Half	35.0	Game	45.3		
FT%: 1st Half	50.0	2nd Half	71.4	Game	60.0		

Halftime: LSU 44, Louisville 36
Attendance: 17,007

and still be triumphant. If you're able to win despite a lot of turnovers, it means you're doing a lot of things really well. For sure, Denny knew that better than the faithful Cardinal followers.

I gave Denny, the Magic Man, my customary "thumbs-up" sign once the post-game show ended and he flashed a nice winning smile at me that meant "nice work, guys." Van, better than any other announcer can do it, told the listening audience "Good night, everybody," and we shook hands. It was time to go home to the Fairmont because the next day would start the routine of practices and press conferences all over again. It was going to be one Easter Sunday, however, when the Easter Bunny would have to give most of the Cardinal followers a rain check, especially those in Dallas. I've already told you about the egg situation in this big cowboy city.

The lobby of the Fairmont was really jumping. Everybody was relieved that the game was over. Even the high price of the drinks was not inhibiting many of the followers. Most were making their eating plans for the evening as many had found a way to escape the hotel prices. That was my goal too, and I lucked out. P.J. had arranged for some of her friends in Dallas — Tom and Rose Marie Snell and their son, David (all who became Cardinal fans during the week) — to pick us up and they took us to a place called Caulfields in Greenville Village. It was very reasonable and very good.

While at this restaurant, I ran into another group of Louisville people and we took a few pictures together. Everyone had a ball and it was a nice way to end what had been a very satisfying day.

When we got back to the hotel after dinner, people were everywhere. I roamed around and visited with a lot of people. Time after time, I'd be standing toe-to-toe with somebody,

U of L president Dr. Donald Swain was very rarely without his western motif.

not knowing their name but feeling a closeness that felt really special. Dr. Swain was roaming around with a big cowboy hat on his head and I tried to envision how he would look on a horse. His hat looked good enough for me to request a side-by-side picture of the two of us. I thought it was terrific for him to bump and rub elbows with everyone else. Yes, sirree, when you can get the University's president to walk around with a cowboy hat on, you're on a roll. And that's exactly what the Louisville Cardinals were then — on a roll. The win over LSU was Louisville's 16th straight and its 20th in the last 21 games. Louisville's record stood at 31-7, and everyone was thinking that winning No. 32 sure would be a nice way to end the month of March.

Spending Easter Sunday in Dallas was a first for me and a lot of other people. Since I was working, the day meant press conferences and practices for Louisville and Duke — the last two teams in the USA still eligible to win the national championship. My first thoughts that morning were about Duke. I had my own opinions about their strengths and weaknesses, and wanted to get them fixed in my mind before listening to the coaches and reading the papers.

Johnny Dawkins, for sure, was the most explosive guard in the nation. He was lightning quick and his moves were frightening. Some of his shots were a little unorthodox (he got them off unusually quick and at times seemed to go off the wrong foot, catching defensive people off guard) but there was no better penetrator in the country. Penetrating guards had hurt the Cards at different times during the season. Dawkins was Duke's all-time leading scorer and that alone said enough. It just seemed that most of his strengths directly attacked the Cards in some of their weaker areas.

His running mate was Tommy Amaker. He was sorta like U of L's Herbert Crook, shunned by the media. Like Crook, Amaker made great contributions to his team but was often overlooked by the media because of the superstars on the squad. Still, Amaker was a picture-perfect point guard. During his junior year he compiled 200 assists, second-best in Duke's history, but his most amazing statistic was that he performed with almost no errors — just 64 turnovers in 31 games. He was very fast, steady, seldom got into foul trouble and was a monster to handle the ball against.

Dawkins and Amaker may have been the best guard duo in the nation. They seemed to have it all. Their weakness, if there was one, was the fact they were only 6-0 and 6-2. Hopefully, I thought, Louisville could take advantage of its height at guard with Milt Wagner and Jeff Hall standing at 6-5 and 6-4, respectively.

Thinking about all the match-ups made me want to roll over and go back to sleep but I let my mind churn a little more. The most encouraging thing I could find was that Duke didn't have the athletes that Louisville had. It doesn't matter how good the execution and the technique are, when being applied against a team that is also very skilled and does a good job of executing, the better athletes will usually prevail. Basketball is basically a game of running, jumping and shooting. As I saw it, Louisville could outshoot and outjump the Duke team, and possibly outrun them. I knew U of L's inside people could outrun their counterparts but I couldn't see anybody outrunning Dawkins and Amaker. Those two guys could make the cartoon character Roadrunner (beep,

classroom. It wasn't going to be an IQ contest but who knew? The Cards may have won that, too. Still, Louisville took some unfair criticism over the academic side of athletics, all unfounded. As a rule, some writers always look for a different, unique way of approaching their topic. In this case, some took the academic approach which, in my opinion, didn't impress any readers. The big question on the following night would be the final score, not the intelligence quotient.

Some of the articles on the day after the press conference pictured Denny as pretty bland, not very humorous. It was probably the importance of the job at hand which made him seem that way to those who didn't cover the Cards on a regular basis, but those close to the program know he's a real entertainer and just as humorous and colorful as the next guy, especially when he's talking about fishing, hunting or golf. This was a time for business, not laughs. One guy wrote, "Give this man [Denny] a personality transplant and he might be like, . . . oh, maybe even Digger Phelps." Obviously, we all know Denny doesn't need a personality transplant. It wasn't time to be funny, it was time to win a national title. After that was accomplished, everyone could be funny in Louisville while it may have been a little hard to get a laugh in Durham, North Carolina.

After Louisville finished at the podium, Coach Mike

Duke coach Mike Krzyzewski and his players became the "darlings" of the media.

Krzyzewski and all five of his starters took the stage. Their approach to the press conference was entirely different, very light and humorous. Jay Bilas was asked about his professional ambitions, and he replied, "I'd give my right arm to play pro basketball, but there's not much call for one-arm players in the NBA." Alarie commented that he "felt like a coach on the court and Coach K doesn't have to tell me anything on the court anymore." The Duke coach followed with, "Does that mean that tomorrow you're not going to listen during timeouts? Is this mutiny, or what?"

Before this particular press conference, the word on Duke had been that they were placid and humorless, about "like a kid finding an algebra book in his Christmas stocking" as one writer described them. Coach K responded to that by saying, "I was shocked when I read that. It must have been started by a couple of guys in New York and what do they know about having fun?" The writer replied, "Good point. The biggest thrill you can get out of a day in Manhattan is making it home on the subway and still have both ears." Someone asked Coach K about the Coach of the Year award, and he answered, "We're still trying to get something passed in the Coaches' Association to let Polish coaches vote."

The Duke contingent put on a pretty good show. They had been funny and answered the obvious questions regarding quickness, player match-ups and Louisville's full-court press. A writer for the Dallas *Morning News* wrote in Monday's paper about the press conference: "Duke was heavily favored in this match-up and, as expected, blew them away easily."

I ran into *Courier-Journal* columnist Billy Reed at the press conference and he felt, like me, that the tone of the conference wasn't fair to the Cards. The whole affair had put down the University of Louisville, sorta like "look how smart and great we (Duke) are." What I really think we saw was a group of players and a coach who had never been at this level before, and it was their way of relieving some of the pressure. They simply stepped out of character for a few minutes. They said nothing derogatory about the Cardinals, but it was their answers to the questions that turned the thing into a one-liner contest. The group from Duke came across as a little cocky, but after 21-straight wins it was easy to feel that way.

After the conference with the masses, the players and Coach K went to several individual podiums so the members of the media could talk to them one-on-one. During this time, they all appeared more serious and gave good, solid answers. Coach K, for example, was asked about being a former Indiana player and coach under Bob Knight. The Duke head man replied, "I totally respect and love Coach Knight, but I do things my way, just as he does things his way." He wanted it known that he was his own man.

I liked Coach K and it was obvious that he had done a terrific job with his group of players. Still, I got the feeling that he was aware he just might be playing this card game with a weaker hand. There's a lot to be said for quickness and jumping ability, and I felt like he knew it would take an extraordinary performance to beat the Cardinals. Sure, Johnny Dawkins could do a lot of damage, but for him to do enough to win would be tough.

Duke was entering the championship game with a tournament average of 69.4 points from its top five players and 77.7 with its two reserves coming off the bench.

On the other hand, Louisville was heading into the final game with an average of 75.6 points from its starters and 82.8 when you added the top two reserves. But the biggest stat for everyone to see was the shooting percentage. The Blue Devils were hitting a weak 48.5 percent from the field in tournament play and just 67.6 percent from the foul line. Meanwhile, the Cards were hitting 56.9 and 79.5 percent, respectively. Another telling stat was the category of assists where the Duke team was averaging 13 per game compared to 20 for the Cardinals.

Through all the hype, these figures really made Duke's chances look slim. But we all know that shooting is like "true love — it's true until it ain't true no more." It's not something you can count on. A good friend of mine had a wife everyone thought was crazy about him. She took $20 to go to the store, kissed him and told him she loved him, then left. That was nine years ago and was the last time he saw her (she cleaned out the bank account that day). Shooting the basketball is not all that predictable either, but taking the right kind of

Easter Sunday was a day for rest and relaxation, although no one forgot the main purpose for being in Dallas.

shots makes it more predictable. Louisville takes those kind of shots because Denny Crum sees to it.

It was time for Louisville's practice to begin, but the NCAA closes practice to the media and fans on this day so Van and I headed back to the Fairmont to salvage what we could of Easter Sunday. I toyed with the idea of going to Southfork with the rest of the media, but was told that what you see on TV each week is not exactly the way it really is. During the introduction of "Dallas" on CBS, the cameras always pan what appears to be a spacious ranch as if it was sitting alone on thousands of acres of land. Not true. Actually it is right across the street from some sort of a housing neighborhood. Still, the invitation included a rodeo, Texas-style barbecue, country band and a tour of the mansion. The media ticket read "Visit the site of dirty deals and torrid romance, and dress western." The only thing I had that was western was an appetite. It was about an hour's ride from downtown Dallas to Southfork and I'm one of J.R.'s biggest fans, but I had to pass on this day. All I wanted to do was get back to the Fairmont for a nice shower and a little R&R.

After thinking about Duke all day and hearing and seeing them up close, I felt even better about U of L's chances. I was confident that Louisville would win so I actually enjoyed my dinner that evening.

The entire crew from WHAS went to a restaurant called "Dakota's." Terry Meiners, the afternoon disc jockey at WHAS, kept us entertained all night. He's something else and going anywhere with him is an experience. Louisville's newly elected mayor, Jerry Abramson, went with us and at one point said, "I sure did pick a great year to get elected as mayor." He wasn't kidding.

We were seated in an outside area that was just beautiful. I looked up and saw a great big guy strolling in. It turned out to be Greg Dreiling of Kansas — the guy I had been leary of as far as the fate of the Cardinals was concerned. I asked him who he liked to win in the final game, Louisville or Duke. He didn't seem to want to answer the question but finally said enough that I knew his choice was Louisville.

At another table sat the officials who would work the championship game along with John Clougherty — Hank Nichols, Don Rutledge and Pete Pavia. Later, as we were leaving the restaurant, they asked P.J. and me to take their pictures beside the built-in water falls.

The day had been a nice one, even though I had hated it because I didn't get to spend much time with P.J. But working on Easter meant the Cards were still alive and taking care of business. That's what we were all doing.

We arrived back at the hotel and fought our way through a packed lobby. When we got to our room, the bad news was stuck under the door. A note said that all rooms had to be cleared by 1 p.m. the next day which meant everyone would have to find a place to loaf until 8 p.m. that evening. That's a long time to hang around, especially in the clothes you have to wear to the game and travel back to Louisville in. We all would need to go through a car wash before we got back home.

Monday had arrived. It was game day, national championship day. It was a day when a lot of people would actually get to the end of that rainbow and collect that pot of gold.

The Cardinals reminded me of a rainbow. The individual statistics were not that impressive but when combined together it was something else. Take a single color from a rainbow, look at it and it's not anything special, but the blending together of all the colors makes it something spectacular. The Cards were the same way.

The clock read 8:20 a.m. and I thought to myself that it wouldn't be until 4 or 5 a.m. the next morning before the U of L contingent arrived back in Louisville. It was going to

Cheerleaders Missy Perkins and Jennifer Haddaway tried their best to get the crowd fired up at Monday's pep rally.

be a long day, one that would last about 20 or 21 tough hours before it would be over. A long afternoon wait was ahead with no place to rest, followed by a tough and emotional game with so much at stake, then a trip home with the bus and plane rides. A win, I thought, would make it all seem like a piece of cake.

I bounced P.J. out of the sack and we started that awful task of trying to pack, keeping some things that would make the day more tolerable for a carry-on bag. Then it was time to carry the luggage to the proper room and get ready for whatever the rest of the day would bring.

As it turned out, having the afternoon without a room was a good deal for P.J. and me. My boss, Bob Sherer, let us have the WHAS van, so away we went to the Anatohle Hotel. The place was unbelievable. We ran into several Cardinal fans who had made the trek over to enjoy the sights and kill some time. The place was a Who's Who of the coaching world. I talked to Wimp Sanderson of Alabama, Glen Clem

Singer Mickey Clark sang his latest version of the "Cardinal Cannonball" at the rally.

of Walker Junior College, Guy Lewis of Houston, John and Betty Bostick of Vanderbilt, Tom Bryant of Centre College (Kentucky) and several others.

Gene Keady of Purdue picked the Cardinals to win it all. He said they had made believers out of him way back in December when Louisville beat his team 77-58. Coach Keady was still angry his team had to play on the opponent's home court for the second year in a row in the NCAA Tournament. He was unhappy about that as he should have been, but he's a fine coach. We all took in a little refreshment together and then it was back to the Fairmont for the pep rally. The time was growing near.

Everyone seemed to be in a great mood, showing no wear and tear on the body. The wear had really been on everyone's pocketbook. It was amazing to me what the Cardinal fans were willing to do to follow and support their team. This trip, as well as the others, had really taken its toll on a lot of people, but no one seemed to care at this point. Many spent more than they should have, punished themselves physically and mentally, yet no one seemed to show any signs of regret. The Cardinal fans are a very unusual group. They get on board and stay on board.

The room where the pep rally was being held filled up rapidly with hundreds of fans, ready and willing to let it all hang out for the cause. The politicians and the entire gang were there. I decided when I talked on this day that I would pick on, with her permission, Lavinia Swain, the wife of U of L's president. She's a great sport and a lady's lady.

The program finally got underway. Mickey Clark sang his latest version of the Cardinal Cannonball and Van Vance went through his usual routine of putting me down before turning the podium over to me. I told the crowd that I had seen Roger Harden, Kentucky's outstanding guard, the night before and he asked me what the main difference between Louisville and Lexington was. "Well," I said, "for me the big difference is that in Louisville the people wave at me using all five fingers." That got the crowd going.

Then I told them about Dr. Swain's and Lavinia's courtship. It seemed that Donald was coming home from a garage sale with items that his mother had told him to carry. He had a

Phyllis George Brown and her son, Lincoln Todd, participated in the pre-game festivities.

pig, a chicken, an anvil and a tub. On the way home he met Lavinia, who was coming from the other direction, and he asked her to reach in his pocket and get him a piece of gum to chew. She said, "I can't do that, you might take advantage of me." He asked her, "How can I do that with my hands full like this?" She looked at him, smiled and said, "That's easy, you put the pig on the ground, the tub over the pig, the anvil on the tub, and I'll hold the chicken."

Wow, the crowd loved it and the joke really brought the house down. My sporting friend, Lavinia, blushed a little but she also laughed. Dr. Swain really laughed. It was just good fun among friends, good friends.

It was time for Van and me to head for Reunion Arena and the big show. While boarding the WHAS van, I spotted Pervis Ellison's family walking across the street. We offered them a ride and they accepted. They were ready. Mrs. Ellison talked about all the money people were offering for tickets and said "mine aren't for sale at no price." It was an enjoyable ride and everyone was really excited. Little did they know, however, what was in store for them and what a great night it was going to be for the Ellison clan.

We stopped off in the press room for some refreshment and food before I started thinking about doing my pre-game interviews. I had interviewed Gov. Collins before the LSU game and for the finals I couldn't think of anyone more appropriate than Dr. Donald Swain. Jeff Hall was my choice for a player. After that was taken care of all I had to do was sit down, settle in and wait for the big show to get underway. I felt real confident and didn't think the Cards could lose, unless they just completely went down the tank. That would never happen, though, at least that's what I thought.

The introductions began and my mind wandered back through the season. We were still calling people like Pervis a freshman, but they weren't the same freshmen who ran on

Tony Branch, a member of the 1980 championship team and now an assistant coach at Lamar, addressed the already fired-up crowd.

196

the court in New York back in November. These people had played 38 games against the best this nation had to offer. I just didn't think of them as freshmen anymore, particularly Pervis. Each player had contributed to what was about to happen. All had sacrificed and fought through a lot of real tough times, and here they were.

It was just like Pervis said, "Coach Crum kept telling us to keep working and it would all come together, and it has."

I thought back to a writer's poll published in the Dallas *Morning News* that day. Fifty-three media members had been polled and 35 picked Louisville to win. Some of the reasons given were: "Too many offensive weapons; Louisville has a big edge inside; Cards' pressure will get to Duke;" and Billy Reed said "Yuppies don't win national championships." Some of those who picked Duke said: "Duke's defense is solid; Dawkins and Alarie won't let them get beat;" and Jay Mariotti of the *Cincinnati Post* said, "for no other reason than brains."

Going into the NCAA Tournament, Duke had finished ranked No. 1 in the nation while the Cards had been ranked No. 7. It was really going to come down to a match between the advantage of Duke's quickness at guard compared to the

The U of L pep band was in full-swing.

inside quickness of Louisville. The shooting percentages couldn't be forgotten either. The experts had spent the past two days trying to match potential performances, impossible to do but fun to talk about.

And the players had done their own talking: "Milt is very quick, especially with the ball in his hands," said Johnny Dawkins. "I don't think I have to score for us to win," said

Cardinal fans milled around Reunion Arena.

Wagner. "Alarie is a smart player who plays position defense. I think he might be the best tight defensive player in the country," said Jay Bilas.

Some of the media saw the match-ups like this: Crook vs. Henderson (advantage Louisville); Thompson vs. Alarie (advantage even); Hall vs. Amaker (advantage even); Wagner vs. Dawkins (advantage Duke, supported by the Coaches' All-American team in which Dawkins led all vote getters with 62 votes); Ellison vs. Bilas (advantage Louisville); Bench

Lisa Wooldridge was one of the few lucky ones who made it inside the building.

Scott Crum, son of the U of L head coach, snuggled up for a short nap before the championship game.

(advantage Louisville); Offensive game (advantage even); Defensive game (advantage Duke); Coaching (advantage even).

That's the way it seemed to some of the media. In summary, it looked like Duke's only advantages came with Dawkins and the defense. Louisville's advantages were with Crook, Ellison and the bench. But I couldn't figure out why they never bothered to mention shooting the basketball as one of the criteria. After all, that's what it's all about.

The big boys in the broadcasting game, Billy Packer and Al McGuire, had different viewpoints. Packer liked Louisville because they were a fresher team and could afford to have more things go wrong and still be able to adjust enough to win. Big Al liked Duke because of Louisville's lack of a true point guard. He also thought that Billy Thompson, who he said had more talent than anyone on the court other than Dawkins, would be the key.

The stage was set. All the predictions had been made and the game had been decided beforehand by a lot of people for a lot of different reasons, but those who would make the final decision were now on the court. The players had respectfully shaken hands and now it had come down to 40 minutes of playing time that would decide who would get to say, without question, "We're No. 1."

The waiting was over, the game had started. It had seemed like a very long day and no matter what you had done, this moment was always in the back of your mind.

Before the old eyes could focus on the action, Herbert Crook scored a quick layup and Louisville was ahead 2-0. It was a good beginning. A few seconds later, Pervis Ellison offered a sneak peek of what was coming the rest of the night when he picked up a basket. Henderson and Dawkins each

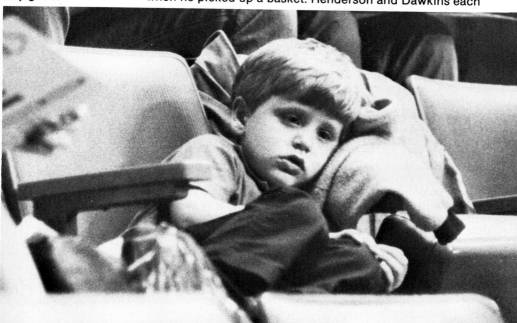

scored and the game was tied at 4-4. You always feel like the early baskets don't matter much but, as we all know, two points count anytime and in a game like this every minute should be played just like it was the last minute.

By the 15:37 mark in the first half, Cardinal fans were beginning to get the feeling that Johnny Dawkins wasn't a fluke, he was for real. Duke led 15-10 and Dawkins had already blistered the nets for 12 points with shots from 6, 16, 6, 19 and 13 feet. At the rate he was going, he would score about 96 points by the final buzzer. Whew!

I thought somebody had better tie his feet together, quickly. I was about to chew the end of the microphone off. As it turned out, the Cards shut him down and allowed him just two more field goals the rest of the first half.

By the midpoint of the first half, Duke led 21-18. The distressing thing at this point was the turnovers the Cards

Much has been said about Duke's fans, but the U of L throng wasn't about to be outdone.

were accumulating. They kept giving the ball back to Duke, giving up plenty of scoring opportunities. I kept wondering how many times could the Cards throw the ball away and have any hope of winning.

The Ice Man, Milt, didn't have a point and Billy Thompson had just four. Man, this was a revolting development. But during the next three minutes, the Louisville bench carried the load. The bench had been one of U of L's strong points all season, a point the media had talked about all week. And they were right because the bench was doing it to the Blue Devils. Before the night ended, U of L's bench outscored Duke's reserves 11-4. You don't have to be a mechanical engineer to figure out that's a seven-point difference.

With the Cardinals trailing 25-18, Mark McSwain and Tony Kimbro took over for U of L and scored the next seven points, three by McSwain and four by Kimbro. It was a big, big contribution.

While Mark and Tony were doing their things, though, Duke's Tommy Amaker and David Henderson were getting four points apiece and Duke maintained a 33-27 lead.

That's when Never Nervous Pervis caught fire. He picked up six points over the next three minutes, with two of his baskets coming by way of the ol' dunkeroo. Milt finally broke the ice and hit two free throws with 2:58 to go, and the Cards tied the game at 33-33 with 2:48 left. It had been a struggle for Louisville as Milt had not scored a field goal and Billy still had just four points. All week long the papers had been full of talk about these two players, but it just wasn't happening for them.

Considering the lack of offensive contribution from the seniors and the team's rash of turnovers, it was amazing that U of L was tied with the Blue Devils. Still, that's what the scoreboard read.

In what was to become a familiar site, Pervis Ellison soared above the Duke defenders for basket after basket.

Before I could catch my breath, Henderson and Dawkins each picked up baskets. Billy T. added a free throw and the half ended with Duke leading 37-34. The Cards had shot a respectable 54 percent, but they had only taken 24 shots, not enough to get the job done considering Duke got off 34 attempts. The reason U of L didn't get off more attempts was because of the turnovers, 14 to be exact. You can't shoot it until you get it to the offensive end of the floor, and the red and black team was tossing it away with regularity. Fourteen turnovers is borderline for an entire game!

Duke had shot the ball at a very poor 41 percent (14 of 34), even lower than its poor average of 43 percent during tournament play. No team could ever win the national title shooting so poorly, or could they? It was 1938 shooting, back when the backboards were fan-shaped and the ball had laces. How could a team shoot 41 percent and still be ahead? It was a simple answer in this case because U of L took just 24 shots and spent the rest of the time giving it back to the Yuppies.

The first-half performance turned in by both teams had not been a "Rembrandt."

It reminded me of the last loss the Cards had experienced, back on Feb. 8 against North Carolina State, especially when the Cards had the ball. There were just a lot of ho-hum turnovers. The thought of that game made me take a big gulp, even though I knew it wasn't Feb. 8, and it was the defensive efforts of Louisville that was keeping them close in the championship game.

On the positive side for the Cards, it had been a half with a truckload of turnovers, not enough shots to fill a Christmas stocking, the senior superstars were coming up shorter than my retirement check, yet they were still in good position. There were a lot of "ifs" but I felt good about the situation. This Cardinal team had been a second-half team for the past

Pervis Ellison was voted the Final Four's MVP for plays like his defense against Duke's Mark Alarie.

six weeks, beginning with DePaul back on Feb. 15. The Cards could get it going when they were hanging over the cliff and looking into the jaws of the meanest, hungriest crocodiles 10,000 feet below. Faced with that type of situation, they could get unbelievably tough.

The rebounding was even at 17 but Louisville's guards had been outscored 21-4, and that was alarming. And that stat would get worse before it got any better. At one point in the second half, Duke's guards had a 30-4 scoring edge over U of L's. I kept complaining about it on the radio, but Van kept telling me the inside people of Duke were getting killed. He was thinking about the positive and I was grumbling about the negative. Actually, this was the way the experts had said it would be. Duke's guards would win and the Louisville inside game would win. That's what was happening, but 30-4! It seemed like a lot.

Dawkins led Duke in the first half with 14 points while the Cards had been led by Pervis with 12. U of L's seniors had a grand total of nine points.

I had noticed that very few people left their seats during the first 20 minutes, even though it had been a quiet game with very few spectacular dunks or plays. But that was history now. The Cards always came out after the half looking like they had been remodeled and overhauled. They were the second-half Cards and this night would be no different.

Duke took the ball out of bounds and Alarie picked up a quick basket to make it 39-34. Thompson countered right back for Louisville. In their next three offensive trips, the Cards hit the boards hard for two tip-ins and a basket by Billy, giving U of L a 42-41 lead at the 17:11 mark. It was Louisville's first lead since the opening minute of the game.

The lead was short-lived, though, as Duke ran off seven straight points, all by Dawkins, to pull ahead 48-42. Boy, that was hard to swallow.

Milt Wagner had still done very little for the Cardinal cause, but I had watched him play for four years and knew that somewhere in this game he'd do his bit. He had said in the pre-game interviews that he didn't have to score for U of L to win, and it looked like he was trying to prove his point.

Joyce Crum was all smiles.

Things got worse when Billy picked up his fourth foul at the 12:30 mark while fighting for a loose ball, and Milt joined him on the bench 11 seconds later when he picked up his fourth personal. Still, the Cards hung tough.

At the 10:08 mark, Pervis turned it on and scored five of Louisville's next seven points, but the Cards weren't gaining because Amaker scored three points and Henderson put in an easy basket. It didn't look pretty for the Cards, even though they had protected the ball a little better in the second half. They were playing most of the game 4 to 6 points behind.

With the clock showing 5:32 and Billy and Milt back in the game, Wagner took off his Halloween mask and showed his real face. Milt would score seven of his team's final 15 points, and Billy hit a terrific shot that only a person with his skill level could produce. Ellison would add the other six Louisville points, despite picking up his fourth foul with 5:03 left.

The Cards took the lead with 3:22 left in the game, 64-63, on an alley-oop pass from Crook to Wagner, but lost the lead

Johnny Dawkins got inside of Billy Thompson to score two of his 24 points.

14 seconds later when Dawkins hit a pair of free throws. Billy answered with an 8-footer to give the Cards a 66-65 lead and Henderson and Dawkins missed attempts, giving the ball back to Louisville.

That set up the play of the game. Following a timeout with 11 seconds showing on the 45-second clock and just 48 in the game, Jeff Hall was forced to put up a shot, under heavy defensive pressure, which fell miserably short. There were nine other players on the court but it was, ironically, a basic fundamental of basketball that drove the nail in Duke's coffin. As Jeff released the shot, all the inside Duke players went into their fundamental routine of blocking off the board. They never figured Jeff's shot would fall short, at least that's the way I saw it. Pervis, who scored 11 of Louisville's final 22 points, snagged the ball and put it into the basket, giving U of L a 68-65 lead and Duke a message. Just 41 seconds remained on the ol' game clock.

Ellison calmly sank two free throws with :27 left, giving Louisville a healthy 70-65 lead.

Duke made one last run at the Cards, but it was too little too late. Bilas put in a missed field-goal attempt and Danny Ferry did the same after Thompson missed the front end of a one-and-one, but U of L led 70-69 with three seconds left.

They immediately fouled Wagner a second later, and he went to the line one last time as a U of L player. It was his moment.

Hitting critical free throws in the final seconds had become routine for the Ice Man. This time, however, he had a little edge with a 1-point lead and the clock about gone. It may not have made a difference, but stranger things have happened in less time. Whatever the circumstance may have been, I'd have bet my partial plate that his free throws would go in. The biggest thing about this moment was that he wanted to be in that situation. It was his specialty. He was the guy who, on numerous occassions during his four-year tenure, had thrown the last shovel of dirt on the opponent. Milt had buried a lot of them, and he'd do it one more time to Duke. It was a perfect ending for a fairy tale that had come true.

The big electronic scoreboard in Reunion Arena flashed the 72-69 score and "Louisville Cardinals, National Champions."

It was a great moment for the fans, players and coaches. It allowed everyone to savor the moment. It had happened, it had really happened!

But it was a tough time for Duke as their emotions and mental frame of mind were being tortured with a sick, deep feeling that goes with the vanishing of a dream. I felt for the Duke team. I could imagine how bad it would be to lose at this moment, with total ecstasy just a shot or two away. I remembered reading a comment by one of the Kansas players (following the loss to Duke) who had said, "I almost wished we had lost in the early rounds rather than lose this close to the end." Losing just happens to be part of playing the game.

I watched the Louisville crowd as the game ended. They

June Turner traveled from California to be in Dallas. Her son, Denny, just happens to be the Cardinals' head coach.

were spent. It was probably the least enthusiasm they had shown in all the days of the NCAA drive. Most stood, applauded and waved their pom pons. I, too, was excited but tired.

I felt really good for the seniors. I felt good for Milt because of what he had done in the final minutes. I felt good for Billy because he had quieted his critics. I felt good for Jeff because he had contributed so much to the championship. I felt good for Robbie Valentine, who had not played much but was always ready when the opportunity came. I felt good for Denny because of the previous year's problems. I felt good for the assistant coaches, Bobby Dotson and Wade Houston, because this was when their work came to the surface — after a lot of very lonely nights out on that recruiting trail. I felt good for assistant coach Jerry Jones because of the important role he plays with the Cardinal

Despite some problem from the local police, th U of L fans were allowe to remain in the arena listen to Coach Crum post-game show.

basketball program. They don't come any more dedicated and qualified than Jerry. I felt a different kind of proud for the other members on the team. As the horn blew signifying that the Louisville team was the national champion, the seniors handed the underclassmen a load to bear, sorta like "We are now the best in the land and what happens from here on in will be strictly up to you." The Louisville program had returned to the perch of the best basketball program in the land.

I felt really good for Dr. Rudy Ellis and trainer Jerry May. They just don't come any better than those two, and the job they do is second to none in the land. I really felt proud for all the Louisville fans. The 1984-85 season had been a disappointing one, but the fans had hung tough and support never faded an inch. Now they had been rewarded for their loyalty. Everyone had found a treasure that would last a

lifetime, something that would last forever, because they had played a part in the Cards' championship. I never scored a basket myself but felt good about the part I played in the triumphant finish. Back during the season, I wrote in a SCORECARD article that to build and maintain a program like Louisville's takes a lot of different kinds of help. We all were a part of the Cardinal family. We all felt pain with each loss and thrill with each win. Now we had all earned a little piece of this terrific accomplishment.

The usual on-floor celebration took place. I was busy doing my thing for Van and WHAS Radio. After roaming around awhile on the floor, I managed to get a quick interview with Pervis. Once that was finished, I headed back to my seat when I felt a little tug at my sleeve. I turned quickly and there was Denny Crum. He looked at me and said nothing, but his smile and quick little wink said a thousand words. All year long during the good and bad times on the post-game shows, or on buses or in the airport, Denny would always talk positive, regardless of the situation. I never disputed any of the things he told me, but there were times when an element of doubt existed in my mind. Now, that smile and little wink simply said, "Jock, if you believe and keep working, regardless of how dim the light may be, good things can happen. Keep the faith. As long as there is effort, there's opportunity. Always dig out the positive and let the negative fall back in the hole."

It was one of the greatest facial expressions I have ever seen, one that I'll always remember of Denny. I felt proud of Van's and my role in the Cardinal family and Denny made me feel even prouder. When looking back, it's funny that in a victory of such magnitude how a few small things that happened are those you treasure the most.

Denny's expression was one of them for me, probably because he took the time to share such an important moment with me.

Introducing Billy Thompson at the celebration the next night was also very special to me. I always felt like he was a very different person and I truly admired his efforts and tremendous determination in a quiet way. A victory hand-shake with one of my very best friends, Van Vance, was also important to me. Van had made a great call during the final seconds on the air. The interviews given to me by Pervis, Jeff and Herbert just moments after the final horn were also important to me. All these were very small happenings, still, they're the ones I remember the most and will never forget.

I got a little melancholy after the game, but that changed when fans began to gather around for the post-game show. I couldn't believe it but the police were running everyone out of the building! I asked nicely, a couple of times, if the fans could remain but each time got that "shut-up, boo boo" look. I was a little firmer the next time I asked and one of the officers finally went to his superior. The boss man, though, was even more demanding than the other officers. I explained that we had thousands of people in Dallas for the

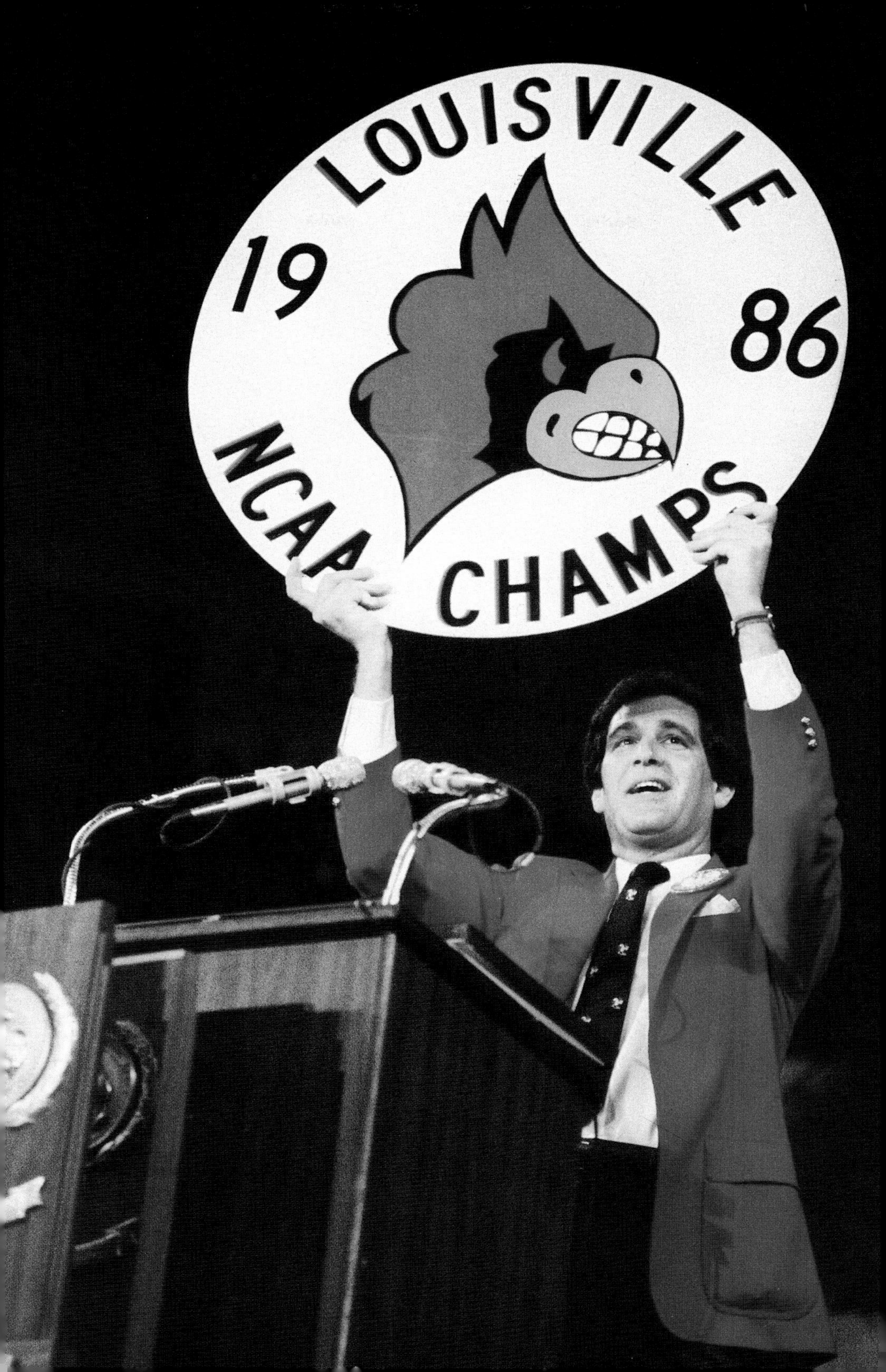
LOUISVILLE
19
86
NCAA
CHAMPS

Billy Thompson scored 22 points in the Cardinals' 88-77 victory over LSU.

Action under the basket, on the sidelines and in the stands was fast and furious in the national semifinals.

Louisville freshman sensation Pervis Ellison, right, eyed his target and scored as Duke's Jay Bilas could only watch.

Thompson soared to block an LSU shot and the Cardinal bench was all smiles. Below, Dr. Rudy Ellis and Milt Wagner talked with LSU's Derick Taylor after the game.

Above, Tony Kimbro, Herb Crook and Milt Wagner surrounded Duke's Mark Alarie. At right, guard Jeff Hall drove the length of the floor to score against Tommy Amaker. Far right, 'Superb' Herb looked over the situation.

The fans cheered as Pervis Ellison put in Jeff Hall's air ball.

Seconds later, Ellison sank two free throws, setting up Wagner's game clinching shots.

Jeff Hall's celebration was delayed momentarily because of a "difference of opinion" with Duke's Danny Ferry. Teammate Chris West and referee Hank Nichols intervened.

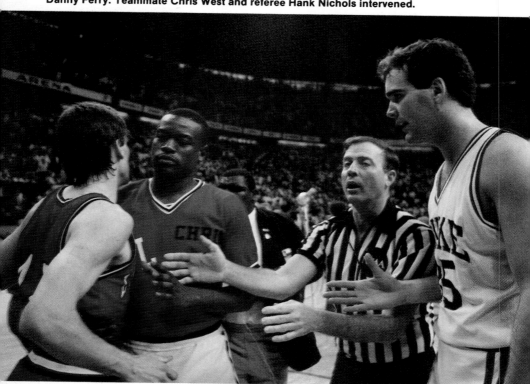

Fans, reporters and photographers swarmed the floor but Mark McSwain managed to find a less crowded place to answer some quick questions.

Coca-Cola
DUKE
69
:00
2
UNIVERSITY OF LOUISVILLE
NATIONAL CHAMPIONS
LOUISVILLE
72
PLAYER FOULS POINTS
TEAM FOULS
reunion arena
FIRSTCITY

The celebration moved from Reunion Arena to Freedom Hall.

had seen a lot of action were smothered by reporters. It was hot in that place and I knew the players were just dying to get out of there. Actually, it took about 30 more minutes to get everyone ready and on the team bus for the trip to the airport.

The ride to Dallas/Fort Worth International was actually pretty quiet, except for the low tone of one-on-one conversations. P.J. and I sat near the back, and it seemed like the Cards had just won a routine game. Darrell Griffith, who led Louisville to its first championship back in 1980, was with us and he said, "It will take a little while for this thing to sink in." I'm sure he was right. At that point the players hadn't really grasped what they had accomplished. They sat there, physically and mentally exhausted. There are times when this sort of conquest can best be appreciated in one's own thoughts and I think they all just really wanted to sit down and think about it some. As some of the players came by, I said, "It don't get no better than this."

They just nodded or gave me a hand touch of acknowledgement.

The team bus was always quieter than the other buses on these types of trips, but I knew the low-key atmosphere would end once we arrived at the plane. It did for awhile, but even the plane ride home seemed to be a lot quieter than I expected. Most of the people on board had been up and going since about 8 a.m., had no place to roost in the afternoon and were pretty much drained emotionally and physically. There were a few "Who Deys" but that was about it.

While waiting for Denny to do his post-game show, we listened to WHAS' "all-night Moose" back in Louisville. He was giving us Cardinal fan reports from home.

We quickly found out that the city had gone bananas. Thousands of people were in the streets and convertibles were being driven around with their tops down in winter. On Broadway Street, every time the stop light turned red, hundreds would yell C-A-R-D-S until the colors changed. It appeared to be like the infield at the Kentucky Derby, except everybody was a winner. Students were on top of the Red Barn, until the campus police ordered them down. One lady was waving the same pom pon she had used in the 1980 championship game.

But it wasn't that way on the plane. The soldiers had fought a tremendous battle and now it was time to rest a little and let the great accomplishment sink in.

I wrote my column for SCORECARD on the way back, so I didn't do much of anything except peck on the computer. As we were about to land at Standiford Field, the stewardess hassled me about putting my tray up. I told her, "Lady, I have no choice but to have this finished by the time we get to the gate." She obviously didn't understand what a deadline was but finally frowned and left me alone.

The pilot told us there would be no people waiting at the airport terminal to greet the team, which wasn't unexpected. We had made that same announcement on the radio several times. The fans had been discouraged from going to the airport. Instead, there was going to be a great celebration in Freedom Hall that night. This was the best way to handle the situation but I sorta wished the players had been greeted with a hero's welcome at the airport. It would have been terrific. There's something unusual about a spontaneous reception and it's a special way to capture the moment. But, for all concerned, it was the best way to handle it.

I was somewhat of a hero myself. Dr Swain had given me the honor of announcing on the radio that there wasn't going to be any classes on Tuesday. Now that's what you call having a president who is "cool, real cool."

We touched down in Louisville soft and easy. Some applauded and others cheered. Everyone was really happy to be home and particularly glad to be unloading the national championship trophy. The Cardinals had traveled to Ogden, Houston and Dallas, and each time they had returned with what they went after.

It was sort of strange going into the empty airport. I didn't think there was any way to keep the people away, but I was wrong. The 4:30 a.m. time we arrived probably had something to do with it because it was a working day for most.

COMPLETE LOUISVILLE-DUKE BOX SCORE

LOUISVILLE

Player	FG	FGA	FT	FTA	REB	PF	TP	A	TO	BLK	S	MIN
Crook	5	9	0	3	12	2	10	5	9	0	0	32
Thompson	6	8	1	3	4	4	13	2	2	2	0	31
Ellison	10	14	5	6	11	4	25	1	0	2	1	35
Hall	2	4	0	0	2	2	4	2	3	0	2	33
Wagner	2	6	5	5	3	4	9	2	5	1	1	30
Kimbro	2	4	2	2	2	1	6	2	0	2	0	14
McSwain	2	4	1	2	3	1	5	2	1	0	1	17
Walls	0	1	0	0	1	2	0	0	4	0	0	8
Team					1							
Deadball												
Rebounds					1							
Totals	**29**	**50**	**14**	**21**	**39**	**20**	**72**	**16**	**24**	**7**	**5**	**200**

FG%: 1st Half 54.2   2nd Half 61.5   Game 58.0
FT%: 1st Half 72.7   2nd Half 60.0   Game 66.7

DUKE

Player	FG	FGA	FT	FTA	REB	PF	TP	A	TO	BLK	S	MIN
Henderson	5	15	4	4	4	5	14	4	5	0	3	28
Alarie	4	11	4	4	6	5	12	0	1	0	1	33
Bilas	2	3	0	0	3	4	4	0	1	0	0	26
Amaker	3	10	5	6	2	3	11	7	3	0	7	38
Dawkins	10	19	4	4	4	1	24	0	3	0	2	40
Ferry	1	2	2	2	4	2	4	0	1	0	0	20
Williams	0	1	0	0	0	0	0	0	0	0	0	2
King	0	1	0	1	0	2	0	1	0	0	0	13
Team					4							
Deadball												
Rebounds					0							
Totals	**25**	**62**	**19**	**21**	**27**	**22**	**69**	**12**	**14**	**0**	**13**	**200**

FG%: 1st Half 41.2   2nd Half 39.3   Game 40.3
FT%: 1st Half 100.0   2nd Half 83.3   Game 90.5

Halftime: Duke 37, Louisville 34
Attendance: 17,007

It was time to hit the baggage dock, and that's where the trouble began. It took forever for everyone to get their luggage, at least 60 to 90 minutes. It really put the old disposition to a test. Everyone had been up at least 20 hours by now and had gone through fatigue and emotional stress. Still, no one seemed to get angry. People just settled back wherever they could and waited for the beautiful sound of the luggage carrier moving. Most everyone had their bags by daylight.

Since the celebration was later on that evening, P.J. and I stayed at a hotel in Louisville. It was 6:50 a.m. when we hit the sack and we stayed zonked until 1:10 in the afternoon.

All my clothes were dirty so I headed out to the Galleria to buy myself a clean shirt. Well, I was amazed when I entered the stores. Everyone was wearing red and black, and T-shirts could be seen everywhere with the magic words written on the front. Large groups of people were waiting in lines to purchase their own versions. Everyone was riding a high. They all wanted to talk about the game and hear about anything I could add. It was a fun afternoon.

I went back to the hotel and rested some more but had to be at Freedom Hall at 5:30 p.m. for instructions. It was going to be a tremendous affair. The athletic department, under Bill Olsen's guidance, and especially Don Russell and Brian Faison, had everything well organized.

Freshman guard Kevin Walls wore a fan's hat on the plane trip home.

For the team, the day had been like a trip to the candy store. Everything there was good, but there was too much at once to be thoroughly enjoyed.

CHAPTER

8

We Are The Champions

Although most everybody on the trip had time to catch a few hours of rest, some of the team had other obligations to fill. Some were bused directly to a local hotel instead of campus while others, like Denny Crum and Billy Thompson, hit the TV studios for appearances on "Good Morning America," "Today," "Daybreak" and "CBS Morning News" among others.

Later that morning, the team and coaches took a trip to Frankfort to be honored by the government officials as the guests of Gov. Martha Layne Collins. I'm sure there were a lot of politicians who were Cardinal rooters, but I'm also sure there were an awful lot of UK followers who were squeezed into applauding the Cardinals. One in attendance said, "If UK had won, this place would have been so crowded you wouldn't have had a place to stand." Well, that was just tough as far as I was concerned because they didn't win.

Rep. Carl Hines of Louisville asked his colleagues to put their feelings on the record by voting to sponsor a resolution honoring the team. After a few holdouts, the resolution was eventually passed unanimously. The resolution had all the expected phrases in it, including a quote from *The New York Times* citing Louisville as the "Ferrari of College Basketball."

Coach Crum took the podium and thanked the General Assembly for taking the time to extend their congratulations to the champions. He also said he didn't think there was any place in the world that appreciated good basketball more than the state of Kentucky and that it made him and his team feel good about being wanted.

It was a visit that needed to be made, but it came at a time when the Louisville party was operating on practically no rest. Gov. Collins thanked the Louisville people for making the trip under the circumstances and allowing the people in the Capitol to honor them.

The Cards loaded up once more and headed back for the great reception which awaited them in Louisville.

Tickets for the the celebration in Freedom Hall were hard to come by. Rumors floated around about people outside the arena scalping tickets, even though they were free. The rest of the city could listen to the ceremony on WHAS Radio or watch it on WDRB-TV.

Those who did attend, all 20,000 of them, were true fans,

not just people who had decided to jump on the band wagon at the last minute.

At 5:15 when I arrived, the building was completely arranged. I didn't understand how it could all be planned so quickly, but was told that it was set up exactly as it is was when there was a rock concert or similar event being held. I guess anything could happen during "Louisville Cardinal Week," as it had already been proclaimed by Mayor Jerry Abramson.

The place began to fill and the sounds of C-A-R-D-S and "Who Dey" could be heard from all angles around Freedom Hall. It was a little scary. I do a lot of speaking, but doing it in front of 20,000 people is something different. I got a little nervous as the starting time grew nearer.

The program had a little of everything in it — short speeches by politicians, music, dancing, cheerleaders, and players' and coaches' comments. As the tension grew, the fatigue which a lot of people were nursing seemed to vanish for a couple of hours. It was time to honor those who had done the work.

The introduction came from assistant athletic director Jack Tennant, "Ladies and gentlemen, it's my pleasure to introduce to you the NCAA National Basketball Champions of 1985-86, the Louisville Cardinals." The background music of "We Are The Champions " began and Denny Crum led the team, coaches and support personnel to the stage and down a long 50-foot runway. It looked like I was watching the Miss America Pageant. Tony Kimbro proudly carried the NCAA championship trophy high above his head. Finally, everyone was seated and the program began.

The cheerleaders and the Cardinal Bird (Beth Mattingly) did their thing. They, themselves, were national champions. Then WHAS Radio's Wayne Perkey took the podium to

Senior Jeff Hall took some time to bask in the glory at the championship celebration.

introduce the governor, Congressman Ron Mazzoli and Dr. Donald Swain, one at a time. There were some embarrassing boos when Perkey intoduced the governor. I didn't understand it at the time, and I still don't. It was one of the rare times I've been ashamed of a few Cardinal fans. For whatever reasons, this wasn't the night to boo anyone.

Mazzoli made a few nice remarks and Dr. Swain was his usual charming self. Bill Olsen, who had been in a similar position as an assistant coach back in 1980, was next. Then it was my turn at bat.

Standing on a raised platform overlooking 20,000 people was an awesome feeling. I told them I felt like Billy Graham and just may ask everyone to rise and sing a hymn, then come forward. The line drew some laughs and helped me settle down. It was then my pleasure to introduce the assistant coaches — Bobby Dotson, Wade Houston and Jerry Jones — and each said a few words. Then I introduced the rest of the basketball support staff — trainer Jerry May, strength coach Doug Semenick, graduate assistant Jeff Van Pelt, volunteer assistant Jack Ford and head manager Jeff Witt.

Van Vance and Jack Tennant had the honors of introducing the non-starters on the team, then WHAS' Terry Meiners introduced Mayor Abramson. The mayor talked about new signs that were being placed around the city that acknowledged the national champions, and commented particularly about one that was being placed at the bank of the Ohio River, facing the Indiana side and the guy in Bloomington who had worn the Duke button to the championship game.

County Judge Harvey Sloane then made a few brief remarks to fit the occasion before crowd favorite Mickey Clark sang his final version of the "Cardinal Cannonball." The crowd joined in the singing and everyone was having a ball.

Pervis Ellison and Jock Sutherland joked around before the celebration began.

It was my time again, but now I was cooler than a "California Cooler." I was really happy to get to introduce Herbert Crook and Never Nervous Pervis. Earlier, one of them had slipped me a note that said they wanted to be introduced together. They didn't want to go up alone. Well, I wasn't going to let them off that easy but sent word back to them that it was OK to do it like that, even though I didn't have any intentions of following their wishes. Here were two guys who had faced all kinds of pressure and handled it with ease, and now they said they needed support from their buddy.

I felt each deserved their moment on stage alone and knew that the massive crowd wanted to pay tribute to them individually. Herbert was first. I introduced him as the guy who was the "other" forward at the beginning of the season but who had reached the point of equal billing. He was a star in his own right and had brought the Cards through some tough spots. I raised my voice and shouted "Herbert Rubber Man Crook." The crowd shook the arena with applause and Herb had to do it alone. He gave me a "you dirty rat" look but handled it well, even telling the crowd, "I hope to see you all in New Orleans next year for the Final Four."

Next came the tournament's MVP, Mr. Ellison. I told the crowd that I had asked his mother what he did the best, and she answered that he was a real good artist but actually what he did better than anything, including basketball, was play the trombone. Then I said "he must be one hell of a trombone player" and the crowd loved it. Pervis walked down the ramp and received a tremendous response, one he deserved. He looked 10-feet tall as he touched all the hands of the fans, wearing a cool-looking striped shirt and sunglasses. He went to the microphone and told the crowd, "I'm sure I speak for the whole team when I say that the championship trophy says 'University of Louisville' but it should say 'City of Louisville.' Thank you all for your support." Hey, it was a piece of cake for an 18-year-old freshman who had only hours earlier been named MVP of the Final Four.

The senior cheerleaders were then introduced by Terry Meiners. They had been an outstanding group all year and it was only fitting they be recognized: seniors Dottie Derringer, Scott Hornung, Karen Smith, Andre Lyons, Scott Greenwald, Denise Zirnheld and James Speed; and underclassmen Missy Perkins, Vonda Goldwair, Jennifer Haddaway, Jeff Bohr, Darrell Willoughby, Lawrence Young and Jeff Stevens. Coach Sherrill Travis' group had won the national title in both the 1984-85 and 1985-86 campaigns.

It was time for Robbie Valentine and Jeff Hall to have their say. Both paid tribute to the fans.

The Pepsi Generation Singers performed and then it was my privilege and honor, and I'm very serious when I say it, to introduce Billy Thompson. I finished my intro by saying, "We all owe Billy the finest ovation this Freedom Hall has ever known. I give you Billlleeeee Thompson!" The ovation was deafening. All the fans had gotten my meaning. They were all there back on that cold night during the winter when some people booed this marvelous athlete. Now they were saying, by their applause, that they were sorry. As Billy made his walk down the aisle, I watched him every step of the way.

A lot of things flashed through my mind, including the beginning of his career four years earlier in Alaska. This was a very special young man, deserving of all the accolades.

Dr. Rudy Ellis, a very compassionate and special man with the Cardinals, got his turn. Doc is the type who touches the heart of everyone he is around. It would be impossible to say how many ex-Cardinal athletes have profited from the expertise of Rudy. He took Milt Wagner to center stage with

Despite overcoming the pressures of a championship game, Herbert Crook and Pervis Ellison felt more comfortable addressing the throng of fans as a duet.

him and watched as Ice walked down his aisle of glory. It was obvious there was a special bond between these two people. They had toughed it out during the previous year when Milt had been injured and Ice had returned to be everything that was expected of him. There was mutual admiration between the two. Milt hugged him and thanked him for everything, then told the crowd, "I'll be back."

Van introduced the No. 1 man and brought him to the podium. It was very fitting that Van had this honor. Van told the crowd, "Denny is not the Coach of the Year, he is the Coach of the Decade." I thought "amen, brother."

Denny touched upon how he had told a reporter before the season began that if his team could survive the schedule, they'd be a legitimate contender by the end of March. He praised his team for its toughness. He praised the four seniors and challenged the returning personnel by reminding them that next year they would be a marked "Deck of Cards." Cool Hand Luke was his usual cool self again.

Throughout the program, a variety of songs accompanied the huge video screens situated around Freedom Hall, songs like "Miracles," "You're the Best," "Moment of Truth," "Second Wind," "The Kid is Hot Tonight," "Nobody Does it Better" and "Believe in Yourself." All were very appropriate for the occasion.

The band played the fight song and the fans filed out as happy as could be. They had bragging rights for a whole year and a national championship tucked away in the hip pocket.

It was a great evening and I considered it a real honor to be a part of it. I'll treasure the night and the memories of the celebration for a long time. After stopping by one of the private boxes that served as headquarters for the production people and getting a couple of snapshots taken of me standing next to the trophy, it seemed to be a good time to head for home. Yes, siree, it had been a great, great day.

Saturday, just five days after the Cards had claimed the national championship, the basketball banquet was held at Ramada Inn's Bluegrass Convention Center. Athletic department officials have gotten into the habit over the years of scheduling the banquet for after the last date of the NCAA Tournament because getting to the Final Four has become the rule rather than the exception.

The banquet was once again sponsored by the Cardinal Athletic Fund, with CAF secretary Opal Newton acting as the official hostess. And, once again, it was a first-class affair.

I always enjoy this final evening because it's one of the few times over the course of a season that I don't have any responsibilities. I can sit back and enjoy.

The site for the banquet was the same as the one the year before, but this time the circumstances were a little different. Just a year ago, everyone was trying to rationalize that the Cards had done OK. After all, they had won 19 games and had made it to the NIT's Final Four.

But this time was different. There was no need to convince yourself of anything. It was there to see. You could read it on the huge banner that hung above the speaker's table — 1986 NCAA National Champions.

Everyone got to the banquet for the "social hour" to brag a little more and have a few "beverage lifters," just to sorta

It was time for the crowd to pay tribute to the team and coaches at the celebration in Freedom Hall.

238

At the awards banquet, seniors Billy Thompson, Robbie Valentine and Milt Wagner took time to thank the fans.

loosen up a little. Everyone looked rested and was dressed out in their best duds.

Assistant coach Jerry Jones acted as the master of ceremonies and tried to get the capacity crowd settled into their seats. The place was packed and tickets to the event were once again at a premium.

The head tables were arranged so the players and cheerleaders were in the front rows for everyone to see. At each table were white caps with red lettering that said "Louisville, National Champions." Bumper stickers with the same message were placed on every chair as were tapes of Mickey Clark's "Cardinal Cannonball." Video tapes of the title game constantly played on the big TV screens located in each corner of the room, putting everyone in the right frame of mind once again.

About that time the members of the team filed down the aisle and took their proper places. The time had come to recognize the seniors and distribute the trophies.

The players who received awards that evening were: Will Olliges (Academics); Jeff Hall (Free Throws) — he shot 89 percent on the season and finished his career ranked fourth on the all-time Louisville list; Pervis Ellison (Rebounding) — he hauled down 318 during the season; Milt Wagner (Assists) — he set a new school record with 165; Herbert Crook and Jeff Hall (Most Improved); Billy Thompson (Best Defensive Player) — a deserving award for him which tells a lot about his desire; Chris West and Mike Abram (Coaches' Award); Pervis Ellison (Best First-Year Player); and Milt Wagner and Billy Thompson (Peck Hickman MVP Award).

I was glad for all of them but found myself thinking that it would be interesting to see who wins the Most Improved award next season. They'll all be aiming for it.

The main speakers were Dr. Swain, Bill Olsen and Denny Crum. Denny, who took the podium to a standing ovation, made about the same comments he had made at the victory celebration in Freedom Hall a few nights earlier, thanking the seniors and challenging the underclassmen.

Jerry Jones, as efficient as he is, made sure that everyone was recognized at least once during the evening. He recognized the parents of the players who were there, thanked the media and even tossed out a couple of nice remarks about the WHAS radio team. No dummy, he even introduced the wives of the coaching staff — Joyce Crum, Alice Houston, Bobbie Dotson, and his own better half, Beverly.

Coach Jones showed everyone just how versatile he really is by throwing in some humor at the appropriate time and keeping the program moving along at the right pace.

The four seniors made their final appearances before the Louisville gathering.

It was a sentimental evening for them, but you could tell that the crowd really cared about each one. Robbie, Jeff, Milt and Billy had contributed so much over the years, now everyone was thanking them for it.

The crowd was treated to some excellently produced video tapes of the season, and everyone cheered at each highlight. The job done by Chris DeMaio and Roy Hamlin in putting the videos together was appreciated by all.

The banquet was the finale of the 1985-86 season but many in the crowd weren't ready to let it end. Some milled around, taking pictures and getting autographs of their favorite team. But as Jerry Jones said to end the night, "That's all, folks."

Still, I couldn't help but wonder if we couldn't just take that huge banner draped across the backdrop and change that 6 to a 7. Oh, well, there was plenty of time for that.

Sixteen days following the big doings in Dallas, the Cardinals took one last bus and plane trip. This time, though, it was of a social nature as the coaches, players and members of the administration flew to Washington, D.C. for a little fireside chat with Ronnie, the guy in Washington who calls the plays for all of us. It was a day in which the Cards had the privilege of meeting the President of our country, Ronald Reagan, even though it was just a few days following the United States' raid on Libya. But the President, being the old actor he is, believed that "the show must go on."

At 7 a.m. on Wednesday, April 16, assistant coach Jerry Jones herded the players out the back of Crawford Gym to the bus driven by Mr. Wells. Milt Wagner, Robbie Valentine, Bobby Dotson and Denny Crum met them at the airport. Everyone wore their best duds for the President, senators and representatives.

The group took an enjoyable Piedmont flight to the

nation's capital. It was a cold day, and the old fox, Coach Jones, was tucked into a big topcoat, ready for "Hawk" (that's what us guys in the low- to middle-income bracket call cold weather). It was more than just nippy outside. Most everyone else wore suit coats.

Along with the usual traveling party, two women, Lavinia Swain and Colette Murray (the University's vice president for development), made the trip. Dr. Swain was already in Washington on University business and was going to meet the group on Capitol Hill. As for media, Bob Domine of WAVE-TV and Russ Brown of *The Courier-Journal* went

Although far from home in Washington, Coach Crum and the team were sought out by admirers for autographs.

242

along. U of L's own television production people, Chris DeMaio and Roy Hamlin, attended. Dr. Rudy Ellis was there but his running buddy, trainer Jerry May, was recovering in Methodist Evangelical Hospital after undergoing surgery for a total hip replacement.

The plane landed at Dulles International where the group was met by a very efficient lady who promptly herded everyone onto a Greyhound bus. It didn't take the party long to meet its first Cardinal fan, the driver of the bus. He had two children who had caught Cardinal Fever, so that meant the players had to sign some autographs for his boys.

The driver took the team on a little tour of Washington that included Arlington Cemetery, the Vietnam Memorial, the Smithsonian Institute, the National Monument, the Lincoln Memorial and other places of interest.

By then it was time for lunch. The Cards ate in the same cafeteria where many of Washington's dignitaries dine. Now this bunch can do some eating, especially when the food is exceptionally good.

The meeting with the President was scheduled for 12:15 p.m., at least the group was supposed to be there by then. The bus took the long way around the White House to let everyone do a little "rubber necking" before stopping in the back to unload. It was at this point when security got real picky. Everyone and everything, including the autographed basketball that would be presented to President Reagan, went through metal detectors and radar screens. The security folks took everything seriously. The media people had to go through a different type of screening process.

The trip to our nation's capital wasn't complete without some sightseeing. But all that just got you inside the door. Everyone was supposed to have a photo ID of some nature for positive identification but two of the players and even the big boy himself, Coach Crum, were without the necessary mug

shots. Coach Jones confessed he had not informed the head coach about this requirement. A member of the President's staff finally stepped in and permitted the group to pass. Needless to say, the man impressed everyone with his power.

That's about the time U of L's wagon master, Dr. Swain, appeared on the scene. He had been waiting patiently for the Louisville contingent to make its appearance.

The Louisville party was divided into three groups. The NCAA's women national champions, the University of Texas, were scheduled to meet the President at the same time, so there was a large group of people congregating on the grounds. One group was divided into players, the second group included the head coaches and the University presidents, and the third group consisted of the remaining people.

President Reagan took group No. 2, which by now included the assistant coaches , into a room near the Rose Garden. Jerry Jones was the envy of all as he stood there in his big, warm overcoat, smiling at everyone else.

A few minutes later, the players from the two schools walked out to the area from two side doors, followed by the

President of the United States and the group consisting of university presidents and coaches. President Reagan then addressed the group as a whole and made some presentations. Billy Thompson did an elegant job of presenting the autographed ball to the President and the Texas people presented him with a jacket.

The main man then made a few remarks to the crowd and

President Ronald Reagan shook everyone's hand in the White House Rose Garden.

Billy Thompson presented the President with a basketball autographed by the team.

singled out Pervis Ellison when he called him "Never Nervous Pervis" and said "that if he was this good at 19, just think how good he'll be when he reaches my age." After the laughter died down, the President went on to say, "I'd like to single out each of you individually for praise, and you all deserve it. I know your victories were the result of many hours of hard work and dedication, individual effort and teamwork."

It was hard for anyone to imagine just how much pressure the man really was under during those few precious moments, yet, there he was in the Rose Garden paying tribute to a few Americans who had made their marks for everyone to see.

Denny and Jody Conradt, the head coach of the Lady Longhorns, each took turns at the podium. Coach Crum's statement was beautifully timed and he said, "On behalf of the University, I'd like to take this opportunity to tell our President that we admire him very much for his willigness and ability to make decisions under stress. As coaches we do that, and we think he does a great job at it."

Later, Denny made another comment which seemed very fitting: "He [the President] has got so much character that he just sparkles."

It was truly a nice trip. Those who had made the same trip back in 1980 (Jimmy Carter was President) after the Cards' first championship said that this trip was somewhat different in that the President spent a little more time with the team. But this trip to Washington was just as special and would long be remembered by everyone.

The groups were broken back down to two and everyone had a chance to take a few snapshots. Then it was off for some touring of the White House. One of the most impressive rooms was where each President who had served through our country's history had left a piece of memorabilia.

Following the tour through the White House, the team boarded the bus for a trip over to the Capitol Building. The bus swung past the area where protestors gathered and the driver pointed out a particular lady who had been protesting against nuclear power at the same spot for six years (I think I agree with her, especially after the disaster in Chernobyl. They tell all us average citizens to be careful with fire-crackers on the 4th of July but look at what that nuclear garbage can do to all of us).

At the Capitol, there was a discussion between Coach Jones and the players about how many steps there are up to the main entrance. The actual count is 82. The tour of the historic building began and the group went through the Senate Chambers, the House of Representatives and the Rotunda. In one big room, every state is represented by a life-size statue of an historic person from that state, so each of the players gathered around their respective monument.

A lot of Kentucky's politicians were with the group and Pervis met up with the representative from his hometown of Savannah, Georgia.

A reception for the Louisville group was held from 3-4:30 p.m. The same banner which draped the wall during the 1980 visit had been changed to reflect the current championship along with the score against Duke. No other team in the country could have made it so convenient for the sign painters in the capital. Only the Cardinals have been there twice in the '80s.

The members of the team signed a lot of autographs for the pages, well-wishers and others in attendance, then it was off to the Crystal Diner for some dinner.

The restaurant was located on the lower floor of a big apartment complex, and the group was supposed to get there before a huge group of kids were scheduled to arrive. It was something to see. It looked like the kids had beaten the Louisville contingent, but as it turned out, it wasn't the group they were supposed to be concerned with. That group arrived a little later. Eventually, the word got around about the national champions being there so the autograph sessions began. As far as the kids were concerned, politicians were nothing compared to the national basketball champions.

Still, everything worked out nicely. Following the meal, everyone was given some time to shop in the small stores

Freshman Tony Kimbro autographed a hat for one delighted fan.

located in the area. Then it was time to cut out for the airport and get on back to "My Old Kentucky Home."

It was a nice flight home and by 10 p.m. everyone was right back where they had started. The Cards had been privileged with a once-in-a-lifetime event and had stood in some high cotton.

Most of the talk on the trip back had been about the President. Everyone had been very impressed with him. For a man of 74-years of age who spends his days facing monumental decisions, Ronald Reagan had looked remarkable. He was alert, very spry and you could detect the sincerity of his words. He was a kind man and a strong man.

The security around the President was also a major topic of conversation. Security had been extremely tight, obviously because of the events going on in Libya. Ronald Reagan had surrounded himself with many young people, including those in the Secret Service. He liked to see young people get involved, which is why he took the time to honor the Louisville Cardinals.

Everyone left Washington with the feeling that our country was in the hands of a very good, very capable and sincere man. It was a day the players would never forget and something they would carry with them forever.

Denny Crum: Coach of the Decade

Denny Crum. What makes him tick? Why is he so successful? Is he really better than his peers?

I've been with the Cardinal program for five years and I've had a lot of time to watch the man operate. We've discussed basketball at length and I've heard him out on several different subjects. These conversations usually took place in an airport terminal, on a plane or bus, or at the dinner table of some hotel or motel. As for comparison, I've had the opportunity over the years to be around a lot of the best Division I basketball coaches in the country.

But how does he stack up against people such as Adolph Rupp and Joe B. Hall of Kentucky, C.M. Newton of Vanderbilt, Dean Smith of North Carolina, Bobby Knight of Indiana and all the others? All of these guys have strong points. Newton is just a great teacher of the game. Coach Rupp was a master at getting the ultimate effort from his players. The Kentucky mentor had an intimidating nature about him that just encouraged effort. I never said anything to Coach Rupp that was arguable. Just saying hello and good-bye took nerve at times. Paul "Bear" Bryant of Alabama football fame had that same quality.

Denny is a very easy person to talk to, but a conversation that would debate a point about basketball was difficult to argue with him about. I totally respect his opinions and ability but I also respect my own judgments concerning the game of basketball. We've talked about a lot of things over the years but seldom does the topic of basketball, in any sort of debatable fashion, pop up. I stay away from it.

His success has been at one level while mine came at a different level, in the high school ranks. For that reason, the game takes on a different picture. For example, I was involved in a 32-minute game where offensive runs weren't that important. I considered myself very capable of teaching "junk" defenses while Denny is a firm believer in the switching man-to-man. I spent a lot of time teaching the running game while Denny favors the corner-break.

I served my time at the college level as an assistant for two years and scouted college games for a number of years. I've always felt one of my strengths as a basketball person was being able to watch a team and really digest what they were doing, their strengths and weaknesses. I thoroughly understand the game at the collegiate level but being in an argumentative situation with Denny Crum on any basketball subject just makes me feel uncomfortable. Maybe it's because I couldn't defend my theories with the same credentials he has.

Most people know that C.M. Newton is one of my closest friends. It's easy for C.M. and me to really hassle around with basketball, but I served on his staff for two seasons and we've been close friends for 35 years. Hey, we lost 36 games together sitting on the same bench. Believe me, that'll either make you very close friends or bitter enemies. But we go back a long way, back to our fraternity days in SAE.

I've observed Coach Crum in a lot of tough situations. The post-game radio shows we do after every game have given me a very good insight into the man. He doesn't change much, whether it's stress or success. He comes to the table in almost the same frame of mind, regardless if it was after a big win or disappointing loss, a poorly officiated game or even after a key injury to an important player. He really handles difficult situations well and seems to keep every-thing in its proper perspective. A lot of people can't do that.

I think a lot of the reason he handles any situation so well is that he's always up front about it. He tells it the way he sees it, good or bad. You always know where you stand with Denny. If he thinks you're wrong, he'll tell you. If he thinks you're right, he'll tell you so.

The most upset I've ever seen Coach Crum came on two separate occasions. The first time was during the 1982 Metro Conference Tournament. Derek Smith, now in the NBA, was a senior at the time and did not make the All-Metro team after being voted co-MVP, along with David Burns of St. Louis, as a junior. Denny just pounced on Larry Albus, the Metro's commissioner at the time, when he walked into Memphis' Mid-South Coliseum.

The second instance was when he came to the table to do his post-game show following Milt Wagner's foot injury against Virginia Commonwealth in the second game of the 1984-85 season. He was visibly upset. I'm sure it was because he knew the impact the injury would have on the season and that Milt needed to have a good year for his own future. He was right because Louisville went on to struggle to a 19-18 record with Milt sidelined.

But as we look back on both of these occasions, they worked out for the better. Derek is a future all-star in the NBA and Milt returned to help win the 1985-86 national champion-ship for the Cardinals. Twice in five years is not a bad record for getting upset and that's why he's been nicknamed "Cool Hand Luke" by NBC-TV's Al McGuire.

When you get into what makes Denny tick, you must go back to the invaluable experiences he had during his days at UCLA with Coach John Wooden. Working under Coach Wooden would have been a dream come true for any aspiring young coach. How would you like to be a young heart specialist interested in mechanical heart transplants and find yourself hanging out with Dr. William DeVries in the operating room as he performed several of these operations?

By reading some of the books written by Coach Wooden, it was obvious this man was different. He just seems to say things in a way that makes more sense. Denny has acquired a lot of the same temperament Coach Wooden has and, judging from what I've read about the legendary coach, has picked some of the same mannerisms and style. Let there

be no doubt that Denny is his own man, but he just chose to follow a very successful example. At least being on the outside looking in, it seems to be that way.

Denny seems to understand what he is trying to get done more than the other coaches. He's always in control. When things don't work out he appears to have the patience to wait for another chance. He seems to understand, without question, what needs to be done and how to get it done.

I've never known anyone who was always right, but Denny is a great teacher and a very intelligent person. He watched and listened in his younger days and, when his opportunity came, he applied this procedure and has gottten better at it with time. That's exactly what he expects from his players. He wants them to get a little better each day. Somewhere along the line, he knows it will all come together. That seems to be his plan and it sure seems to work for him.

He knows what it takes to win, keeps on teaching it and lets it happen. It's easy to say that a lot of coaches don't have the luxury of waiting for things to happen, they have to do it now. But Denny has earned his right to that attitude and now it's his to work with. You reap what you sow. Denny Crum is a very good farmer.

The thing I envy most about the Louisville coach is his ability to line up priorities. He does a terrific job of getting his "ducks" in line. I just wish I'd have known him when I was still in the coaching business. I was one of those guys who carried every loss home with me. I'm sure I let the losses influence my life at home, which wasn't fair to my family.

Denny, on the other hand, seems to be able to walk in, do his job and, no matter what the results, walk out and move along. I'm sure he doesn't erase everything completely from his mind but I believe he buries them to the point where life for the people around him carries on.

Granted, he's in the catbird seat with a 10-year contract that guarantees him a $1 million bonus if he stays the duration, but he's earned it with his success.

I don't know how many times I've heard him say, "We'll just put them out on the court, work hard and see what happens." And he'll follow that up with, "If we get beat, we'll go back and work some more and hope to do better the next time out." Now that's a great attitude to have, one you can live with and have peace of mind. I truly believe Denny is at peace within himself, something a lot of us cannot say.

Denny Crum, without a doubt, is the Coach of the Eighties. Four trips to the Final Four and two national championships in this decade alone speak themselves.

And the 1980s aren't over yet. There's more to come. There's just too much "hay in the barn" along with farmer Crum for it not to be that way.

Denzil (that's his real name) is a fierce competitor at whatever he's doing. He wants to catch the biggest fish in

Denny Crum has compiled some impressive statistics in his 15 seasons at U of L and seems destined to be in the Hall of Fame by the time his career is over.

To be successful, you must have good help. Crum's coaching staff (Bobby Dotson, Jerry Jones and Wade Houston) is one of the best.

the water, hit the golf ball the farthest, destroy you in a card game and shoot the biggest bear in the woods. Ask any of his golfing buddies. When the friendly stakes get high enough, there's no way to beat him. He'll simply find a way to win.

Crum's teams use a switching man-to-man defense. It's a unique defense and, to my knowledge, the Cards are the only team around that switch on everything, particularly going away from the basket. This defense has more holes in it early in the season than the worst and oldest pair of socks in my drawer. It's a defense that really requires a lot of player communication and alertness. It's a costly defense in the early season games, but it's something else when it all comes together, usually in February and March. The finished product forces an opponent into a one-game preparation.

Come tournament play, there's no time for opponents to make the adjustments.

Another asset of Denny's is that he doesn't believe in the quick fix. He's a man of patience, at least on the basketball court. His attitude with Billy Thompson is a perfect example of his patience. Several times over the past four years he came to the post-game show and defended his star forward, even when Thompson's performance was below the quality you'd expect from a player with his ability.

After one game when Thompson was 1 of 5 from the field and had five turnovers, Coach Crum wanted to talk about his 10 rebounds and the fact that he had led the team in scoring, rebounding and assists the entire season. He wouldn't talk about the turnovers.

Denny refused to let anyone criticize Billy. He seemed to know that Billy's time would come and that he'd do the ultimate for the University. He knew that down the road Billy T. would more than fulfill all the dreams of the Cardinal faithful. And he was right once again.

Denny never panics. Many times after seeing a player make a goofy mistake, I'd look directly over at the coach and his facial expression would never change. For an example, I remember watching the Cards in the Final Four back in 1983. The site was Albuquerque, New Mexico and the opponent was a very tough Houston team led by Akeem Olajuwon and Clyde Drexler. Louisville was making a desperate attempt to come back in the late stages when Thompson, a freshman at the time, broke loose and headed down court on a breakaway. It should have been an easy basket but Billy attempted a one-handed pick-up slam, a la Dr. J., and bobbled the ball. The television camera zoomed in on Denny. Instead of being in a rage like I would have been, he gave Billy T. a clinched fist of encouragement. Now that took some self control.

He gives players opportunity after opportunity, providing they work hard and wait their turn. Denny always talks to them in a tone of voice that's instructive, not destructive or derogatory. He advises and points the way in such a manner that the players aren't intimidated. He truly is a super teacher of the game of basketball and the way he wants it played.

The players on his teams usually never break any scoring records because in his system no player gets that many shots. He teaches a team concept and that's the way it's played at U of L. It takes a special touch to get these hot-shot high school stars to accept this style and not be able to "shake and bake" at every opportunity. But Coach Crum gets it done by showing them that by playing team basketball, the rewards will be greater in the end.

During the actual 40 minutes of a game, Denny's biggest asset is his ability to totally concentrate. This is what makes him the best in the business when the clock is turned on. The total picture is always on his mind and he's able to read the opponent's weaknesses, then close in for the kill. In today's arenas, that's not an easy task. Still, that's why Louisville was able to outscore its opponents 3 to 1 in the closing minutes of the six NCAA Tournament games.

All these assets are a reflection of his training at UCLA, blended in with his personality, temperament, attitude and desire to win. If you think about it, just hanging around UCLA with year-after-year championships is enough to give you a terrible hunger for victory. The trick comes in having the desire, ability and intelligence to get it all executed. Obviously, Denny has done just that.

In my opinion, Denny is better than his peers at this stage of his career. But no one does it alone and Coach Crum has great help. Jerry Jones is his right-hand man. He's at all the practices and seems to be the second man in charge on the court. Coach Jones has a good basketball mind and is a guy

I don't mind arguing with in regards to the game. He's the perfect assistant. He loves his position and has no desire to do anything other than what he's doing.

J.J. has great rapport with the players. They all listen to his every word. He stays current on all the rules and what's happening in the world of college basketball. On the road, Coach Jones acts as a trouble-shooter.

My only criticism of Jerry is that the man doesn't need any sleep. Regardless of where we are, when the dining room opens in the morning he's there waiting for the first cup of coffee to come off the line. The man reads the morning paper before the ink gets dry.

Few people in this world have a job that's perfect for them, tailor-made as if it was the perfect fit. Jerry Jones is one of them. Besides, he's the best interview around.

Recruiters. Nobody, not even Denny, could get much done without the road runners smelling out the talent and trailing them down whatever route it takes. Louisville has two of the best, Wade Houston and Bobby Dotson. The proof is running around the Louisville campus year after year.

Both of these guys have the ability to do their own thing as a head coach, but it's a situation where they need to be very selective. Actually, being an assistant at the University of Louisville is a better position than being head coach at a lot of Division I schools. Recruiting is a very tough job and basically a young man's game. But it's a price that has to be paid in order to get the opportunity of being a head honcho.

As for Wade and Bobby, I'll leave you with this thought: All schools have recruiters but few of them have the Ellisons, Thompsons, Halls, Wagners, Crooks and Kimbros on the same team.

As for Denny, I find the man to be modest and confident. Let's face it, there's no way anyone could achieve what he has done and receive the applause without realizing he was a little special. But Coach mixes with everyone. At times he'll take the floor, especially when the conversation is about golf or fishing. Actually, he's more cocky when he talks about his recreational activities than he is in the world of college basketball. His face just shines when he gets somebody to listen to his fishing conquests.

For sure, he's a man who knows how to do his work in the winter and how to play when it's leisure time.

Yes, without a doubt, Denny is the Basketball Coach of the 1980s. But he'll be the first to tell you once you get to the top of the mountain as champion, you automatically become every opponent's primary target. You'll have to spend the future trying to hold on to that mountain top. It may be a tough assignment, but it sure is a beautiful view.

CHAPTER

10 The 'Crunch Bunch'

The Crunch Bunch — that was a label the Cardinals had tagged on them. Time after time after time, they seemed to move to another level of play during the closing minutes of a game and would simply put the opponent away. The errors and missed shots would just go away and down the stretch they became flawless.

It was a somewhat ironic nickname because what had buried the Cardinals during the early part of the season had become their strong suit during the stretch run. The Cards eventually lived by what had brought them death in the beginning.

Each game became a team effort. Each night brought to the front another Cardinal to make the big play, giving U of L an edge. When they once got the edge, they became doubly tough for the opposition. It became almost uncanny watching this team become a viable force. It got to where you could see it in their faces, especially during critical points in critical games.

This group of Cardinals was not much for pats on the back, hand slapping or cheering on the court. They did it with cool, icy confidence. When it came time to end it, that's exactly what they did — end it.

I remember looking at the U of L roster back in October as I sat in my family room. As I gazed at the list of players available to Denny Crum for the 1985-86 season, I made mental notes of the shortcomings of this team.

Pervis Ellison was a newcomer. What could you count on from him? Nothing for sure. Billy Thompson had seemed to struggle through the past three seasons, looking brilliant at times and just barely adequate at others. The other forward, who would it be? No way to know for sure. What about the guard positions? Milt Wagner would be back, possibly in only body and maybe not with the same skills. You can never tell for sure how people will respond following an injury that sidelined them for an entire season. Would the quickness be there? How about that beautiful shot, would it still be around? How about Jeff Hall? He could shoot and had improved his ball handling and defensive skills a lot, but would that be enough? With this lineup, who would play the point? How could you beat the good pressing teams without a good point man? How about the bench, would it be anything? Would the depth be there? What about the other freshmen, could they contribute? Would Kevin Walls' return make a difference? Would Mark McSwain be more consistent this year? Was this team going to struggle like the 1984-85 team? Why was Louisville opening in the Big Apple NIT with this bunch?

Those are the things that went flashing through my mind, and I'm sure the Cardinal coaching staff had entertained some of the same thoughts. Still, there were even more questions. Would this group be able to press effectively? Would Billy Thompson have his best year ever?

As I looked at these questions, I took an optimistic viewpoint. I felt good about the roster, certainly not national-championship good but at least good. I felt like they would hold their own in the Metro.

In an early column for SCORECARD, I picked the Cards to win 3 of 4 games in the preseason NIT and went on to write they'd finish the regular season with a 25-7 record. Well, I was exactly right. I did have a couple of differences, however, such as beating Cincinnati at home and losing to Houston on the road. Those were reversed but my numbers were correct, proof enough that I took the optimistic route.

When Jerry Jones saw what I had picked, he told me, "Jock, you must be out of your head. How can we win 25 games with a gym full of freshmen, a wounded returnee and our returning post man (Barry Sumpter, who started every game last year), ineligible?" But I know Coach Jones, and he was probably really thinking about possibly 26 wins instead of 25 but would never admit to it. You see, these coaches have to play that "Po' Us" routine. Jerry had seen the summer games and knew something about Pervis. He knew Milt's physical condition. But he didn't fool me because I knew what he was thinking all the time.

My hopes for a good season increased during the trip to New York. The Cardinals were in both games right up to the finish before something happened to take them out of it. I thought at the time, and even said it on the air, that if Louisville could give away as much as they had in this game and still be in contention to win right up to the very end, then that was a very good sign. Kansas and St. John's picked up a bundle of easy baskets against the backside of the press and, to make it worse, Milt Wagner had shot the ball from everywhere in Madison Square Garden in both games, and nothing had gone in. Still, the Cards were hanging in 'til the end. It was then that I thought to myself, "Hey man, we were going to be all right!"

Now, I wasn't thinking about a national championship because I wasn't that optimistic. But as the season progressed, so did that optimism. The Cards posted some really good wins against a good Western Kentucky team and a good Indiana unit. The victory over Syracuse was a biggie and I was encouraged with both wins over Virginia Tech. I was also proud of the victory over DePaul and, for sure, the win against Memphis State. They were all regular-season victories which kept the hopes alive.

Coach Crum and the "Camden Connection" of Billy Thompson, Milt Wagner and Kevin Walls.

There were down times, too, the worst coming against Kentucky. I was really discouraged with the rebounding totals in that contest. The loss at Memphis was a downer because the Cards had outplayed them all night. The loss to Cincinnati in Freedom Hall hurt because I felt it might push the Cards out of the conference race and it's never a good feeling to lose to an inferior team, especially at home.

Following what turned out to be the last loss of the season at North Carolina State on Feb. 8, I left Reynolds Coliseum feeling glum about some things.

The Wolfpack had beaten the Cards easily, and Mark McSwain's return seemed to be very iffy. But that's one thing about being a Cardinal fan — the Louisville team usually makes a quick move to arouse the spirits as they did just two days later by blitzing Virginia Tech in Blacksburg.

My hopes were on just getting into the NCAA Tournament and having a legitimate shot at making it to Dallas. I didn't feel as optimistic about the Final Four, but there came a time when that changed. It was about the time people started calling them the "Crunch Bunch." It's true, I did falter a little by predicting a loss to North Carolina in the NCAA Tournament, Crunch Bunch or not. But when I looked at the Tar Heel roster with all that size and experience, it got the better of me. My heart thought "Cardinals" but my head said "North Carolina." To make matters worse, I was stupid enough to say it publicly.

Following the victory over North Carolina, I had no doubt that whoever was going to win the championship would have to beat the Louisville Cardinals. To me, defeating North Carolina was the final confidence lift this team needed. Dean Smith's squad had lived at the top of the polls for 13 straight weeks while Louisville was hanging somewhere between 15 and 20 for most of the season. Everyone knew about Brad Daugherty and his Tar Heel teammates.

In the back of a lot of people's minds, the game between Louisville and North Carolina was the game for the championship. The Cards won and from that time on they seemed to take the court as if they already were champs and were

259

simply defending their title. It was an attitude sort of like "it's ours, now let's see you take it from us."

Denny Crum deserves a lot of credit for the newly found attitude the Cardinals seemed to have had. He put his team together a little at a time and got everyone to accept their roles and pull for a common cause. After all, if things got tough he could always call a timeout and put the unit together again. I truly believe that when the players return to the bench and see that picture of Denny standing on the sideline waiting to set up the next couple of minutes of play, they get new life before the next horn blows. They always came out after timeouts and made things happen during their stretch run for the championship.

For sure, there was an aura of confidence and supremacy of being the best. I even had the feeling that following the win over North Carolina, Louisville's opponents felt like they were playing the eventual champions. Coach Sonny Smith

The heralded freshman class of Pervis Ellison and Keith Williams (both sitting), Avery Marshall (33), Kenny Payne (21), David Robinson (25) and Tony Kimbro (44), was instrumental in the Cards' success of 1985-86.

of Auburn said, "Louisville is the kind of team you should play to win it all." His statement set the tone for the remainder of the playoffs. When U of L took the court, people looked at them as the team to beat. I must have asked 100 strangers in Dallas who they liked in the finals, and not one single person picked Duke — nary a one. Personally, I was still concerned about playing Kansas again, but when Duke eliminated the Jayhawks I felt a national championship would return to the home of the Kentucky Derby — Louisville.

Following the NCAA Tournament, I found myself sitting in the same room where I had asked myself all those preseason questions, but now I had all the answers. I read the papers following the championship game again and found myself still marveling at all the things the Crunch Bunch was able to accomplish. I realized then that this Cardinal team had battled their way through the NCAA Tournament and seldom did they put together 40 good minutes of solid play. Mercy, how good they would have been if they had played all 40 minutes like they always seemed to play in the second half!

I admit that I had dreams for this group of players, but dreams are free and they make you feel good. My dreams would usually blot out at the end with the "No Way Will This Happen Syndrome." There's a lesson we can all learn from the 1985-86 Louisville Cardinals — no matter what adversities you might face or how overwhelming the odds are against you, everything has to happen before it becomes a fact. Sometimes we all look at a situation and immediately think we better not get our hopes up. But with hard work, proper direction, perserverance, attitude and faith, miracles can become reality. We all discovered on the last day of March 1986 that dreams DO come true.

Billy Thompson

Billy Thompson, who hails from Camden, New Jersey, signed at the University of Louisville as the nation's most sought after high school basketball player back in 1982. Every conceivable adjective was used in describing his talents and what his future would be in Cardinal country.

I remember his first game in the red and black. It was on Nov. 26, 1982 in the Great Alaska Shootout. It was that night that I started calling him Billy T.

At the time, I was working with Dave Conrad on WHAS-TV. I felt within myself that night that this guy was special, very special. He just handled himself differently and he did things in a different way. Actually, coming in with the hoopla that he did would make it almost impossible to be what the media had told everybody he would be. I think some of his teammates began calling him "World" and the word is that name was given to him by either Rodney or Scooter McCray.

Well, for sure, he was the new kid on the block. In his first few games he would miss a shot and the crowd seemed to gasp. He didn't get every rebound and they would gasp. Naturally, I'm exaggerating some, but that's the way it seemed to be. No matter what he did in his career it was never enough.

There were times that I told Van, in private, that I was disappointed in Billy's performance. It looked like he just made mistakes at critical times. But I never doubted his talent.

Over the past four years, I really learned to respect this young man and admire his mental toughness. I have truly watched him come alive as a great college talent.

Many times on the radio show, I stated that he would be a first-round draft choice in the pros. This was during some of his tough times while Kentucky's Kenny Walker was astounding the world with his play. I said, "He would have more early success in the pros than Walker" and "would probably go higher in the draft."

Just this past year, I was speaking at the Quarterback Club in Louisville and made some of those same statements to them. I even told them that before the year was over Billy would be playing exceptionally good basketball.

I was immediately challenged by some of the membership. One member laughed and said he wanted to see me after the season because he wanted to hear me say that I had been wrong. I wish I knew his name now, but he knows mine and I'm still waiting for him to talk to me.

Another thing fans need to remember is that in Denny Crum's system of basketball, you are never going to get 20 shots a night. He believes in the team style of play. The 1985-86 squad was a perfect example of how Coach Crum likes his teams to play. All of the starters averaged in double figures. There were no weak spots. They all had to be defended.

In one sense, Cardinal players are victims of the system. But, in the long run, they always come out better because of that same system.

Billy was special. If they ever make a new Tarzan movie, Billy's their man. He has a perfect body and is exceptionally strong. Billy is an excellent leaper with extraordinary ability to get any rebound. He has good hang time on his shots and does an excellent job of positioning the ball away from the defender. The forward is a master of using English on the ball and the banking board. He has the ability to play outside or inside and has terrific basketball senses.

Simply stated, Billy has all the qualities that any coach could ever want in a player. And that includes mental toughness.

Away from the game, Billy seemed to be pretty much of a person who liked to have a lot of time to himself. I traveled a lot of miles with this young man, by all means of travel, but seldom did I ever get the chance to really talk with him. The one time I really wanted to talk to him was following the loss to Kansas in Lawrence.

He had a tough last couple of minutes in that game and

I think he carried the burden for the loss on himself. During the trip home and the time spent waiting to change planes, he kept to himself. I could see Billy was hurting and I wanted so badly to talk to him. I'll always regret that I didn't do just that.

He always had his radio and his earphones in place, and that alone discourages conversation. Sometimes, I think he did it so he could have time for his own private thoughts.

Billy Thompson accepted a lot of criticism during his four years at the university, but it never influenced his effort. I had an opportunity to talk to his father one night in Freedom

Thompson scored a new career-high when he poured in 30 points against Wyoming.

Hall, and I've always understood Billy a little better after that conversation. "Billy has always been taught to be a team player and that's what he is," his father told me. You could tell his father felt very proud as he spoke about his son.

At times, Billy was asked to do a lot of things that still required improvement to match the skills which made him so special. In the learning process, he made some errors. In his case, though, that was not allowed by the fans in the stands. I feel like he knew he was doing the best he could at the time, and that's all he could do.

I respect him because he stayed tough and we all know how he performed when the "Really Big Show" got underway. I always felt, and said so publicly, my only criticism was his lack of concentration for a long period of time. That was just my personal opinion. It appeared, at times, Billy felt the situation didn't merit his top effort.

He is very intelligent. I want to go on record as saying it will be a long time before the Cardinals can replace the talent and accomplishments of Billy Thompson.

Billy was tough enough to do the job when it came time to do it and is a very special person. I will always cherish the privilege I had introducing him at the giant championship celebration in Freedom Hall.

Milt Wagner

I don't know what the exact definition of the slang word "cool" is, but I do know that the word "cool" means Milt Wagner. Not because of his ability to step to the foul line under all pressure situations and circumstances and rifle the ball in, but because of his natural way of just being Milt. Hey, the man walks cool, he talks cool and he is cool.

I have always been a fan of Milt, from the moment I met him back in the beginning of the 1981-1982 season. Milt and I started with the Cardinals together down in Bowling Green, Kentucky at the Wendy's Classic Tournament.

From the first moment I watched him shoot that feathery shot, the one that barely moves the nets as it passes through and looks like a precious gem or a fine piece of silk, he was special. Watching Milt shoot the basketball was like looking at a beautiful painting, or possibly watching a refined ballet dancer go through her routine of perfection.

Milt was a very coachable athlete. He had to be put down by the coaches occasionally, but accepted it and came back with more determination. Always, he was exceptionally friendly and made you feel like he enjoyed talking with you.

In the many interviews we had over the five years, Milt would speak like he shot the ball, taking his time and enunciating every syllable. He'd explain, in his way, whatever question had been presented to him.

Many times I saw him get on the bus, in the wee hours of the morning when we would be heading out for the airport, and it appeared he was walking in his sleep. Only small

openings of the eyelids were visible. As he passed, he would somehow manage a little smile that seemed to say, "Hey Man." During the daytime hours, he usually had the shades on and the smile was a lot bigger. The Ice Man, for sure, was warm and compassionate. He was a favorite of all who gathered around him.

It took a man with a lot of heart to spend his fourth and supposedly his senior year watching his friends move on, watching his teammates play and knowing, if his services had been available, things for the Cardinals would have been a lot better. This all happened because of the broken foot suffered against Virginia Commonwealth in the second game of the 1984-85 season.

With that obstacle overcome, it was 1985-86 and time to see if the silky shot was still there, if the courage to jump and make the cuts right and left would be a problem, and to see if the confidence was still there. As time would tell, it was all still there, but it did take a little while to get it back together like it had been before.

Through the first eight games, Wagner was shooting a very unfamiliar 35.6 percent, hitting on only 36 of 101 shots. In the first and third games of the season, Wagner was 3 of 16 and 2 of 15 from the field. It was a terrible thing to watch, so you can imagine how he must have felt.

I think his game returned for the first time against Indiana in Freedom Hall. Ice hit 7 of 12 field goals and 8 of 10 free throws for a solid 22-point effort. As usual, he was the deadliest at the end of the game.

A lot of folks, including me, were beginning to wonder if it was ever going to come together for Milt. The professional scouts, who were always around at game time, had no doubts. The head talent scout for the NBA, Marty Blake, said, "I wouldn't worry about his shot. Your shot never leaves you." The other pros all seemed optimistic about the return of the Ice Man, so why should we be concerned?

They were right because he came back as strong as ever, averaging 14.9 points per game and hitting 49.5 percent of his attempts.

I know that I have never seen a deadlier free-throw shooter at crunch time than Milt Wagner. You just never thought about him missing a "must" free-throw.

One time, he even apologized for missing a freebie that would have iced the game. It was against South Carolina and the score was 74-72 with the Cards in the lead and four seconds left on the clock. His shot would have put the game out of reach but it hit the back of the rim. Later he would say, "I regret that I missed the free-throw. That's my specialty. I knew it was too strong as it left my hand."

The kicker here is that it wasn't a game-winning shot, it simply would have eliminated any chance for a South Carolina win. Had it been a game-winner attempt, I would have bet my winter underwear that it would have hit nothing but bottom.

Being able to perform when the pressure is on takes a special quality within a person. It takes inner courage and total confidence, complete concentration and the sensitivity to be able to put the feathery touch on the release of the ball. Milt had all these qualities as a Cardinal and will carry those same qualities on down the road with him in his future. It just won't seem the same out there without having the Ice Man to call upon to decide who will win or lose.

It was a fitting tribute for Milt to step to the free-throw line in Dallas with two seconds remaining in the final game. Successful free throws would lock up a national championship for the Louisville Cardinals.

What was going through the minds of the millions of basketball fans as he toed the line for this dramatic moment? I can't speak for them but I knew there was NO DOUBT. That's why we call him the "Ice Man."

Jeff Hall

This is the story about a supposedly slow-footed white kid from Fairview, Kentucky, who would play on a national championship team.

If Hall was indeed so slow-footed, how could he play such an important role on the 1985-86 national champions? There are three simple answers to that question: he never was that slow; he had the heart of a lion; and he developed his own technique for dealing with the quicker people.

It was that heart of a lion part that hurt Jeff at times during the early portion of his career at Louisville. He'd often let his temper get to him some, which would affect his performance. But as time passed and he matured more and more, Jeff learned to handle that problem and play under control, regardless of what was happening.

It's ironic but during his senior season, Jeff rarely, if ever, showed a trace of his temper. At least not until the final second of the final game with the championship net already fitted for his neck size. With the clock ticking down to zero, Hall picked off a pass and headed for the basket to stamp the win with a rousing dunk. But Duke's Danny Ferry clotheslined him. Hall, angered, turned and threw the ball at Ferry.

But the flare-up lasted just momentarily and everything turned out OK. Jeff had a lot to feel good about at the moment and I was worried about him ending his fine four-year career on a sour note.

Also, it was this slow-footed white boy who had been assigned to guard Duke's All-American guard, Johnny Dawkins. He was as quick as any college player in the nation.

But why would the U of L coaching staff create such a matchup?

Crum and his staff were well aware of Jeff's heart of a lion, an ingredient he carried around inside his strong body. They knew he would accept the assignment as a personal challenge. When Jeff makes that kind of commitment, you could bet he'd give it every ounce of effort he could muster.

Louisville used a 1-3 zone defense with Jeff shadowing Dawkins. He hawked him like Dawkins was satan himself and the Duke guard hardly sniffed the basketball after the switch was made. Jeff put this player, who had lightning feet, in a box and mailed him home to mother. With Dawkins shut down the game belonged to the Louisville Cardinals, with all the glory and everlasting memories. It was a terrific moment for Jeff.

When the final horn sounded, Van shoved a tape recorder in my hand and told me to "get out there and get me something." Away I went and found Jeff standing at midcourt, slumped over and trying to find some air among the hordes of fans, cheerleaders and media. I was afraid he was hyperventilating so I asked him if he could say anything. He gasped out, "Hold on a minute, Jocko, I just need a

second." He quickly regained his breath and gave me what I needed, just as he always had. I had talked to him before the game so it was only fitting that we talked after the victory.

Jeff was physically spent. There was nothing left. He had gone after Dawkins with energy he just didn't have, but that's the type of thing people who have the heart of a lion do. When the hunt starts, it's not over until the kill. I was so proud of him that I wanted to hug him right then and there. This was the same guy a lot of people thought would be better coming off the bench during his four seasons, but not anymore.

It was during his junior year that Jeff got better at being a starter. He was forced into handling the ball a lot more than he was accustomed to and against the opponent's better players because of Milt's injury and absence in the lineup.

In his first two seasons, Jeff was stripped of the ball, picked clean in embarrassing fashion, more than once. He got much better at protecting the ball as a junior, increased his stamina and learned to do a lot more than just shoot. He became a complete player the hard way, under fire.

When his senior season rolled around, Milt was back and many thought Jeff would be on the bench again. No way, not this guy with the heart of a lion. Those type of people don't let things like that happen to them. He was right there with the rest of the starters, just where he belonged. He may have become the "other" guard with Milt back, but that's a role he could accept.

Jeff was a deadly shooter from the outside with absolutely perfect hand action on the release of the ball. He was picture-perfect as a shooter and probably had the best range of any of the guards on the team. The new 3-point goal being put in for the 1986-87 season would have been meat and potatoes for Jeff.

One theory was that Milt's return to the lineup would free up Jeff a lot more, which it did. But the opposite was also true. Jeff's presence on the floor forced every opponent to honor him. Milt would be the first to tell you that Jeff opened up a lot of opportunites for him.

In the six NCAA Tournament games, Jeff committed only nine turnovers. That was a super job for somebody who had to handle the ball as much as he did under pressure situations. That's an average of 1.5 per game. Remarkable for a guard. He finished his four-year career hitting 51.7 percent of his field goals, mostly from long range.

Yes, it can be said this slow-footed white boy had made his mark in the four years he spent with the Cardinals.

I had a lot of opportunites to talk to Jeff during that time. I remember how homesick he had gotten as a freshman, but he toughed it out. It didn't take long to realize this country boy had a lot of stuff inside him, good stuff.

Before the championship game, I asked Jeff if it had been worth the hard work and if he'd enjoyed it at the University of Louisville. He replied, "It's been great. I just wish I could do it all over again."

All of us wish Jeff could do it over again, too. But that can't happen. However, we all know that anyone with the heart of a lion will always be a winner. Jeff Hall is certainly that.

Robbie Valentine

The first time I ever saw Robbie Valentine was back in 1982 during the Kentucky High School State Tournament. Robbie had led his North Hardin team to a 37-2 record and it looked like it was going to be 38-2 seconds later in the state championship game. It looked like his team was a cinch to win when a youngster from Laurel County by the name of Paul Andrews let go a desperation shot from near midcourt. The ball went in, turning ecstasy into doom for Robbie and his teammates.

It was during that tournament while broadcasting the game with Van Vance that I made the remark that Robbie, in my opinion, wouldn't be as successful in Division I college basketball as he had been at the high school level. His shot was hard and flat.

On the other hand, no one played harder or had more enthusiasm than Robbie. I also thought he was the most exciting player in that state tournament.

Robbie went on to sign with Louisville where he really worked hard to soften his shot. But the old injury plague got him before he had a chance to do much.

No one expected him to do a lot as a freshman, especially with the likes of Lancaster Gordon, Scooter and Rodney McCray, Charles Jones and Milt Wagner around.

He had to deal with knee problems as a sophomore. As a junior it was a hand injury.

Finally, after his junior season, Robbie was healthy. He surprised everybody by leading the Louisville Developmen-

tal Summer League, a league loaded with great Louisville players of the past, in scoring.

Bad luck always seemed to follow Robbie. Injury after injury kept him on the sidelines in his first three seasons at U of L and now, even though he was healthy, Coach Crum was forced to play a talented group of freshmen. Their years were ahead of them while Robbie's were about over. Still, nothing seemed to dampen his enthusiasm.

Robbie volunteered to be taken off his athletic scholarship and put on a Pell Grant just so Crum wouldn't be over his allotment of 15 scholarship players. He quickly became the crowd favorite in Freedom Hall and the chant "Ro-B, Ro-B, Ro-B" became a common theme. He even joined in with the crowd during one late-season game.

Healthy for the first time as a senior and in almost perfect shape (his knees were OK), Robbie was still relegated to bench duty. Too many Cardinals who had not been injured and forced to miss valuable practice time and games received most of the available and precious game minutes. He simply had been denied his chance of lots of playing time because of his earlier career injuries.

But Robbie never pouted. He became the Cardinal on the sideline who gave constant encouragement to his teammates on the floor. In those rare instances when he was called upon, the forward was always ready. He made some good things happen.

It's awfully easy and tempting to just give up when something stands between you and where you want to go. Robbie wasn't like that. He continued to give the effort. As a result, when the championship watches and rings were passed out, he could claim one for his own. He deserved it and probably appreciated it more than any other player on the team. The ring made it all worthwhile and probably even eased the pain of that unlikely shot back in 1982.

Herbert Crook

Herbert Crook began his practicing way before the official first day of practice on October 15. His preparation for the 1985-86 season began in an area where there were no baskets, no courts and no basketballs. His season began in the weight room.

During his freshman year, Herbert had shown moments of real potential. Still, like most freshmen, there were other games when his presence was hardly noticed. No one knew

better than Herb that he needed some additional strength if he was going to hold his own inside against the caliber of competition he would face every night. Plus, the new freshman class coming in was loaded with talent and Crum's newest members had been ranked as the top recruiting class of any of the other schools in the nation.

All summer long, the raves of the Louisville fans had been about the super performances these incoming freshmen were having in the summer league. They were already making their marks in a league loaded with many of Louisville's past heroes — Derek Smith, Rodney McCray, Darrell Griffith, Scooter McCray and Charles Jones, plus a lot of other real tough and talented players. With all that NBA talent playing in the league, the folks were still talking about the play of the incoming freshmen. Wow, those guys must really be something!

Herbert was not a regular in this league. In fact, he played very little in this league, opting instead to improve his skills in his own way. For sure, his overall game needed some improvement. His stats for his freshman season were just barely mediocre, especially his shooting accuracy. As a rookie in 1984-85, Herb attempted 179 shots and canned just 80 of them. That's 44.7 percent, which wouldn't win the hearts of many basketball fans, much less the coaches. It was just plain ol' almost-bad shooting. At the foul line as a frosh, Herb wasn't much better. He took 66 shots and made 43 for a percentage of 65.1.

Now, coaches are faced with a big problem with this kind

of shooter in the lineup. The opponent won't respect that player as an offensive threat and, therefore, they'd play a sagging defense to help out on the more potent offensive players. In short, they'd jam everything up inside.

As a freshman, Herb had done a respectable job on the boards, getting 3.9 rebounds per game with an average playing time of 15.8 minutes. Offensively, he finished the season with 203 points, good for a 5.3 average.

Before the season began, I wrote an article in SCORECARD about who I thought would probably be the starters in 1985-86. This list did not have Herb's name on it. In fact, I had him figured to be no better than the second forward used coming off the bench. My exact words were, "The forward spots will go to Thompson and Payne. McSwain will be the first replacement, followed by Crook."

Obviously, I was wrong. You can't measure determination and pride.

But I wasn't the only one surprised with Herbert. When practice began in October, Denny Crum was as surprised by Herb's play as much as anyone. The forward had returned for the 1985-86 season as the team's most improved performer. Whatever it was that Herb had done in between the seasons, it had worked.

As the season progressed, it became obvious that before the year would end, Herbert Crook would no longer be just the "other" forward. Sure, an All-American candidate, Billy Thompson, was playing opposite Herb at forward, but the "Rubber Man" would make a mark for himself. By the end of the season, Herbert commanded the respect of all U of L's opponents. When the opposing coach put the names on the board as a player who needed close attention, Crook's name was up there.

In the season opener, Louisville took on Miami of Ohio in the first round of the NIT. Herb, as a surprise starter, got 15 points and six rebounds in just 24 minutes of play. Even more amazing was the fact that he hit all six of his free throws. Herb looked good, to say the least, and Cardinal fans were shaking their heads in disbelief and wondering if that was, indeed, the same Herbert Crook.

The answer was no — it was an older, more mature and a new Herbert Crook. It was a Herbert Crook who would have a lot of terrific games as the season progressed and who would be as important to the Cardinals as ANY player on the court.

Herb was just a pleasure to visit with this past season. He's basically a quiet person but always handles himself in such a way that it's obvious he is a class person. Throughout the year, I'd ask him for a couple of minutes on the mike. He'd always oblige but I could tell he'd just as soon I'd interview someone else. The Louisville native didn't seek any head-lines, he just went out and played. He was a coach's player because he made the effort to do exactly as he was told.

Superb Herb was named to the All-West Regional team in Ogden. He was first on my ballot and, had there been an MVP award, it's my opinion the announcer would have blurted out Herbert Crook's name. He would have definitely deserved it.

No one can doubt Herb's improvement over such a short span of time, but it happened. The question now is what can he do to improve next year?

All players need to get a little bit better defensively each year they play and there's always room to improve the shooting, from both the foul line and the field. From my point of view, Herb needs to come up with some offensive moves where, with his back to the basket, he turns to his left. He's already deadly turning to his right with a good, natural motion, but needs to be able to go to his left a little better when he's posting up. He's got to keep that defensive man guessing some. But regardless of what Herb needs to work on, I'm sure the coaching staff will have a few suggestions and Herb will do whatever it takes.

Well, it was just a terrific year for the Rubber Man, and the proof is in the numbers. During the championship season, Herb raised his shooting percentage to a 52.8 clip, an increase of almost 8 percent. His shooting from the foul line went up by 3.5 percent. When the whole show was over, Herbert had averaged 11.9 points during the regular season and, get this, 16.2 points during NCAA Tournament play.

Yes, it's a fact that Herbert won't fool anyone when practice begins for the 1986-87 season, but one thing is for sure — Herbert Crook will never ever again be called just the "other" forward.

Pervis Ellison

Remarkable — that's the word that tells the story of Pervis Ellison.

When trying to understand how a young man of 18-years of age, a freshman, could become the MVP of the Final Four, a feat that hadn't been duplicated since 1944, it's obvious that you are dealing with a young athlete of intelligence. His high school records revealed that he graduated with a 3.5 grade-point average. That's very, very good.

Following the LSU game, a win that set up the Duke-Louisville championship game, much of the talk of the media was about the intelligence of the Duke players.

Pervis calmly suggested that maybe it would be wise for them to check the transcripts of the Louisville players.

Actually, it was Pervis' intelligence that played a big part in his accomplishments. It took a very level-headed and strong-thinking individual to cope with the many difficult situations he faced as the season progressed. Sometimes, keeping your own emotions and fears under control in the face of adversity is the most difficult task of all. Pervis had the very unusual ability to properly keep himself on an even keel all the time. He accepted instruction and criticism well, and had the intelligence to learn quickly the many different offensive patterns in Crum's arsenal, executed his part with a quality performance and always gave it his best.

That covers the mental aspect of Pervis Ellison, but how about the playing part? Before his senior year in high school began, Pervis' name was not on the top of recruiting lists of the major schools. He wasn't physically awesome looking, being of a very slight build. His face had the look of an

adolescent and his voice was very soft and gentle. His moves on the court weren't powerful looking. At the time, he wasn't even mentioned in the Who's Who of *Street & Smith's Basketball Yearbook*. He was listed 71st, however, by Bob Gibbons' Blue Ribbon Scouting Service. In other words, Pervis Ellison started his last year of high school with the credentials of a so-so prep player.

It was during his senior year that the 6-10 center began to make his move. He averaged 27 points, 19 rebounds and seven blocked shots per game as a senior while leading his Savannah (Georgia) team to a regional championship. He was no longer a secret and by the time players started signing letters-of-intent, Pervis had become a hot potato. He signed with Louisville in April, following his participation in the McDonald's Derby Classic All-Star game. By then, he was on fire. But it was too little and too late for the other recruiters as Pervis chose U of L over Georgia Tech. The trained eye of Wade Houston had seen something in Pervis before the other recruiters had seen it in the young man. Lots of college recruiters had seen Pervis at the summer camps, but perhaps Sonny Smith of Auburn said it best, "You could see that he would be a player, but it looked like it would take a little time."

Well, Sonny missed on that opinion.

It only took about six weeks of preseason practice before it became obvious to all concerned that Wade Houston had returned with the catch of the year. Pervis, in deciding between Louisville and Georgia Tech, said his final decision was made because of the state of Kentucky's basketball reputation. I'm also sure that Wade's personality and recruiting style had left their marks on Pervis.

Basketball is very important in Kentucky, just as Pervis had expected. With that in mind, he checked in at the Louisville campus, spent the summer working at a lumber yard during the day and shooting hoops at night. He played in the summer league with his freshmen teammates and got excellent reviews from the ex-Cardinal greats.

"He's great," said Wiley Brown, a member of U of L's 1980 championship team. "I think he will fit right in at the University of Louisville."

"He's a beautiful big man," added Derek Smith, now a member of the Los Angeles Clippers of the NBA. "Pervis just needs to play basketball."

Ellison, by no means, was the MVP of the summer league. In fact, one or two of the other freshmen had looked better than Pervis. But summer leagues can be foolers for the simple reason the games consist mainly of shooting and scoring. Team discipline is absent, there are no awards for assists and the quality of defense is not even close to what is found once the real games begin. The extra pass is never made and shot selection is poor. The people with the best one-on-one abilities are the ones who really make the best showing. At least that's the way most summer leagues have appeared to me.

Ellison arrived at U of L weighing in at 190 pounds. For a player who stands right at 6-10, that's downright skinny. But this brings me to the next reason why Pervis got the "remarkable" tag hung on him. He simply fooled people all year.

No one could see the quickness or his ability to anticipate. He just didn't look like he could or would do any damage to anyone.

The big, bad man from North Carolina, Brad Daugherty, said, "I've heard the name, but I don't know anything about him." Needless to say, by the time it was all over, Daugherty

Pervis Ellison was just a freshman but he showed St. John's All-American Walter Berry that he is capable of playing with the big boys.

had met, bowed and surrendered to Mr. Ellison with respect. The North Carolina center did outscore Pervis 19-15, but it was the type of duel that left both players well acquainted with each other.

With Barry Sumpter's academic problems, Pervis had an open lane to the starting position. He was the best post man prospect in the building, even though the word is he was recruited to be a forward. That's a possibility in the future with the signing of 7-2 Felton Spencer from Louisville Eastern High School. After all, after being the MVP as a post man in the Final Four, playing forward would give him the challenge of being a MVP at a different position. Just joking, I think!

Pervis started at center in his first collegiate game against Miami of Ohio. It was the beginning of what would be a remarkable year for a remarkable young man. In his first game as a Cardinal, Ellison scored 11 points, grabbed seven rebounds, dished out two assists, made four blocks and had one steal in 33 minutes of play. Amazingly, he had only one turnover. That's a pretty good night's work for a mere college boy of only two months.

In the semifinals and finals of the Big Apple NIT in New York, the youngster faced two post men who were loaded with experience. They were beefier and older than Pervis, but neither were more confident of playing quality basketball than the young man from Savannah.

Against Kansas, Pervis faced 7-1 Greg Dreiling, who probably weighed over 250 pounds. No problem. Pervis outscored him 18-12 and had no turnovers to Dreiling's three. Louisville lost but Pervis had done well in the Big Apple game.

In the consolation game against St. John's, "Never Nervous" Pervis faced a man who was one of the leading candidates for Player of the Year. The U of L freshman came out second in this battle, but not by much. Walter Berry, who

was at least 22-years-old, had been getting raves from all over the Big East when Pervis was still a high schooler in Georgia just trying to get his name in *Street & Smith's* list of talented prep players. But on that night in New York, Berry outscored his younger counterpart by only 22-16. Actually, Pervis scored one more field goal than Berry but the St. John's star was 8 of 10 from the foul line. In the rebounding department, Berry gathered in 13 to Pervis' seven. Overall, Ellison had held his own against a man with outstanding credentials. Louisville lost the game again, but it was competition against players like Dreiling and Berry that, by season's end, would make Pervis mentally tough. He went on to accept challenges from everyone and performed his skills in a fashion that would make all the experts wonder aloud, "How could this be happening?"

I met Pervis Ellison's family at the South Carolina game in Columbia. It was obvious that they were very proud of their son. "I've known a long time that he would be something special," said his father. And his mother called him "her baby." Pervis has two sisters, one who was at the game. She was most outspoken and said, "He needs to get stronger and then he will really be something." She was a beautiful young lady and it was obvious that she, too, was very proud of her 6-10 brother — Pervis Ellison II. Little did they, or any of us, know just how much they would have to be proud about when the season ended.

I'm really not sure what this young man can do to top his performance of the 1985-86 season. For sure, he set a new standard for freshmen in their rookie year of play. When coaches say what they always say, like, "You can't expect freshmen to do this or that" or "They have to learn so let's not expect too much," you can bring up the example of Pervis Ellison. They'll no longer be able to say "Freshmen just don't become MVP's of the Final Four." Instead, they'll have to modify that to "Freshmen SELDOM become MVP's of the Final Four." It happened in 1944 by Arnie Ferrin while playing with Utah, and it didn't happen again until 1986 by Pervis "Never Nervous" Ellison. That's a difference of 42 years!

Pervis finished the year shooting 55.4 percent from the field and 68.1 percent from the free-throw line. He averaged 8.2 rebounds and 2.0 assists per game and blocked a total of 92 shots, four more than all Louisville's opponents combined. He averaged 13.1 points in 30.6 minutes of action per game. His NCAA totals improved to 15.5 points and 9.5 rebounds per game while averaging 33.8 minutes in the six contests.

He wanted nothing but what was his. Against North Carolina, there was a critical tip-in during the final minutes of the game, just before Louisville stretched out its lead. He had been given credit for the basket but spent the entire post-

but he refused. I did what Denny Crum did with Mark. I made no scene and simply let it pass, thinking I would settle it later. I settled the dispute with my player and he returned in the finals to score 25 points and lead our team to the championship. It's just a fact that these athletes are temperamental and it takes understanding by all parties to keep the boat from rocking.

And that's exactly what Denny did with Mark — he settled it later. From that time on, Mark made a new committment to himself and to the University of Louisville Cardinals. He decided he'd wait his turn and be ready when it came, which is exactly what he did. Mark's play down the stretch was ever so valuable.

Following that incident, Mark began to build on his performance. He got tougher and tougher and was beginning to play his best ball of the season when, during a game in Raleigh against North Carolina State, Mark went down. He made no effort to get up and it was obvious he was hurt. The next day the papers read, "McSwain out indefinitely." Boy, what a hole that made in the reserve situation!

But, as time passed, Mark recovered from the strained ligament in his knee. The Cardinals continued to hang on to victories and Mark made his return to the lineup. Having his services off the bench played a very important part in the drive for the national championship.

During the six-game winning streak it took to become NCAA champions, Mark posted some real good numbers. From the field, he hit 13 of 20 shots for a very good 65 percent. At the free-throw line, he canned 10 of 14 for 71 percent. He finished the tournament averaging 3.0 points and 4.2 rebounds, with the points and rebounds usually coming during the tough times. Even more, Mark clocked in 94 minutes of quality time during these six special games, averaging 15.7 minutes per contest. Dr. Rudy Ellis and trainer Jerry May had used their magical powers once again when they patched up Mark for the final run to glory. Mark not only ran, he ran well.

As you look back at the entire picture, Mark had served the role that was laid out for him. His mental toughness entered into his new committment and improved play down the stretch. The upcoming season will have new goals for Mark to conquer. With the graduation of Billy Thompson, there is a forward position open for any of the players to grab. You can bet ol' No. 10 will be applying his newly found committment to make that vacant spot HIS home and only a place for others to visit.

Tony Kimbro

Tony Kimbro, when he signed at the University of Louisville, said, "My goal for choosing the University of Louisville is simple — I want to start and win a national championship."

Well, one out of two ain't bad for a beginning freshman. After just one season, Tony already has the coveted ring on his finger and the starter's role is just waiting for next season to come around.

Kimbro entered the Louisville program with all the accolades one could carry, including being named "Mr. Basketball" in Kentucky, which by itself is a bundle of roses. He made the All-State team three straight years, something not done very often. He was picked by *USA Today* as one of their "Elite Five" and made *The Courier-Journal's* "Super Five." Tony was invited to play in all the major all-star games.

It was obvious to everybody that "this guy could play." It was reported that Nevada-Las Vegas, DePaul, Kentucky and others were on his mind, but when it came time to sign on the dotted line there was only one logical choice. Why go anywhere else when the country's basketball program of the '80s was right in town? The fact he wanted his family to be able to see him play made his choice even easier. Besides, with a family close by, there's always that chance for a little home cooking and the clothes seem to stay cleaner.

Kimbro, at 6-8 and 190 pounds, spent his freshman season at U of L as Denny Crum's first choice for relief of the starters at both the guard and forward positions. That alone is an indication of his ability. His hands are quicker than a New York-second and his shot is deadly. Looking back, I'm sure the task of trying to learn the responsibilities of two positions hurt his early season performances, but the end result was certainly worth the effort.

Tony did well in the preseason Red-White scrimmages and when it came time to open up with the NIT game in Cincinnati, he was ready. He got the call for 18 minutes in relief in his first collegiate game and hit four of eight field goals for eight points, had four rebounds, two assists, one steal and no turnovers. That was a pretty good beginning!

"I was a little nervous," Tony said after the game, "but it went away. I really didn't expect to get to play that much, but I'm not complaining. I really like playing guard but I need to do some more work on my ball handling and my ability to see the whole court."

It will be a tremendous advantage for Tony if he can be converted to guard. Big guards, in the mold of Magic Johnson of the Los Angeles Lakers, are scarce. Tony could become that type of player. I doubt he will ever be as effective a passer as Magic, but he could come close to his other qualities.

I firmly believe that in the 1986-87 season, he will evolve as the most improved player of the year. I talked with Tony often and interviewed him a couple of times, but with the type player he'll eventually become, I imagine Tony will keep my microphone hot in the future, even though he is a little shy of the mike.

With the starting guards and forwards the 1985-86 team

had, Tony didn't have the "green light" to, as they say, "go for it." It wasn't a restriction placed on him by Denny Crum, it was a restriction that being a reserve and a freshman automatically brings a halt to what you can and cannot do.

Still, Tony became looser and looser as the season progressed. It reached a point that when Tony entered the game, there was no loss of the quality of play on the floor. He always came in and contributed.

For awhile, the Louisville team went six-deep. There was no doubt about the six, which included Tony, but after that there was plenty of doubt. Later, that figure went to seven when Mark McSwain got it together and then eight with the cool play of Kevin Walls, but for the longest time Kimbro was the only consistent help off the bench.

Tony reached a level of performance that was just about ready to really blossom when the injury bug jumped up and grabbed him with a pinched nerve in his shoulder. That's a painful injury, especially when it's in the shooting shoulder. It took him a few games to get it back together, but he did indeed get it back.

One of Tony's biggest contributions came in that bizarre game in Columbia against South Carolina. Louisville had to have a win in order to set up the climactic home finale against Memphis State. Most of the Cardinals, especially the seniors, had run across hard times that night. Tony, Pervis Ellison and Herbert Crook carried the load, but it was Tony's play which really put the Cards over the hump.

"Tony played his best game of the year tonight," said an obviously pleased Denny Crum.

The freshman picked up seven first-half points that helped keep the Cards within reach of the Gamecocks.

In the championship game against Duke, Kimbro hit 2 of 4 from the field and both of his free throws in 14 important minutes of action, and he played errorless ball in a game which saw his Cardinal teammates turn it over 24 times.

At the banquet, one week after the championship game, I was somewhat surprised and a little disappointed that his name was not included among the award winners. This may have been the year to have an award for "Best Sub." There were just so many nights that Tony came in and really contributed, giving the Cardinals a lift off the bench. Coaches really don't expect reserves to do anything spectacular because it's their role to hold the fort and circle the wagons, but in Tony's case he usually did more than that.

Tony had compiled some excellent stats for a freshman reserve once the season came to its glorious ending. He shot a super 57.2 percent from the field and averaged 5.3 points, 2.5 rebounds and 1.3 assists while having the distinction of being the only reserve on the team to play in all 39 games. His biggest weakness was at the foul line where he shot only 59.0 percent. During crunch time, however, Tony improved that percentage to 83.0.

Tony Kimbro will go on to have a terrific career at the University of Louisville. This past season he kept his foot on the brake, but opponents had better beware of Tony when it becomes "green light" time.

Tony Kimbro was one of the team's better defensive players in his rookie season.

Kevin Walls

The third member of the Camden Connection to join the U of L basketball team was Kevin Walls. It was a big disappointment when, as a freshman, it was announced he'd have to sit out the 1984-85 season with a knee injury. Louisville fans were crushed, so you can imagine how he must have felt. Here was a young man who had come out of the main stream of high school basketball with the title of the nation's leading scorer and he wasn't even going to get to play!

Kevin had ripped the nets at a pace of 44-plus points per game as a prepster and did it in a very tough league. His Camden High team, the same school that sent the Cards Billy Thompson and Milt Wagner, always played the best competition, so Kevin's performance in high school wasn't just a fluke. In fact, just this past year, Camden finished the season ranked as the nation's No. 1 high school team.

Mercifully, Kevin's red-shirt season passed and it was time to look ahead to the 1985-86 campaign. It was going to be a new beginning for Kevin Walls. But just how would he be used with Wagner and Hall both returning for their senior seasons?

It was my guess he'd see a lot of action against teams that were really applying down-court pressure. Everybody understood it would take Milt some time to get his act back together again after being off for a year with a bone injury to his foot, but I don't think anybody gave Kevin that same grace period.

I remember the first time I saw him on the floor wearing a monstrous knee brace. I couldn't imagine anyone being

Kevin Walls left the team for five days in midseason but ironed everything out to contribute to the championship drive.

able to move with that thing on. I watched his movements very closely and always thought I could see a slight limp, or swinging of the leg, and a loss of quickness on that very important first step.

He had played some in the summer league and in the preseason Red-White scrimmages as well. In the first public scrimmage at Jeffersonville High School in southern Indiana, Kevin scored 19 points. He tallied eight points in the second public exhibition before 13,547 fans in Freedom Hall. But during the third scrimmage, in Charlestown, Indiana, he injured himself early and didn't even play in the team's last scrimmage of the season.

The first time I saw Kevin play was in the Derby Classic All-Star game in Freedom Hall after his senior year of high school. At the conclusion of the game, it was announced that Kevin Walls was chosen as the game's Most Valuable Player. You could see that scoring came easy for the 6-1 guard and he was a master with the ball. I was really impressed and excited, as was any U of L fan, that he would attend the University of Louisville.

I'm still excited about what Kevin will do before he finishes his career with the Cardinals. Early in the 1985-86 season when he was put into games, it just wasn't the Kevin Walls I had seen in that high school all-star game — the sure-handed ball handler and shooter who could fill it up. At that point in time, I don't believe he had faced the fact that his leg was not fully back to what it had been before the injury.

As the season progressed Kevin saw less and less action, but seemed to be handling it very well. Then, it all hit the fan. Kevin chose not to attend practice and even missed the game against LaSalle because of remarks made by Coach Crum to a newspaper reporter in Camden. There's one thing I know for sure about Denny Crum and that is he's up-front with everyone. I'm sure whatever he said to the Camden *Courier-Post* was a true evaluation of Walls' progress as he saw it. Denny was quoted as saying things like, "He has trouble handling the big guards. He's got to earn his right to play." From what I had seen of Kevin thus far, he wasn't physically capable of earning his right to more playing time. He just didn't do things as he had done when building up his impressive high school credentials. Even if the knee was perfect, an athlete still has to deal with the mental aspect involved following an injury of that nature. The brain has to know that there is no pain, no hesitation. I didn't see the pain but I did see the hesitation. It was, just as Denny had said, going to take some time.

Walls rejoined the squad after a talk with the head man and eventually began to get his game together. He received a little spot duty off the bench and responded. Kevin looked better on the floor and his movements seemed to be more natural.

It was in the game against DePaul when he got his big chance. Milt Wagner got himself into early foul trouble so Crum started Kevin in the second half. After getting over the shock of starting the second period, Kevin performed like the player I had seen in the Derby Classic. He played 15 minutes against the Blue Demons and connected on 2 of 3 field goals and 4 of 6 free throws for eight points. It was a comeback effort for himself and the team as Louisville was down by five, 31-26, at the half. The previously little-used guard also contributed two assists and three big steals while fueling the Cardinal attack.

He had shown everyone that the forgotten man was still alive and kicking, and was only going to get better. There were several instances after the DePaul game when Kevin would find himself looking at a one-on-one situation. Reading his mind, I just knew he was thinking "I'm going to take you, sucker" and he'd give it a little shake and bake before backing off to stay in the scheme of things. He knew he could do it but, in this situation, it was best to back off. The time will come, however, when there will be no backing off — the defensive man will be history. I know it will happen down the road.

I kept a close eye on Kevin throughout the season. He's a very sensitive person and a young man with a lot of pride. It had been embarrassing for him to return to eligibility status and still see little playing time. He was looking at a healthy

Jeff Hall, Milt Wagner and Tony Kimbro, all with two good legs supporting their frames, and he just hadn't accepted the fact that he still had to wait a little longer.

As the season headed for the stretch run, I noticed that Coach Crum didn't hesitate to use Kevin in any situation. I found myself feeling good when he entered a game. He really played tough 'D' when he got down into that stance and looked 'em in the eyes. You could just sense he was daring his opponent to do something. You could see his confidence swell each time he took the court.

Kevin is a smart player who understands the game of basketball and has the best floor-vision of any of the Cardinals. He's one of those guys who has the "eye of the tiger."

In the upcoming season, he'll have his eye on one of those starting guard spots. There will be a lot of shuffling people around at guard, but I just have the feeling that Kevin will get his playing time in. There's one thing about people with pride and sensitivity — they are fighters. But playing with confidence on only one leg makes the fighting hard. From what I saw as the season ended, Kevin Walls has just about got the knee problem whipped. And, you must remember, Kevin is not used to losing.

Mike Abram

When I traveled with the Cardinals throughout the year, I think I felt more compassion for Mike Abram than any of the other players and their situation on the team.

Mike had a good freshman year in 1984-85 and even started in seven games, including the final five in the post-season NIT. As a rookie, Mike hit 50 of 103 shots from the field and 17 of 22 free throws. He turned in some good games against good competition.

The 1985-86 season, however, wasn't that good for him. Since enrolling at U of L, Mike has been caught between a rock and a hard place. He's not quite big enough at 6-4 to hold down a forward spot and hasn't had enough experience at the guard position to feel comfortable with the jobs that go along with playing in the backcourt. It's a tough situation to be in.

There's no better athlete in the Louisville camp than Mike Abram. He would make a great decathlon participant. When the Cardinals got involved with the use of weights in their strength and conditioning program, Mike quickly came to the front. Louisville's strength coach Doug Semenick said, "Pound for pound, Mike Abram is the most powerful player on the team." That was a pretty big compliment, especially considering the raw strength of Mark McSwain.

Physically, despite his height, I think Mike could hold his own with just about anyone. He is an exceptionally quick jumper. His natural position at the collegiate level would be at a No. 2 guard, an off-guard. With Kevin Walls, a true point guard, healthy, and red-shirt prospect Keith Williams ready for duty, Mike might just settle into that position. In the past, he's been thrust into the ball handling guard spot, by necessity, against cat-like quick people. It's been tough on him.

In retrospect, a red-shirt year during the championship season might have been the best thing for him. It would have given him time to really work on the skills needed to play at guard, but I'm sure he wouldn't trade anything for the championship stroll through Ogden, Houston and Dallas. He pretty much lost a year of eligibility because of his limited playing time (99 minutes in 17 games). Mike is an outstanding young man who's loaded with natural talent. I want to be there the day he gets the opportunity to unleash some of that ability on a Cardinal opponent.

During the Final Four in Dallas, I ran into his parents, Dr. Sam and Millie Abram. They were just like everyone else, ecstatic about the opportunity Louisville had coming up. They were really class people and were having a ball. I mentioned to them that I was anxious to see Mike do his thing somewhere down the road. His father responded with, "Mike has time left to make the grade. He has always made it and I think he will do it again."

I probably talked with Mike Abram as much or more than I did with any of the players throughout the course of the season. He's a very easy and pleasant person to talk to, but he's a quiet person who spends a lot of time with his own thoughts.

The reason I felt so compassionate for Mike during this past season was because he had moved up and received a lot of playing time in the later stages of 1984-85. After battling your way up and getting used to playing, it's awfully hard to have to sit back down. I'm sure there was a tendency on his part to think, "Well, I had my chance and blew it," but that's not the way it was. It was just a situation of Mike having to learn the guard position after he'd spent all his previous playing days at the inside positions. Ex-Cardinal Lancaster Gordon, now with the NBA's Los Angeles Clippers, had the same obstacle to overcome at Louisville. Mike Abram will also make the adjustment.

Any time a person chooses to be an athlete, he's taking on something that throws a lot of hills and valleys at him. Learning to deal with these adversities while maintaining a good attitude is one of athletics' biggest rewards to the individual participant. I like what Dr. Abram said about his son. Mike has always done it and he will do it again. You can look in his eyes and see that Mike thinks so, too. As they say, "Like father, like son."

Chris West

For one athlete on the Louisville team to parallel Mike Abram's athletic talents, it would have to be Chris West. Since arriving at U of L, Chris has been on a constant roller coaster ride.

As a freshman in 1982-83, Chris played in all 36 games. After a red-shirt season in 1983-84, the Louisville native came on as a sophomore and got the starting call 12 times. Playing in all but three of the games a year ago, he averaged 2.9 points, dished out 50 assists and came up with 17 steals.

When 1985-86 rolled around, I'm sure Chris had his goal set to be in a position to get plenty of playing time. But it didn't work out that way for several reasons.

Mainly, there was a lot of quality competition for game action with Milt Wagner, Jeff Hall, Tony Kimbro, Kevin Walls and Mike Abram. Somewhere along the line, Chris had been tagged as a defensive specialist, which he is, but for every time you're on the defensive end there will be a return trip to the offensive end of the floor. It's at this end where Chris lost the battle.

His offensive stats after three seasons as a Cardinal are not impressive. He's attempted 120 shots and connected on only 43 of them for a meager 35.5 percent. He has a tendency to shoot the ball out of his range (or at least out of the range the coaching staff prefers him to shoot from) and he hasn't been too accurate from within his range.

Still, nobody works harder, or tries harder, or has a better attitude than Chris. He has cat-like quickness, all the stamina in the country and does a good job of advancing the ball down court in the running game. But during the championship season, he had little opportunity to even be on the court.

Chris was always friendly and wore a smile. When he got on the bus, though, you could tell he was bursting inside to play.

This past season's stats were a far cry from his first two seasons. He only averaged 3.5 minutes in the 22 games he saw action and took just 12 shots from the field, making six. He hit half of his 14 free-throw attempts in 1985-86 and was credited with 10 assists.

During the NCAA playoffs, I couldn't help but notice that Chris was mentally into every game and each play, always encouraging his teammates. He sat patiently waiting for Denny Crum to call his number and appeared to be ready for action. Chris had accepted his role.

I wouldn't have been surprised to see him enter the Duke game to take a try at dealing with Johnny Dawkins, but it didn't happen. No one would have given it any more effort. I think if the spread of the game had been wider and Dawkins had continued his offensive rampage as he did in the early minutes, Crum would have looked to Chris for some help. But the Cards in the game were able to keep things under control. Let's face it, with the talent Louisville had this past season there were a lot of very good players who spent time on the sidelines.

Chris has one more year of eligibility remaining and he'll wear out a few nets over the summer working on that shot within his range. He's that type of player. One thing is for sure — he'll never quit trying.

Kenny Payne

Kenny Payne, the last of the six recruits to sign at the University of Louisville last May, hails from Laurel, Mississippi. He's an offensive threat each time he touches the basketball and possesses perfect hand position on the ball on his jumper. Kenny's a young, friendly man who's always flashing a million-dollar smile. He's the type who could walk into a room of 100 people who had been condemned to die a horrible death, smile at them and, I promise you, they would all smile back.

The 6-8 forward was the talk of the summer league in 1985.

He had squared up against all the big names and shot the ball through the hoop with ease. He finished the summer averaging about 20 points per game.

Kenny did not become a target of the Louisville recruiters until his junior year, normally too late for a new school to get involved and have any legitimate chance of signing a high school player. As it turned out, however, he passed up opportunities to play at Kentucky, Mississippi and Alabama to sign with the Cardinals.

After many successful high school accomplishments and further success in the summer league against quality players, Kenny entered his first season of college with great expectations. He had the size along with super shooting ability, so there's no reason why he wouldn't have a very good freshman year of college. Unfortunately, that wasn't what happened.

As the 1985-86 season slipped away and his playing time became less and less, I'm sure there were times when he would find himself wondering if he had made the right college choice. That's a normal reaction for any player to have when it becomes obvious you're going to spend a lot of time on the bench and you're not going to have a great year, at least not as far as personal accomplishments are concerned.

Back at the beginning of the season, Kenny had done well in the games in New York. He continued to do some good things afterward. But, as game after game passed, you could see he needed some more time to get other necessary skills on an even par with his shooting ability to play at this level. Besides, having Billy Thompson, Herbert Crook, Tony Kimbro and Mark McSwain fighting for playing time at the same spots he was after made it tough on the young man.

Nobody disputed his magnificent looking jumper, but there were times when he had problems deciding what was a shot and what wasn't. His final shooting statistics for 1985-86 showed Kenny hitting a mere 52 of 119 attempts for a poor 43.7 percent. His inability to make good shot selection was the reason. Regardless of how good a shooter you are, no one makes many bad shots. If anybody should shoot in the high 50's on Louisville's roster, it's Kenny Payne.

Besides his poor shot selection, Kenny had trouble protecting the ball and his passing game was a little short of being good many times. He seemed to hold his own on the boards but defensively Kenny needed to get better, much better.

It's just a fact that when a player's playing time begins to slip away, he has less time to make something happen when he's on the court. It becomes a "Catch 22." A player wants to stay within the scheme of the game plan when he enters a game, but he also needs to do something good to make a mark for himself. Then, perhaps the next time, his call to play would come a little sooner. That's about the way it goes for a player until he learns that as a reserve he doesn't have to doing anything spectacular.

Substitutes need to do the routine things well, such as playing defense, rebounding and running the patterns.

These are the things Denny Crum wants to see from his bench. The scoring could come later.

There were many times when Kenny tried to make something happen, just as he had always done as a player. But that wasn't his role anymore.

At the Division I level of college basketball, it's extremely important that players understand their roles, regardless of whether it be as a starter or as a reserve. Kenny had a hard time with this, as have many other players who entered into a top-level program bringing with them a ton of shiny credentials.

In the preseason Red-White scrimmages, Kenny did really well. In three games, he hit 39 of 67 shots and pulled down 30 rebounds. He scored 26, 35 and 25 in the three outings. Obviously, he could score. But like a lot of players who sign with a top Division I basketball school, Kenny found out early that there's a lot more to playing the college game than shooting.

Kenny is going to be a terrific player at U of L before his time is up. He has natural offensive movement around the basket and he does a good job of posting up. He has the size and, even though he's not the quickest guy on the block, his speed is adequate.

It was on the night when Louisville returned to Hattiesburg to play Southern Mississippi that Kenny had his biggest nightmare. Many of his friends had driven in from Laurel.

Signs decorated Green Coliseum. But it was a terrible evening for Kenny, who had just two points and three big turnovers in 13 minutes of action.

It's times like that night when character is important. A player's mental toughness is tested. He swallowed the evening, as bad as it was, and just kept on smiling.

Natural and pure shooters are hard to come by. Kenny has that ability. Now he has to get the other parts of his game in line, which will happen because he now realizes what it takes to play for the best basketball program in the country.

I watched Kenny closely as the season progressed. I watched him have some good times and I saw his disappointment when things went badly. I thought he reached a stage where he really withdrew a little, but then I saw that smile return. It was then that Kenny Payne had accepted his role, knowing exactly where he stood. Coach Crum gave him every opportunity to perform, but when this performance lacked the quality that was expected, the head man had to settle on who he was going to have to go with. It was getting down to "crunch time" and the experimentation days were over.

When a player of Kenny's ability looks around and sees other talented athletes, all good friends, having to wait for their chance, there comes a time when accepting becomes easier. Kenny's time will come and the waiting will be over.

As the Cardinals headed down the stretch in their quest for a championship, Kenny Payne was happy. He was alive

and active on the sideline. He knew that Denny had made the right choice, and he now accepted it.

No one was prouder when that final horn sounded. He celebrated as much as the starters because he was now a member of a national championship basketball team.

I know, in my heart, he was thinking about how great it was and he felt proud for the seniors who had waited four years for this to happen. Perhaps someday he would do the same thing with his class and he'd be on the court playing during a Final Four. He was thinking, in the back of his mind, that he'd make it all happen once again. He knew he had the determination to make himself a better player.

Kenny Payne is a talented basketball player. Now that he knows what it's going to take, I feel a lot better about the Cardinals' chances of making it all happen again down the road. The future looks good at the University of Louisville and it's my bet that Kenny Payne will play a big part in that future.

David Robinson

David Robinson, like his teammate Avery Marshall, traveled north to Louisville from a place where sunshine is abundant. U of L fans got their first glimpse of the Gainesville (Florida) native when his high school team, Eastside, participated in the King of the Bluegrass Tournament in Louisville during Christmas vacation. It just so happened that his team was paired against a team from Laurel, Miss. that had another future Cardinal on the roster — Kenny Payne.

David averaged 13.1 points and 11.1 rebounds as a prepster, not impressive stats, but he played on a well-balanced team. After visiting DePaul, Miami of Florida, Jacksonville and Southwestern Louisiana, he signed on with Louisville during the November period and became the Cards' first signee of the season.

He's one of the best jumpers on the Louisville squad, but didn't get to see a whole lot of playing time in his freshman season. David played in five games last season and had his best outing of the year against Wyoming when he scored two points and grabbed three rebounds.

In last year's media guide, David listed his personal goal while at U of L as "to win the national championship." How quickly some people's dreams come true!

With three seasons ahead of him, David has a chance to

make it happen again. He's a gifted athlete who just needs to build up his upper body strength some. He didn't get much playing time as a freshman, but the future is still his.

Will Olliges

Big Will Olliges, a 6-9, 205-pound center, joined the team out of Louisville St. Xavier High School in 1982-83. He spent his first year on the U of L campus as a red-shirt and had little chance to play during the past two seasons.

As a freshman in 1984-85, Will saw action in only eight of the 37 games. As a sophomore during the championship season, the native of Louisville saw 28 minutes of action in 12 games. That's not a whole lot of court duty.

I'm sure Will had a lot of moments of disappointment in his first two seasons, but it never showed. His competition for playing time is very talented, something he's accepted. Going through a championship year like 1985-86 helps erase a lot of the bad times.

Will still has time left as a player at U of L. He works hard

and has continued to improve daily. The mystery of what lies ahead for any of us is what keeps life exciting. It always gives you something to look forward to. Will is always looking ahead, trying to do the best he can with anything he attempts.

In the Louisville basketball media guide, he listed as his personal goals to get his degree in electrical engineering and better himself as a person. For sure, he's moving right along toward both of those goals. He received the academic award at the basketball banquet and, just for good measure, picked up a national championship ring while traveling toward his goals.

Maybe he'll even get a second one.

Avery Marshall

Avery Marshall signed on with the University of Louisville back during the NCAA's early signing period in November. The 6-7, 210-pounder put up some impressive statistics in high school, averaging 20.2 points, 11.4 rebounds and 5.4 blocks per game. That's not bad coming from a place like Myrtle Beach (South Carolina) where basketball is the furthest thing from most people's minds. Man, I sure would have loved to have grown up in a place like Myrtle Beach with all that white sand and water just around the corner!

But Avery found time to hone his basketball skills and went on to make all-state and honorable mention All-American as a senior.

Like many athletes when they enter college, they're forced to learn a new position. Avery played center in high school but will have to learn to handle the ball and play defense against faster people as a forward at U of L.

Avery missed most of the championship season because of a fractured fibula suffered on Dec. 26 in practice. Up to that point, the forward had only played in one game, and that was for just two minutes against Purdue. Still, he managed to pull down one rebound.

His injury, however, was probably a blessing in disguise. He qualifies for a red-shirt season and will have four big seasons of eligibility remaining. Avery is talented, and I expect him to make his mark before the next four seasons are over.

Keith Williams

One member of "The Crunch Bunch" who you didn't hear much about was Keith Williams, a 6-4, 180-pound point guard from Louisville Seneca High School. Keith was often overshadowed in high school by the tremendous amount of publicity received by Tony Kimbro. But, quietly, he averaged 16.9 points, 6.5 rebounds and 7.0 assists while helping Seneca to a 32-2 record. To show that he could really play the game, Keith went out and gathered MVP honors in the first game of the Kentucky-Indiana High School All-Star series.

An early season injury and the reality of not getting much playing time forced Keith to red-shirt this past season. He spent the year working in practice to better his game. The left-hander fits Denny Crum's mold of a big guard and he has the quickness and intelligence to get the ball to the right person.

With the graduation of both Jeff Hall and Milt Wagner, Keith is a strong candidate to get a lot of playing time in the next four seasons. A starting spot in 1986-87 is not out of the question. He has all the tools necessary to be a big-time college guard.

CHAPTER

Final Thoughts

And they lived happily ever after. That's the way I remember most fairy tales ending.

The 1985-86 University of Louisville basketball squad had been a fairy-tale team. It was a team that had lost its center, a 7-footer who had started 33 games in 1984-85, before the 1985-86 campaign even began. It was a team forced to use a freshman as Barry Sumpter's replacement, even though he had been recruited as a forward. At one starting forward position was a player who had never really lived up to expectations in his previous three seasons. At the other forward spot was a guy who fooled everyone, including Denny Crum, when he earned a starting berth in 1985-86 after a freshman season in which he averaged just 5.6 points and 3.9 rebounds per game, not exactly stats that would impress your favorite cousin. At one guard spot was a guy who everyone claimed was a good shooter but had slow feet and was a very mediocre defensive talent. At the other guard was a senior who was trying to make a comeback after suffering a major injury that had kept him out of action for an entire season.

That was the starting group, as unlikely as it may have seemed. They were backed up by two players who became frustrated and unsettled during the year, and even toyed with the idea of throwing the whole thing into the can. The other primary reserve suffered an injury just as the team entered into post-season play, and he had a hard time getting it back together.

Now I ask you, does that sound like the lineup of a team that earned the right to wear national championship rings? No way.

Back in early January, just winning the Metro Conference seemed very remote. But it happened, the same way the Chrysler Corporation came back under Lee Iacocca's direction. It happened the same way Jack Nicklaus came back at the age of 46 to win the Master's Golf Tournament. It happened just like a one-armed Louisvillian golfer by the name of Don Fightmaster refused to give in to his handicap and won the World's One-Arm Championship and national title seven times. It happened for the same reason that Milt Wagner was able to come back and play like he did before his injury of last year.

All these examples say the same thing. There are just some people who have a quality that's within them. When challenged, these traits surface.

Many times, the group as a whole becomes the motivator of the individual. That's the way it has been with the U of L basketball teams, particularily in the 1980s. The Cardinal program has been built on solid ground and by quality people. Coaches Peck Hickman and John Dromo got the ball rolling for the University of Louisville and Denny Crum kept it rolling. Now, it not only rolls but grows and grows.

The Louisville Cardinals play a brand of basketball that is appealing to young people all over the state and country, and fans keep growing in numbers. Everywhere I go, people tell me about listening to Van Vance and me doing the radio broadcasts of the Louisville games. They talk about the Cardinals, their schedule and how they enjoy the fact the team plays all the tough opponents — conference games and national TV games every other day, it makes no difference. They like to be associated with a team who has that kind of grit. They ask questions about the players and the coaching staff.

I've seen the Cardinal Bird on T-shirts in Daytona Beach, New York City and Lawrence, Kan. Cardinal fans are popping up everywhere. Granted, WHAS Radio with its 50,000 booming watts along with all the national television exposure has helped put the Cardinals within the reach of people, but it has been the performance of the players on the floor that has made the basketball team so popular.

The Louisville teams take no prisoners, are willing to gamble, press, use the entire 94-feet of the floor and are just exciting to watch. U of L is quickly becoming one of America's favorite basketball teams. It's not just luck that the Cards appear on national TV week after week — five straight weekends in this past championship season alone. It's unheard of, but it happens constantly with the Louisville program. They're there because the networks want viewers and the Cardinals have their followers.

This tradition has been established by many quality people and great athletes, people who have set the standards for others to follow. Players out of the deep past like Charlie Tyra, Phil Rollins and Bill Darragh of the 1956 NIT championship team. Players like Butch Beard, Wes Unseld, Jim Price, Junior Bridgeman, Allen Murphy, Phillip Bond and Wesley Cox have made their marks as All-Americans. The players of the 1980s have carried that tradition in fine fashion, players like Roger Burkman , Darrell Griffith, Wiley Brown, Tony Branch, Lancaster Gordon, Derek Smith, Charles Jones, Rodney and Scooter McCray, Rick Wilson, Jerry Eaves and Manual Forrest.

These and many other ex-Cards have set high standards of performance. Nowadays, the determination of the young players who enter the U of L program is like the bite of a mud turtle that doesn't ease up or let go once it clamps those teeth down. The new players want to be the next Darrell Griffith or Billy Thompson.

This past season's seniors have left high plateaus for the returning players to reach, just as their predecessors did. They left challenges for the incoming people to accept. No, sirree, success just doesn't happen, it's cultivated through example and great direction.

The Louisville Cardinals are, without a doubt, the "Basketball Team of the Decade." It's in the facts. For seven seasons since 1980, just 16 different teams have made it to the Final Four. Only one team has been there four times — the Louisville Cardinals. Only one team has won two national titles — the Louisville Cardinals. There are only two active coaches in the country who have won the big one even twice, Indiana's Bobby Knight and Louisville's Denny Crum. No other school, including U o f L's rival neighbor in Lexington, can boast about doing any better than the University of Louisville. No way, not in the '80s.

One super U of L fan, Lewis "Sonny" Bass, spotted a T-shirt that read on the front: "Duke, 1986 National Champs." On the back of the shirt it read: "I bought this shirt at halftime." Sonny said, "If the University of Kentucky had a shirt that read 'UK Is The Greatest' then the back of the shirt should read 'I bought this shirt many years ago.' "

The top five NCAA Tournament appearances of this decade look like this: Louisville (four appearances and two titles); Georgetown (three appearances, one title and two second-place finishes); Houston (three appearances and two second-place finishes); North Carolina (two appearances, one title and one second-place finish); and Virginia (two appearances, no titles or second-place finishes). Three teams have made just one Final Four trip in the '80s and won the tournament — Indiana, North Carolina State and Villanova.

Teams pop into the limelight here and there, but to stay at the top year after year takes a special kind of toughness. This past year's team was an example. I watched those guys crawl onto the bus on those mornings of the early flights after late games the night before. I watched those guys sleep wherever they could find a chair. I watched them plow through the month of February when each game was important, and they had very little time for practice or rest but they toughed it out. I saw the disappointment on their faces many times during the year, for a variety of reasons, but I also saw the determination in their eyes and the tremendous effort they put forth.

I remember talking to Milt Wagner while waiting for the elevator in the New York hotel right after he had made just 2 of 15 field goals against Kansas in front of his family and friends. In his mind, he was blaming himself for the loss, so I told him, "Milto, all you need is a good dose of Freedom Hall. Take two aspirin and everything will be better in the morning." It was hard for him but he flashed one of his great big smiles and said, "Yea, the Hall will bring my jumper out."

I watched Denny Crum put the pieces back together many times during the year. He reminded me of someone working on a jigsaw puzzle, except the pieces didn't fit. Some of the pieces needed a little added on or a little taken off here and there in order to make them fit properly. It took time and patience. It was then that I saw a lot of John Wooden (10 titles) in Denny. He had the gift of patience and could make the mechanical parts of the puzzle work in unison.

But that was easy compared to the mental aspect of the puzzle which needed to be dealt with. All players have different dispositions and breaking points, something the person putting the puzzle together must figure out. Each piece has a certain place where it fits within the scheme of things. That must be understood and accepted or the pieces will never fit together and you'll never have a completed puzzle. A puzzle missing just one piece doesn't get the job done.

Dealing with people's minds is a very difficult task, but Denny handles it well with his honesty. He tells his people the way it actually is and convinces them that his way is the best way and will benefit everyone, in time. And he has the results to back up his words.

This year's team was a perfect example. As the season progressed, it became obvious who the starters would be and even the less-observant fans knew about when to expect a substitution and which player it would be. The players became the same way. They learned to accept their roles. Once that happened, they were determined to play their roles as best they could. Actually, I think the 1985-86 Cardinals came about as far mentally as they did physically. After the 1984-85 season, there was some loss of confidence. You have to learn how to win but it's also possible to forget how to win following a few setbacks, especially when things aren't going so good.

The Cards had a wealth of success to look back upon. History and tradition are great motivators. Nobody wants to be remembered as the one or ones who let the program slide back to the status of just another good team. So they picked up the pieces after 1984-85 and put the puzzle together again.

The University of Louisville basketball program is a class act and there are many factors why it's been so successful. The program is sound, but it goes beyond the players and coaching staff. A packed Freedom Hall is so very important to U of L's success. Over 19,000 fans plan their days around the games. It may have meant skipping a meal or not doing the dishes, or missing the bowling or card night with the gang, or the bird cage may have had to wait another day to get cleaned, because the University of Louisville basketball team came first.

Watching the Cards has become a family affair for some. The Lewis family — Manville, Mary Manetta and Melissa — for example, go to all the home games. Many times, they'll come by to talk to Van and me. They're also there at the airport when the team returns from a trip. Sometimes William Swafford is with them. They are perfect examples of the types of people and families who put the Cardinals right at the top of the list.

There are many families just like them, families who seldom get to make an NCAA trip, but these are the type of people who are the backbone of the Louisville program. The Cardinals are a team which, in one sense, belongs to the hundreds of families who live and die with each win and loss.

One group of men always stops by the press table following the broadcast. They are terrific fans and loyal to the end. But the stands in Freedom Hall are loaded with those kinds of people. Minnie and Joe Dotson, the parents of assistant coach Bobby Dotson, happen to be that way. They were big Cardinal fans before Bobby became a member of the U of L staff.

There are all kinds of people who never miss a game, even though their seats aren't great. Dr. Wes Farnsley and his wife, Gail, are good examples. The bathroom in their home looks like the U of L bookstore. The walls are loaded with Cardinal pennants, plaques and just about everything else imaginable. Like many others, they are top-flight, dedicated Cardinal fans. With them, the Louisville team is a priority.

Their seats in Freedom Hall aren't that good but they want to be there and be part of it.

It's the same way with thousands of Cardinal fans because these people expect a quality show and they know the effort will be there on the floor. I admire and respect the Louisville fans. Lousy weather means nothing to them. As far as they are concerned, game night means Freedom Hall and that's where they intend to be. It may have been too cold to take the dog out for a walk or ride up to the store to get a loaf of bread, or the roads may have been slick, or maybe they were just too tired to do anything, but there's nothing that can keep these people away from Freedom Hall. Hell, man, it's game night and the Cards are in town!

A little piece of the national title belongs to many, many people who never fired a shot or grabbed a rebound. It was a family championship, belonging to all the thousands of people who follow the Cards.

Personally, I'm not sure I could ever be a hardy die-hard fan if I had to fight the traffic, parking, weather and seats in the clouds, as many do. Then again, maybe I could. It's quite possible that I've gotten spoiled in my old age, mainly because I know I have the best seat in the house, right next to the guy who wears the "dancin' and romancin' pants."

Time will quickly pass and it will be time to do it all over again. There will be the same tough nights and days, the same tough schedule and the same emotional highs and lows, but before that time gets here the Cardinal Family will be anxiously waiting for new challenges to conquer. The players will be eager and the fans will be revved up for another great season.

The decade of the '80s has thrust the Louisville Cardinal basketball program to the top of the mountain. They are like the mighty lions, the kings of the jungle, and they conquer with style. Basketball at U of L reminds me of the story about a safari group which was crossing the great plains of Africa. One master hunter became separated from the group and found himself alone, faced with the many treacheries of the jungle. In just a short time, a great African lion faced him, eye to eye. The hunter fell to his knees where he pressed his hands together and prayed. But to his surprise, the lion also fell to his knees and pressed his mighty paws together in the same praying position. The master hunter was shocked. He looked up and said, "What a relief, my prayers have been answered!" The lion calmly replied, "Unh unh, man, I ain't praying, I'm saying grace."

That's what I call style. The story sorta parallels the position of the Cards.

They will be the hunted next season. They will be the prized trophy for the opponents. They'll be the target of each team that can be squeezed onto that schedule. Every opponent who takes the court against Louisville will be out to make their season. Beating the Cards will be front-page news in the sports section of any paper.

When Louisville takes the floor for the first time in 1986-87, the Cards will most likely be ranked No. 1 in the preseason major polls. For most programs, that would be a lot of added pressure for starting out the season, but it won't make any difference to the Louisville team. Denny Crum will start building all over again. He'll use different combinations of players, regardless of the opponent or score. It'll just be another puzzle to put together. But he'll do it the same way he always does, piece by piece.

Two of my favorite quotes from the championship season came from Denny and Pervis Ellison, the youngster known as "Bubba" to his friends in Savannah. Denny's words emphasize effort, priorities, family and understanding, and he said it over and over, before the big games and the meaningless ones: "I'll work as hard as I can and the players will work as hard as they can, and we'll just throw the ball up and see what happens. If we win, that's good. If we lose, we'll just go back and work some more to improve. Whatever, life goes on."

To me, that says it all. Life doesn't end after a basketball loss. Enjoying the wonderful gift of being alive and healthy is more important, and Denny believes just that. It's the way he is. Win or lose, when his young son Scott comes over to the post-game show as he does sometimes, Denny's eyes light up with excitement. It's the same when his son Steve or his lovely wife Joyce gets within touching distance. It's very apparent that winning is not the most important thing in this world to him. It just so happens that he is good at it.

Oh, yea, about that quote by Never Nervous Pervis. Following the championship game, Pervis was asked repeatedly about being chosen MVP of the Final Four as just a freshman. His reply reflected the entire spirit of the team and accentuated "we" instead of "I" when he stated, "WHO CARES ABOUT BEING THE MVP WHEN WE'VE GOT THE NATIONAL CHAMPIONSHIP!"

How sweet it is.

UNIVERSITY OF LOUISVILLE
1986 NCAA Tournament Statistics
(6 GAMES)
RECORD: 6-0

PLAYER	G-GS	MIN-AVG	FG-FGA	PCT	FT-FTA	PCT	REB-AVG	AST-AVG	PF-D	TP-AVG
Thompson	6-6	191-31.8	45-65	.690	20-27	.740	47-7.8	24-4.0	22-0	110-18.3
Crook	6-6	178-29.7	32-57	.560	18-25	.720	49-8.2	17-2.8	16-0	97-16.2
Ellison	6-6	203-33.8	40-68	.590	13-20	.650	57-9.5	6-1.0	20-1	93-15.5
Wagner	6-6	202-33.7	29-67	.430	33-36	.920	14-2.3	34-5.7	12-0	91-15.2
Hall	6-6	192-32.0	29-56	.520	5-6	.833	9-1.5	15-2.5	10-0	63-10.5
McSwain	6-0	94-15.7	13-20	.650	10-14	.710	25-4.2	6-1.0	9-0	36-3.0
Kimbro	6-0	73-12.2	8-16	.500	5-6	.830	8-1.3	8-1.3	9-0	21-3.5
Walls	6-0	44-7.3	5-11	.450	2-2	1.000	2-0.3	5-0.8	4-0	12-2.0
Valentine	3-0	4-1.3	1-1	1.000	1-2	.500	3-1.0	1-0.3	0-0	3-1.0
Payne	3-0	8-2.7	1-3	.333	0-0	.000	1-0.3	0-0.0	1-0	2-0.7
Abram	3-0	7-2.3	0-2	.000	0-0	.000	4-1.3	3-1.0	0-0	0-0.0
West	2-0	2-1.0	0-0	.000	0-0	.000	0-0.0	0-0.0	0-0	0-0.0
Olliges	2-0	2-1.0	0-0	.000	0-0	.000	0-0.0	1-0.5	0-0	0-0.0

	FG-FGA	PCT	FT-FTA	PCT	REB-AVG	AST-AVG	PF-D	TP-AVG
Louisville Totals	203-366	.550	107-138	.780	229-38.2	120-20.0	103-1	513-85.5
Opponent Totals	190-398	.491	62-100	.620	191-32.8	107-17.8	125-7	442-73.7

U of L Steals (27) Opp. (39): Ellison (8), Wagner (6), Thompson (5), Hall (4), Crook (2), Kimbro (1), McSwain (1).

U of L Blocked Shots (28) Opp. (5): Ellison (11), Thompson (9), McSwain (3), Wagner (3), Kimbro (2).

U of L Turnovers (91) Opp. (82): Wagner (18), Crook (18), Thompson (16), Ellison (11), Hall (9), McSwain (6), Walls (6), Kimbro (3), Payne (2), Abram (1), Valentine (1).

UNIVERSITY OF LOUISVILLE
Final 1985-86 Basketball Statistics
(39 GAMES)
RECORD: 32-7 (overall): 12-2 (conference)

PLAYER	G-GS	MIN-AVG	FG-FGA	PCT	FT-FTA	PCT	REB-AVG	AST-AVG	PF-D	TP-AVG
Thompson	39-39	1216-31.2	221-384	.576	140-196	.714	304-7.8	151-3.9	126-2	582-14.9
Wagner	39-39	1312-33.6	220-444	.495	137-159	.862	122-3.1	165-4.2	92-2	577-14.9
Ellison	39-39	1194-30.6	210-379	.554	90-132	.681	318-8.2	78-2.0	117-3	510-13.1
Crook	39-39	1124-28.8	171-324	.528	119-173	.688	252-6.5	83-2.1	117-1	461-11.9
Hall	39-39	1190-30.5	168-317	.530	65-73	.890	68-1.7	113-2.9	81-3	401-10.3
Kimbro	39-0	696-17.8	91-159	.572	26-44	.590	96-2.5	51-1.3	78-1	208-5.3
McSwain	28-0	321-11.5	32-57	.561	38-53	.717	80-2.9	24-0.8	35-0	102-3.6
Payne	34-0	303-8.9	52-119	.437	17-22	.773	58-1.7	11-0.3	20-0	121-3.6
Walls	27-0	191-7.1	16-36	.444	24-32	.750	12-0.4	19-0.7	14-0	56-2.1
Abram	17-0	99-5.8	12-23	.522	5-13	.385	19-1.1	13-0.8	11-0	29-1.7
Valentine	16-0	41-2.6	9-17	.529	2-4	.500	9-0.6	4-0.3	8-0	20-1.3
West	22-0	77-3.5	6-12	.500	7-14	.500	9-0.4	10-0.4	16-0	19-0.9
Olliges	12-0	28-2.2	2-5	.400	2-2	1.000	7-0.6	2-0.2	2-0	6-0.5
Robinson	5-0	6-1.2	1-3	.333	0-0	.000	6-1.2	0-0.0	2-0	2-0.4
Marshall	1-0	2-2.0	0-1	.000	0-0	.000	1-1.0	0-0.0	1-0	0-0.0

U of L Team Rebounds:	89-2.3	Opp. Team Rebounds:	88-2.3
U of L Deadball Rebounds:	93-2.4	Opp. Deadball Rebounds:	99-2.5

	FG-FGA	PCT	FT-FTA	PCT	REB-AVG	AST-AVG	PF-D	TP-AVG
Louisville Totals	1212-2281	.531	672-917	.733	1450-37.2	724-18.6	720-12	3096-79.4
Opponent Totals	1067-2336	.457	560-823	.680	1220-31.3	543-13.9	802-34	2694-69.1

U of L Steals (256) Opp. (305): Wagner (52), Ellison (50), Crook (40), Thompson (33), Kimbro (25), Hall (23), Walls (10), Payne (7), McSwain (6), Abram (5), West (2), Olliges (2), Valentine (1), Marshall (0), Robinson (0).

U of L Blocked Shots (216) Opp. (88): Ellison (92), Thompson (63), Kimbro (25), McSwain (12), Wagner (10), Crook (7), Hall (4), West (1), Robinson (1), Payne (1), Walls (0), Valentine (0), Abram (0), Olliges (0), Marshall (0).

U of L Turnovers (632) Opp. (606): Thompson (142), Wagner (124), Crook (86), Ellison (60), Hall (53), Kimbro (52), Payne (31), McSwain (26), Walls (24), Abram (14), Valentine (9), West (8), Olliges (2), Marshall (1), Robinson (0).

U of L	Opp	Opponent	Site	Margin	Top Scorer	Top Rebounder	Attendance
81	65	Miami (Ohio)	N	+16	19 Thompson	17 Thompson	10,416
80	74	Tulsa	N	+ 6	21 Thompson	10 Ellison	6,720
78	83	Kansas	N	- 5	18 Thompson, Ellison	8 Thompson	14,225
79	86	St. John's	N	- 7	16 Ellison, Wagner	9 Crook	8,598
77	58	Purdue	H	+19	13 Thompson	9 Thompson	19,265
88	75	Iona	H	+13	19 Ellison	13 Ellison	19,038
73	70	Western Kentucky	H	+ 3	20 Crook	10 Thompson	19,308
65	63	Indiana	H	+ 2	22 Wagner	11 Ellison	19,493
64	69	Kentucky	A	- 5	19 Wagner	8 Thompson	24,180
94	62	Wyoming	H	+32	30 Thompson	8 Crook	19,037
86	55	Eastern Kentucky	H	+31	19 Thompson	8 Crook	19,235
71	73	Memphis State	A	- 2	14 Crook	8 Thompson	11,200
59	54	Southern Miss	A	+ 5	18 Ellison	9 Ellison	8,053
85	64	Florida State	A	+21	27 Wagner	10 Thompson, Crook	7,198
83	73	Syracuse	H	+10	24 Wagner	7 Ellison	19,318
82	84	Cincinnati	H	- 2	16 Wagner, Ellison, Hall	9 Thompson	19,304
69	71	Kansas	A	- 2	23 Wagner	8 Crook	15,000
72	60	LaSalle	H	+12	14 Crook	10 Thompson	18,908
91	72	UCLA	H	+19	20 Wagner	10 Ellison	19,384
74	72	South Carolina	H	+ 2	16 Wagner, Hall	12 Thompson	18,981
103	68	Virginia Tech	H	+35	21 Thompson	11 Ellison	19,406
64	76	N.Carolina State	A	-12	21 Thompson	9 Thompson	12,400
93	83	Virginia Tech	A	+10	25 Thompson	13 Crook	10,000
74	58	Cincinnati	A	+16	23 Thompson	9 Ellison	12,683
72	53	DePaul	A	+19	28 Crook	9 Ellison, Crook	15,754
83	74	Southern Miss	H	+ 9	19 Thompson	13 Ellison	19,240
89	67	Florida State	H	+22	26 Wagner	14 Ellison	19,157
76	59	Houston	A	+17	25 Ellison	9 Thompson	5,125
66	55	So. Alabama	H	+11	13 Crook	6 Ellison	19,063
65	63	South Carolina	A	+ 2	18 Ellison	11 Ellison	6,071
70	69	Memphis State	H	+ 1	18 Wagner, Ellison	9 Crook	19,582
86	65	Cincinnati	H	+21	19 Crook	7 Thompson, Ellison	19,452
88	79	Memphis State	H	+ 9	31 Wagner	13 Ellison	19,611
93	73	Drexel	N	+20	24 Thompson	10 Thompson	9,037
82	68	Bradley	N	+14	16 Ellison, Wagner	8 Ellison	10,061
94	79	North Carolina	N	+15	24 Thompson	9 Thompson, Crook	10,936
84	76	Auburn	N	+ 8	20 Crook	11 Crook	9,650
88	77	LSU	N	+11	22 Thompson, Wagner	13 Ellison	17,007
72	69	Duke	N	+ 3	25 Ellison	12 Crook	17,007

LOUISVILLE HIGH PERFORMANCES

Individual

Points	31	Milt Wagner vs. Memphis State
Field goals made	13	Billy Thompson vs. Wyoming
		Milt Wagner vs. Florida State
Field goals attempted	19	Milt Wagner vs. Memphis State
Free throws made	13	Billy Thompson vs. Virginia Tech
		Herbert Crook vs. Cincinnati
Free throws attempted	17	Billy Thompson vs. Virginia Tech
Rebounds	17	Billy Thompson vs. Miami (Ohio)
Assists	11	Milt Wagner vs. Louisiana State
Steals	6	Milt Wagner vs. Eastern Kentucky
		Milt Wagner vs. Florida State
Blocked shots	8	Billy Thompson vs. Virginia Tech
Field-goal percentage	1.000	Billy Thompson (8-8) vs. Cincinnati
Free-throw percentage	1.000	Milt Wagner (9-9) vs. Kansas
		Herbert Crook (10-10) vs. North Carolina

Team

Points	103	vs. Virginia Tech
Field goals made	45	vs. Virginia Tech
Field goals attempted	75	vs. Virginia Tech
Free throws made	39	vs. Virginia Tech
Free throws attempted	54	vs. Virginia Tech
Rebounds	54	vs. Virginia Tech
Assists	28	vs. Virginia Tech
Steals	19	vs. Eastern Kentucky
Blocked shots	13	vs. Virginia Tech
Field-goal percentage	.619	vs. Iona (39-63)
Free-throw percentage	.857	vs. Kentucky (6-7)

GAME LOWS

Louisville

Points	59	vs. Southern Mississippi
Field goals made	24	vs. Western Kentucky
		vs. Indiana
		vs. Southern Mississippi
		vs. South Carolina
		vs. Cincinnati
Field goals attempted	44	vs. Cincinnati
Free throws made	4	vs. North Carolina State
Free throws attempted	5	vs. North Carolina State
Rebounds	24	vs. Kentucky
Assists	12	vs. Cincinnati
Steals	1	vs. Kentucky
		vs. Florida State
Blocked Shots	2	vs. Memphis State
		vs. Cincinnati
Turnovers	9	vs. Bradley
Field-goal percentage	.387	vs. Western Kentucky (24-62)
Free-throw percentage	.476	vs. Iona (10-21)

Without his outside accuracy and penetrating skills, the defense crashed inside and doubled Jeff Hall, pushing him farther out on the court. Without his ball-handling skills, there were times when it looked like "Federal Express" would have to be called in to deliver the ball upcourt. Without his stigma on the court, it became obvious that opponents no longer feared the Louisville Cardinal basketball machine.

Simply stated, the hunter became the hunted.

All the adjustments were tried, the press abandoned, rightfully so, and the Cardinals had the look, a lot of times, like they were trying to keep from losing rather than thinking about winning.

The record should read U of L, 14 wins; opponents, 18 wins; and Freedom Hall fans, 5 wins. The home crowd actually lifted the Louisville team to victory that many times, along with help from Coach Crum's game savvy and use of timeouts.

Adversity is a word that, according to Webster's Dictionary, means: "*a stroke of ill fortune.*" Some important man, whose name I cannot recall, said, "Adversity is the best test of a man's silent strength."

Facing adversity is certainly not a pleasant task, but as bad as it was without Milt, there are a lot of positive points we can look back on that will help "the return of the high-flying Cardinals" in the 1985-86 season.

Let's start with the coaching staff. I promise you that Denny Crum spent a lot of sleepless nights and uneasy times trying to come up with something that would allow his Cardinals to "hang in there" or "circle the wagons." He most certainly reached into his bag of tricks, all the way to the bottom, and that's how they were able to scratch out 19 victories with a team that had no chance to go .500 for the season. He and his staff did a lot of note comparing and had a lot of conversation that included phrases like "maybe we could" or "if we did this." In other words, they all had their thinking caps on, made suggestions and let the boss man make the decisions. Let's call it "food for thought."

I personally think this pulled the staff very close and they all came out of the 1984-85 season fully tested with answers to those "ifs" and "maybes." They most certainly will be a better coaching staff for the experience.

The press, which is Coach Crum's bread and butter, had to be abandoned. He now had to play without the easy baskets that Louisville had thrived on in the past. Denny and his staff had to employ a style of play that was not to their liking, but it kept them in a lot of games that might have been out of reach had they continued pressing.

Billy Thompson went to the guard position, which was a new experience. He had some good and some bad moments, but he improved as the season progressed. The guard spot, where you face the basket and have to make your offensive moves with the ball in motion, is totally different from playing the forward spot where you can pivot or dribble while in possession of the ball. Playing the guard spot will most certainly improve Billy as a player. This year when he's caught in the guard position, he can say: "Hello, friend" instead of "Hello, stranger!"

Abandoning the press meant playing a lot more set, half-court defense, and at times last year, Louisville's half-court defense did a fine job. That experience will most certainly be an asset to this year's team.

The Cardinals were forced into playing a lot of zone, certainly not a pleasant choice for Coach Crum. But, nevertheless, there is a place in the Louisville defensive scheme for use of the zone. When you coach the zone you broaden your skill in adusting to the zone. This year the zone will be another weapon that the Cards can use with authority.

Last year's adversity forced a lot of playing time on players who expected to do a lot more sitting than running. All the Cards got their chance at bat. They gained game experience that can be achieved in no other way. As a result, entering a game in the upcoming season will be a lot easier.

When you don't get the steals out of the press, you have to work for everything you get on the offensive end. This meant the Cardinals had to spend a lot more time in the half-court set offense. Running a lot of offense against a real, live defense can't be anything but helpful. Let's just leave it by saying "proper repetition equals proper execution."

The Cards were forced into a lot more do-or-die timeout situations, not to mention ball-control situations. All these things will offer positive results for U of L in the 1985-86 season.

I think Cardinal fans had to toughen up a little with the disappointments that happened, such as losing to Cincinnati (twice), Southern Mississippi and Tulane. Obviously, they handled it OK because every time they opened the doors at Freedom Hall there were 19,000-plus fans waiting anxiously for another Denny Crum miracle.

I think adversity in the case of the Cardinals and the 1984-85 season is sort of like the "chicken and the egg." The pain can be real bad, but the egg can be real good.

No way did the joy of the 19 wins overcome the agony of the 18 losses. I think we need to remember one very important point and that is: the pain of adversity has already been dealt with while the advantages are yet to be enjoyed.

Personally, I admired the Louisville program for the grit and hard work it took to win 19 games.

I can remember being in a similar situation in my high school coaching days. We lost a key player and could never recover. Things got so bad that I had to ask for volunteers to get a starting lineup.

As Van and I walked out of Madison Square Garden last year after being handled easily by Don DeVoe's Tennessee Volunteers, I looked over and said, "Hey, man, what do you think?" He took a few more steps and said, "Hey, bro, just wait until next year."

Well, it's next year now and time to enjoy some of the lessons that were learned.

Next week we'll take a sneak peek at the 1985-86 team as I see it. By the way, since the chicken has done her painful part, it's time to enjoy the egg. Make mine well-done.

The schedule

reprinted from SCORE**CARD**
(Nov. 16, 1985; Vol. 3, No. 12)

Schedule — meaning who, when and where the Cardinals will be doing their thing. It used to be that coaches and athletic directors spent hours planning a schedule that would allow for a couple of easy sisters to open up with, then a big game, then back to another "easy sister." No more is it that way!

Seems a creature named national TV came strutting onto the scene bringing, as a companion, the old proverbial green, meaning "money," and that now decides the who, when and where, especially if you have a top-notch basketball program like the Louisville Cardinals. People like Rodney and Scooter McCray, Darrell Griffith, Lancaster Gordon, Charles Jones, Milt Wagner and Billy Thompson, just to mention a few, have made the Cards more popular on TV than M*A*S*H*.

There is just no way that the universities can turn down the big money of TV, plus the exposure is really a terrific recruiting tool. Louisville will be on national television at least 13 times (including ESPN) this year, which is amazing. They will be playing weird times such as on Sundays at 8 p.m. and Saturdays at 2:05 and 3 p.m., and so on.

These weird times certainly change the routine on game day. These times mean early wake-up calls and a change in the pregame meals. Who cares? It's national TV time. Showtime, man! Louisville is on TV more than Howdy Doody or Captain Kangaroo! Mark that down as a compliment to the Louisville basketball program. Let's face it — the TV people put the teams on that the public likes to watch.

Well, the schedule begins on Nov. 22 in the NIT. What? Outrageous! Starting the season with a big-time national tournament . . . No problem. Denny Crum would play anybody anytime, in a snowstorm or on a floating iceberg.

The reason — from the start of Day 1, he is preparing for the conference and NCAA Tournaments. A little inconvenience here and there doesn't seem to matter — like chili, it's the end result that counts. So "Sorry, Charlie," it's off to Cincinnati and a tussle with Miami of Ohio. Don't giggle because, believe me, they have upset more folks than Chaminade.

Back in the '70s, I was on a scouting assignment for the University of Kentucky. I was working Marquette, easily the favorite in the first round of the NCAA. I made enough notes on Marquette to fill the trunk of my car and then, with two minutes left in the game, it dawned on me that Marquette was going to lose. I had nothing on Miami of Ohio. Only a tape from a local TV station saved me.

Miami of Ohio can beat you, but the Cards should win and would probably play Dayton after they eliminate Tulsa. This means Louisville vs. Dayton. I'm going with Louisville but it will be nip and tuck. Dayton's coach, Don Donoher, does a terrific job and he will have to be beaten. At this point, Louisville stands 2-0.

Now it's off to the "Big Apple," New York City, for the semifinal showdown in Madison Square Garden. This is no bargain of a trip. Too many weirdos to suit me. Last year, I asked a guy what time it was and he told me it was "none of my business."

In New York, I see Louisville with a split — winning one and losing one — making the four-game record 3-1.

Now it's back to Freedom Hall for the home opener. No way would the Cardinals lose the home opener — a win for Louisville.

Next comes Iona, which is another Card win. Add a Western win to this and by the 18th of "Joy to the World" month, the Cardinals are 6-1.

Oh, oh. Here comes Mr. Bad Guy himself, Mr. Knight, bringing his super guard Steve Alford and a truck load of junior college players in. Sorry, Bob, that won't be enough. I give the nod to Louisville. Incidentally, when a man throws large objects wherever he chooses, you always call him Mister. (I thought chairs were for sitting.)

The next opponent is Athletes in Action, and it's hard telling who will be playing for them. It's a church-affiliated team and anybody who might get that religious feeling just might show up. Nevertheless, this is Louisville's turn for a win.

Here it comes — the trip to Lexington to take on the Kentucky Wildcats . . . oops, make that Kentucky Ugly Shoes. No respectable Wildcat would wear those ugly things — he would be run out of the jungle. Hey, man, I like the Cardinals in this one. Kentucky's recruiting was shorter than my worst golf shot — no way can superstar Kenny Walker do it all. Well, it's time to sing Auld Lang Syne at the stroke of midnight and kiss somebody. The Louisville Cardinals made it this far and they stand 9-1.

It's January and in comes Wyoming — the home where the buffaloes roam. A win. Next comes Eastern Kentucky with a good team, but the 19,000 Freedom Hall fans will help give Louisville another win.

Now the trouble begins. It's off to the land of troubled Dana Kirk for a game with nasty ol' Memphis. The only good thing that ever happened in Memphis was Elvis Presley. Nevertheless, it's a win for Memphis, but only one time this year will the Memphis Tigers get the best of Louisville.

Let's keep traveling and head down to the hot spot of the South — Hattiesburg, Miss. — for a conference tussle with Southern Mississippi. That place is deader than last year's petunias. Another Louisville win — lightning will not strike twice in the same place!

Next comes a quick flight to Tallahassee, Fla., and a battle with Florida State. Mr. Ugly, Alton Lee Gipson, is gone, thank heavens. Another win for the Cards and, hopefully, this time without a fight. Last year the Cards won the game and the fight.

Now it's time to take it back to the city of Louisville, but guess who's coming to town — Earl "The Pearl" Washington. This will probably be trouble and could be a loss for the home team. Syracuse got a lot of tough experience last year in the Big Eight Conference, plus the Pearl can be real tough.

It's Metro time again as Cincinnati comes to town. This year, the Louisville team will not lose two games to the riverfront team. A win for the Cardinals. Coach Tony Yates is doing it in Cincinnati, but he loses this one.

Now it's off to the wheat state of Kansas. This just might be a little too much for the Cardinals. At home I think the Cards would win, but at Kansas and with Danny Manning, give this one to the Jayhawks.

Thank heavens, it's back to the classiest basketball house in the country, Freedom Hall, and a good win over LaSalle. Well, now, the longest, darkest and coldest month of the new year is over and the Cards have 15 wins and four losses.

Sweetheart month is next and guess who's coming to dinner — UCLA. Give this one to Louisville. It's a tough trip from Los Angeles to Louisville. The time difference and fatigue catches up quickly. Sorry, Coach Hazzard, but your old buddy, Denny Crum, nailed you.

Following UCLA will be Bill Foster's South Carolina Gamecocks — the home state of this year's Miss America. They won that contest but they will lose this one. A win for Louisville.

Now, the nicest coach in the Metro, Charlie Moir of Virginia Tech, will try his luck with the Cards and his luck will be bad. A loss for VPI.

Oh, oh, it's time to hit the road again and go to Raleigh, N.C., for a round with Jim Valvano and N.C. State. Believe me, that's a tough place to park, get in and get out, much less talking about a win. The Wolfpack will win in a close one.

Travel, travel, travel — the next three stops are Virginia Tech, Cincinnati and DePaul. This is a very dangerous stretch. I see the Cards getting wins in two of the three games with the loss coming in Chicago, another tough spot to come in first.

Home again. Whew, that was a tough trip. Freedom Hall will host the next two games — Florida State and Southern Miss. Two wins for the Cardinals.

Now for a quick trip to the state of J.R. and Miss Ellie for a tussle, probably a brawl, against Houston, the "almost home" of Tito Horford. Houston is coached by Guy Lewis. He has many critics but a lot of athletes — certainly more important than the critics. This one is a tossup, but could easily be Louisville's last regular-season loss. Hopefully, the McCrays will be in town for a little talk about "the good ol' days."

Let's put a win down against South Alabama at home and slip down to Columbia, S.C., for another win.

Well, you know what they say . . . you should always leave the best till last. It's Memphis State time again. Wonder who let them out of their cage? This will be a biggee — Dana will want this one badly. But, tough luck Coach, get these animals out of here. You're beat!

It's time to add the columns up. I say 25 wins and seven losses, including an 11-1 conference record.

Hey, that would be terrific with two, and possibly three, freshmen playing a prominent role. Keep in mind this look into my crystal ball sees this record with all the key people remaining healthy.

The Metro Tournament Conference is in Louisville and, without hesitation, I like the Red & Black.

Coach Denny Crum will read this, shake his head and smile, but Coach Jerry Jones will be more verbal . . . such as, "How can that rubber lip hooker with the yips pick us to win 25 games playing freshmen?" Hey, man, "Silk" is back and, besides, we know what a great job you guys do.

Incidentally, since I have bragged on you, do we have to leave Hattiesburg at 6:10 a.m. this year? OK, please, pretty please.

Traveling has its good and bad moments

reprinted from SCORE**CARD**
(Jan. 25, 1986; Vol. 3, No. 22)

Traveling with the Cards is a real experience, and it all starts like this. The team usually arrives at the airport about 45 minutes before the scheduled departure. This huge pile of luggage sorta takes over the corridor. Most of it is player equipment, along with various other supplies.

Normally, the plane tickets for the players have been pulled early. The players have been assigned the aisle seats, which gives them a place to put their long legs. This is taken care of by the manager, who also handles the boarding passes for the entire traveling party. Believe me, this is really a big help.

Van Vance, my colleague, and I always sit together. We usually laugh the whole way, normally about the one-liner contest we are having. I usually win. Jerry Jones is normally reading with one eye and keeping tabs on the overall situation with the other eye. Denny Crum can usually be found beating Coach Bobby Dotson in a game of gin. Denny loses just enough to keep Bobby on the hook, but so far Coach Dotson hasn't figured that out. Coach Wade Houston can normally be found in the snooze position.

For sure, the players all look like telephone operators with their headsets on, listening to a slight resemblence to music.

Billy Thompson can be found with his sound box , which is about the size of a small apartment refrigerator. Milt Wagner won't be very far from the box.

The plane is reasonably quiet, except for the laughing between Van and myself.

Believe me, airplanes always seem to have a problem of arriving or leaving anywhere on time. A couple of years ago, we were stuck in Atlanta's airport for 12 hours. Coach Crum got a little impatient. It was a silly situation where one plane had a crew and no passengers while another plane had passengers but no crew. He asked, " Why can't that crew fly this plane, since it's the same type of aircraft?"

That seemed reasonable to me, but red tape eliminated this from happening. Denny offered to fly the plane himself, only to learn that his faithful followers said, "No, thank you!"

We were working our way down to Mobile to take on the University of South Alabama.

The problem was a terrible ice storm had stopped anything from happening in the South. It so happened that Dick Vitale, the announcer for ESPN, was traveling with us. He drove us all bananas! This guy can do some tall talking, but he can also say some interesting stuff.

Another time, we were in Hattiesburg, Miss. On this trip, we were using a charter flight. When it came time to land, the pilot sorta let the plane fall out of the sky. Everyone was holding onto their ears. Jeff Hall really suffered some severe pains from it, and Coach Dotson had a little bleeding from his ears. It was two weeks before I could hear anything. That's when I discovered that being a little deaf wasn't all bad. The hotel housekeeper with all her banging around and the big trucks zooming by outside had no effect on me. I slept like a hobo with a hangover.

We were scheduled to leave following the game. We loaded up and the stewardess passed out some food that would never pass the Mississippi Food Inspector's standards. But we all gobbled it down while anxiously waiting to take off and head for home. It was about 1:30 a.m. when it was announced that the plane needed some sort of cranking device to start the engines. This thing was locked in the hangar and the guy with the key was AWOL.

Well, now it was back to the motel that we had checked out of before the game for a long four-hour sleep. We actually got airborne the next day at about 7:10 a.m.

I gotta say this, though — the Louisville group is a real bunch of troopers.

Everyone sorta goes with the flow and just laughs their way through these little inconveniences.

That pretty well ended the charter flights. There is an advantage to the charter in that the players can go to class the next day, if they can return following the game. I'm always concerned about flying when the chief pilot is wearing a bowling shirt and baseball cap. Maybe the charters will surface again in the future, and it will be a good experience. But for now I say "hooray" for commercial flying.

There are a lot of real nice flights, but it seems that the bad ones linger with you. Just this year, the Louisville party headed for the airport to load up and head for home on a jet charter. But it was discovered that the plane was still in Atlanta. It seems that the plane had traveled to Atlanta to correct some sort of mechanical problem. Well, now, I'm all for that, but it was a little disappointing to discover that there would be a two- or three-hour wait. The team, the group of fans and all concerned just laughed it off.

For sure, it was not my day. Upon arriving at the Louisville airport, pretty well bushed, I discovered that my car had a dead battery. It was 6 a.m. by now. At 6:45 I finally headed out for Lexington. But about the time I hit the Shelby County line, I heard this big boom. One of my tires had just given to cuss. Still, I made it. Now that I look back, it wasn't so bad. The worst part was that we lost to St. John's.

The ususal Louisville traveling party includes the players, the coaches (sometimes coaches Houston and Dotson are out recruiting but they always show up at the game site), trainer Jerry May (who is in charge of the traveling party), sports information director Kenny Klein (who has rapidly become very efficient in his duties and the name of the former SID, Joe Yates, is seldom mentioned), Jeff Whitt (team manager) and Danny Hass (student trainer). The media is also usually represented by *Courier-Journal* writer Russ Brown and *Louisville Times* writer Jim Terhune, along with the radio team of Van Vance and myself. At times, the TV crew of Don Russell and Jack Tennant are also with the group.

It's really a fun group of people. Regardless of the little problems that happen, it's always a great time.

Normally, upon arriving at our destination there is always a prearranged bus, or sometimes vans, waiting to take the group to either shooting practice or the hotel, depending upon the time. The University goes first class with the team. They stay in real nice places and eat good, well-prepared food. Wherever they stay, the rest of us stay. That makes it nice.

Like any group that travels together, there is a lot of kidding going on. Van is always loaded down with shoulder bags that just might have anything in them from an electronic chess game to a six-week-old banana. This guy would make a great safari man because he can carry more than a medium size camel. Me . . . I travel with the bare minimum. It's for sure that Van will have whatever I might need.

Coach Dotson, meanwhile, is always being harassed about losing all the time to Denny, which he continually denies. Everyone else is usually harassed about something.

A normal game day looks like this:

9:00 a.m. — Wake up
9:45 a.m. — Breakfast
11:00 a.m. — Shooting practice
3:30 p.m. — Pre-game meal
5:00 p.m. — Taping
6:30 p.m. — Depart hotel
7:15 p.m. — Pre-game talks
8:05 p.m. — Game
Midnight — Bed check

Van and I always arrive at the game site two hours prior to tipoff to check out the lines and get any interviews that we feel might enhance the broadcast. Surprisingly enough, there is not a lot of free time on these trips. It's mostly airplanes, airports, vans or buses, motels and arenas. One of the nice parts of the travel, however, is eating out the night before the game. Either all or part of the group, excluding the team, will come up with what is rumored to be a great eating place. For sure, there are a lot of tall tales told at this gathering.

The recent Memphis trip included a real nice affair at the "Folks Folly Prime Rib Steak House." In attendance were Denny and his guest, George Lapides (who is the boss man of the Memphis Class AA baseball team), Bill Hardwick (who was a national champion tour bowler at one time), Klein, Terhune, Brown, Vance, PJ (my wife) and me. This was a great treat because Denny got into fishing stories. When he gets on this kind of subject, he really gets enthused and becomes very relaxed and talkative. Boy, did he tell some wild tales.

I heard him say 20 and then I heard the word "feet" tied to rainbow trout. I thought to myself, "Wow, a 20-foot trout." Naturally, I heard wrong. He talked about the art of presenting the different lures to the different types of fish at different times of the year. He said, "Fish are either moving around looking for food or hiding under a rock, and you have to fool them or make them mad." I could already see that the sea creatures of the deep are too smart for me. Golf drives me cuckoo; fishing would finish me off.

Next came the bear stories. It seems that these fish go up stream to spawn, which brings out the bears. Your guide has to stand guard with a big elephant gun because the bear might just turn the fisherman into a "Bear Burger." The story goes on with putting the fishing tackle away and hunting the bears. That did it for me! The only bears I'm interested in are the Chicago Bears and their quest for the Super Bowl.

After all that talk about fishing, I was about ready to go out and buy myself a boat. But the bear story ended that. Besides, camping out for me is Holiday Inn. Tents and that stuff just don't do it.

Now comes the time to pay the check and Denny comes up with this thing called "the numbers game" to decide who has to pay and who gets out free. He volunteers to pay for part and out of nine people, three will get out. Guess who survived — Van, my wife and myself.

The game went like this: You start with numbers between one and 500. People keep guessing with the instructions "higher or lower" until the numbers squeeze down. Somebody hits, and they lose.

Nice game, Denny. I loved it, as well as the evening featuring stories from " Field and Stream."

It so happens that Denny is a fisherman with lots of experience. He started with his father and fell in love with the sport at a very early age. He has caught bass weighing 8.5, 10.6 and 11.2 pounds. And I'm told that this is special.

Two of these were caught in Tallahassee a couple of years

ago. I saw them myself. No fish story here; it's a fact. They looked like the Abdul-Jabbars of the fishing population to me.

The word is out that Denny and Dana Kirk of Memphis were involved in a fishing contest this past summer. Denny sorta hints that it was no contest and Dana said it was so bad that Denny had his picture made with "my" fish. Fish stories are always like that.

Following the recent Memphis game, the road trip continued on to Hattiesburg with a one-night stopover in New Orleans that included a practice session at the University of New Orleans and, for sure, the normal eat out. This one took place at Morans Riverside Restaurant, which is supposed to be one of Denny's favorite restaurants anywhere. The meal that the Louisville folks enjoyed looked like this: turtle soup, shrimp scampi, crab fingers, oysters and Fetttuccine Alfredo with an entree of lamb with broccoli and carrots, plus a touch of wine. Hey now, how's that sound for a New Orleans meal!

This was followed by another Denny Crum session of entertainment — this time the topic was golf. That's the good news. The bad news is that I stopped off in Nashville to visit with my friend C. M. Newton, the coach of Vanderbilt. I was able to watch the Vandy-Georgia game but, as you can see, I missed a nice evening in New Orleans.

The players had a chance to take a stroll through Bourbon Street. It was just a nice break for everyone.

As a rule, the players do most of their eating at the hotel under the watchful eye of Jerry May. Coach Jones is always close by to deal with anything that needs attention.

The bottom line of "Life on the Road" is still influenced by winning or losing. The more time you spend with the Cardinals the more you get involved, and losing sorta puts a damper on the old attitude. You just sorta feel disappointment. We all play the "Mr. Cool" game of saying "Life goes on," but, for sure, a little pain is felt by all the traveling party.

Traveling with the Cards is certainly something that I will always treasure. I've taken lots of pictures and, when it comes time for my rocking chair, I'm sure I will enjoy looking back on those good old days with the Louisville Cardinals.

For now, though, I can still say, "Could I have a menu, please" and laugh at my colleague, Van Vance, as he struggles up the halls of the airports with pounds and pounds of shoulder-bag luggage, plus ask Coach Dotson, "How much did you lose this time, Bobby?"

Tough? — I reckon

reprinted from SCORE**CARD**
(Feb. 8, 1986; Vol. 3, No. 24)

Whoever made the statement, "It's a tough job but somebody has got to do it" must have been looking at the Louisville Cardinals' 1985-86 basketball schedule. It's certainly not a pleasure walk in the park on a beautiful autumn afternoon.

Maybe it's time to talk about the schedule, keeping the fans happy and, in the process, being able to win enough games to qualify to participate in the NCAA Tournament.

Just for the heck of it, I got interested in comparing Louisville's schedule to the other top teams in the nation. These comparisons truly indicate the task which Louisville faces is a little above and beyond the call of duty. This comparison is based only on the January and February schedules since this is when conference play starts almost everywhere around the country. It's also the time when teams need to fare well against conference opponents.

So let's look at the schedules of the nation's top teams and compare them to Louisville's schedule:

Beginning with January, North Carolina plays only two worthy opponents outside the ACC — Notre Dame at home and Marquette on the road.

Duke plays St. Louis, Harvard, Miami and Oklahoma, all at home. Only the Sooners can be considered a top-flight team.

Georgia Tech? They play only one legitimate opponent outside the ACC — Illinois.

Now let's take a look at some of the teams closer to home.

Kentucky plays only one game outside the SEC — North Carolina State.

Indiana doesn't play a single opponent outside the Big Ten Conference.

Now, I'm aware these are large conferences and there isn't room for much outside competition. And, granted, some of this conference play is tough. But with basically all conference play to plan for, the highs and lows are much more predictable. In going against conference opponents, you're familiar with their style of play along with their personnel.

But throw in a tough opponent from outside your conference every weekend and see what happens.

It makes the job of preparation exceptionally tough for a simple reason — there is NO time for preparation. And when this outside opponent is going to play you on national television, you MUST find some time for preparation.

That probably means letting preparation for a conference opponent slide. Obviously, you can lose a few league games and finish second, third or whatever. But you can still win the conference tournament, receive the automatic bid into the NCAA and come out smelling like honeysuckle on a warm summer day. Or even if you should fail to win the conference tournament, the NCAA would have to take a very close look at the super, super-tough schedule you played. At least it should work that way.

Now, let's take a look at little ol' Louisville's patsy schedule. For six consecutive Saturdays that began back on Jan. 18, the Cards will face six opponents on national television. Those opponents are Syracuse, at Kansas, UCLA, at North Carolina State, at DePaul and at Houston.

During the weeks of these games, Louisville will be knocking heads against all the Metro Conference teams.

LaSalle and South Alabama also make stops in Freedom Hall during this period.

Personally, I think it's a little much to expect any team, much less a team that is playing three freshmen a lot, to post a big, impressive record that'll only show three or four losses. I think it's great to play the best competition, but only to a point. The main goal is still to work hard and make every effort to win the regular-season conference title.

What does all this mean?

It means the Cardinal fans are being treated to the toughest Division I schedule in the nation. You can take pride in the fact the networks think this much of the Louisville basketball program.

You say, "That's great!" It's OK to say that but don't expect any team to survive that schedule without some disappointments.

Louisville came back off an eight-day road trip and had just one day to prepare for the nation's No. 4 team — Syracuse. The good news is that they won. The bad news, however, is that two days later it was Cincinnati in Freedom Hall and they lost.

Four days after that they traveled to Kansas to take on what I think is the second- or third-best team in the country. And there is no tougher place to play in the nation than Allen Fieldhouse. Still, the Cardinals almost ran the Jayhawks out of Lawrence, only to lose 71-69.

Then it was at home three days later against LaSalle, a game which the Cards managed to win.

How many times can a major college team generate that high pitch of intensity?

Do you go to work everyday with a fever-pitch desire to die for your job?

No way.

The Cards will play at home against Virginia Tech on Feb. 8. The Hokies have been ranked in the top 20 all year. The very next day it's off on a four-day trip to Raleigh, N.C., to play Jimmy Valvano's North Carolina State Wolfpack on national television at Reynolds Coliseum. And then over to Blacksburg, Va., for another game against Virginia Tech at Cassell Coliseum, another tough place to win.

Believe me, these are tough assignments. I'll even continue that four-day story by saying that it's only a half day at home before it's off to Cincinnati to play. Then it's back home a day before heading to Chicago to tackle DePaul on the road in another national TV game.

Now that's 10 days that are strictly going, playing or returning. Keep in mind that all these games are important, either for conference play or national exposure. But in no way can a group of college athletes come out "ready for bear" in every game.

Now, you ask, why is the schedule the way it is?

That's an easy answer. The Louisville Cards are America's favorite TV team. That's a real compliment to the Cardinal basketball program. No team is on the tube, and I mean the tube seen everywhere, more than the Louisville Cardinals. And, I might add, no team plays better on the tube.

valuable person. These are people who are willing to do this type of thing in order to be a part of the program and spend some time in the pit.

The trainer and team doctor are also there. To them, the pit is just another place to take care of emergency situations. These are professional people. They watch the game as spectators, but always with an eye out for the injury and exactly how the injury occurred. Their work really begins when they leave the pit and get involved with the rehabilitation of the injured player.

I can remember when I used to think about how great it would be when I could have my own team on that bench, sitting there dealing with whatever. I sat there for a lot of years and suffered through a lot of painful experiences as well as celebrating a lot of exciting times. I never really thought about the pit being a terrible place until one day, out of the clear, it came to me that I was always anxious to get out of the pit, win or lose.

I'm convinced I felt that way because it was a place where I had to deal with so many different emotions, none of them predictable. I think most of us like to stay pretty much on an even keel. Dealing with peaks and valleys continuously is a very tough way to go. But it seems that coaches like it that way.

In a recent interview with Ray Meyer of DePaul, he said, "Jock, I honestly miss it." He only did it for 42 years at the same school. As I looked into his eyes, I knew he meant it.

The other day I heard a story about this guy who went to a market that dealt in body parts and transplants. He came to this row of jars that contained the brains of scientists, computer experts, surgeons, lawyers, etc. Finally, he came to a jar labeled "Coach." It was empty so he asked the clerk where the coach's brain was. The clerk replied, "We haven't found a coach yet who had any!"

With all the agony and displeasures that go with the job, the clerk just might be right.

The goal: quality minutes

reprinted from SCORE**CARD**
(Mar. 8, 1986; Vol. 3, No. 28)

Talking with Kevin Walls recently, the young man used the term "quality minutes." I was really struck by the term.

I had asked Kevin about what was on his mind as he entered a Louisville game. He answered, "I just want to go in and get some quality minutes that will help our cause."

We have all heard the word used in a lot of ways, but I had never heard it said that way in regard to performance minutes. But if you think about it, what better way could it be said?

I guess the next thing is to establish exactly what a quality minute of play is.

Does it have to be a perfect minute? I say no.

In my opinion, a quality minute would be a minute of play that your personal opponent would be held in check, making no contribution to his team's cause; would be a minute where a player would make no ball handling errors, or if he did turn it over was able to recover and get the ball back; offensively, a player would have good shot selection and make sound mental judgements; and, the player, in striving for the quality minute, would perform in both the team offense and defense, carrying his fair share of the load and not be guilty of poor performance and execution.

It wouldn't be necessary to make the shot to be considered a quality minute. The player would contribute in some way to his team's winning effort, doing nothing to damage his team's chance of winning.

Maybe we should discuss the other type of performance minutes that happen from time to time. Let's put minutes played into four categories: (1) suberb minutes; (2) quality minutes; (3) zero minutes; (4) minus minutes. These categories are pretty much self-explanatory.

The superb minute would be a minute of near perfection, going beyond the quality minute boundaries to include stunning plays and dazzling dunks. The quality minute has already been defined.

The zero minute is where the player is in the game but does nothing to help or hurt his team, a minute where the player never makes a mark on the charts.

Recently, a Cardinal player played a 7-minute stretch in a game and never made a mark. He was trying hard but it just wouldn't happen for him. Defensively, he was no better. He was flirting with the zero-minute category. Keep in mind when a player is performing in this category, the team can be said to be operating at 80 percent efficiency. This will get you beat, unless the opponent is doing the same.

In the college game, there are 200 minutes of playing time. From the first day, the goal of any coach is to improve his group to the maximum number of solid-play minutes possible and eliminate the number of zero and minus minutes. A good question would be, "How many quality minutes does a team need to reach the acceptable level of performance?" No one knows the answer because it would all depend on the opponent and how many quality minutes they could put together.

The last category, the minus minute, is where a player seems to do everything wrong and takes away from his team's chance of winning. He performs at a level that deducts from his team's opportunity to succeed.

This happens to all players, particularly young players. Most of the time, these people will be replaced in the lineup before too much damage is done. These athletes need to really work to achieve the category of quality minutes the next time the opportunity presents itself. The skills are there, it's just a matter of time.

Billy Thompson, Milt Wagner and Pervis Ellison seem to

have a flair for performing at the superb level much of the time, getting a lot of quality minutes. But even these multi-talented players will occasionally dip down to the zero and minus levels. Thank heavens these are short visits.

When these moments of poor play surface, we, as fans, are quick to criticize. That's because we know what they are capable of doing. Maybe we need to remember that we all have our moments of poor performance and be a little more understanding. Somebody has been doing something right or Louisville wouldn't have over 20 wins at this point in the season.

Let's get back to the quality minute.

As a starter who will normally play 30 to 35 minutes, there is no way this player can give his team that same amount of quality minutes. Either a break in concentration, shortness of breath or just being human will take its toll somewhere.

The coach who is skilled in recognizing these tell-tale signs of performance failure will get these people out for a short breather, which will restore the player back to the quality of possible superb performance. Performance will normally break down with an experienced player when he is fatigued.

I really believe the quality-minute category is what the substitute should strive for. If I were a sub, I'd concentrate on this team and make every effort to give the quality time for every minute I was on the court. Naturally, the longer you played the harder it would be to maintain this standard of play, but that would be my goal.

I wish I had used that term in the many times I've sent a substitute into a game. I probably said something like, "Play hard and don't screw up." It (quality minutes) just seems to be the perfect term to use when sending in someone to do a job. It seems to identify with words such as success, accomplishment and contribution.

The term, to me, seems to make the task a lot easier. Just think about yourself going into a game and your coach has said to you, "Son, get on in there and give us some quality minutes." To me, that would be motivating and I would play each minute with a goal. And each minute I would have a new goal.

The improvement you've seen in Louisville has been the result of more quality minutes being played by the Cardinals. Herbert Crook, for example, has really been playing solid lately. Even when he isn't scoring, he's working hard in all the other phases of the game.

Jeff Hall, in my opinion, has become a quality-minute player. Jeff's minutes are not as spectacular as some of the other Cards, but he has reached the level of performance where he is always contributing. There have been many games where Jeff has had no turnovers, or maybe just one. Keep in mind that he handles the ball as much as any of his teammates. Defensively, he's learned to honor his opponent's speed and allows for this in his defensive position. His shot slection is excellent and his accuracy even better.

To me, one of the glaring weaknesses of the Cards has been the poor minutes that some of the players have put in during substitution roles. The reason, however, is Louisville's first three substitutes, as of late, have been freshmen.

Tony Kimbro is the exception. He's been able to come in and really contribute. In fact, now I feel as comfortable with Tony in the game as I do with any of the starters.

I was beginning to feel that way about Mark McSwain when he injured his knee. I think it's just a matter of time before Kevin Walls will be reaching his goal, consistently giving the Cards some quality minutes. Hopefully, Kenny Payne will do the same.

To me, the Cardinals have reached a plateau, defensively, where they make it difficult for the opponents to succeed in their offensive schemes. They are able to sustain this for most of a 40-minute game. But this has not been the case on the other end.

Offensively, they are lagging in consistent quality minutes. They have had a tendency to go from spectacular to zero as a team. But the good news is they go back to quality and spectacular. They play in streaks, including nonproductive streaks.

Lately, the Cards have been a second-half team. They've survived with this but, as the NCAA progresses, it's going to take more offensive consistency throughout the entire 40-minute game. This means the individuals will need to produce more quality-minute performances. I believe the very importance of the tournament will cause this group to go from quality to superb and back no lower than acceptable quality.

Looking back to the Big Apple NIT, these Cards have done a lot of playing and have improved tremendously. Personally, I feel good about their progress and their opportunity. They are what I call "travel tough," which I'll discuss at another time. They've faced all challengers, all over the country.

Personally, I think they are about ready to face whatever lies ahead and make us all very proud BIRD LOVERS.

Recently, prior to a game in Freedom Hall, I did a pre-game show and took it to Van (Vance) at the table. He listened to it and said, in a loud voice, "Bones! This is just bones. Don't bring me bones without the meat."

This was Van's way of telling me I had just spent a couple of minutes out of the quality-minute category. There are times when we all need to be reminded.

P.S. — Many thanks to Kevin Walls for the term "quality minutes." I just wish I could have heard it 20 years ago.

'Travel tough'
and 'game tested'

reprinted from SCORE**CARD**
(Mar. 15, 1986; Vol. 3, No. 29)

The old guy on the television commercial put it nicely, "They do it the old-fashioned way. They earn it."

How many times did you hear your mother or grandmother say, "Take your medicine and you will be all right," or how about, "The harder you work the luckier you'll get." My favorite is, "If you want to learn to play good hardball, you gotta play with the boys who play good hardball."

These are cliches we've heard over the years that tell us in order to achieve something, you have to pay the price.

The Cardinals have paid that price for what they want to achieve — qualify for the NCAA post-season tournament and be as completely prepared as possible to succeed to their maximum potential.

I doubt if many teams ever succeed to this limit; however, Villanova did it last year as they came from nowhere to win the national championship.

This preparation all really started back on Oct. 15 when practice began. The first test came in the Big Apple NIT, first against Miami of Ohio and Tulsa in Cincinnati and then against super tough Kansas and St. John's in Madison Square Garden in New York City.

That was some test.

Louisville took the challenge with old-timers Jeff Hall, Milt Wagner (who was still untested following the broken foot) and often talked about Billy Thompson. There was an improved Herbert Crook and Mark McSwain, along with a barnyard full of "guppies" — something I call freshmen.

The test was really tough, sorta like asking sophomores in high school to take the college entrance exams . . . particularly so if you were expecting high marks. For sure, Cardinal fans always expect high marks. Needless to say, they have been spoiled by the wins and wins and more wins the Cardinals have given them over the years.

You might say, "So what! There were other teams that took on the same challenge."

My answer to that as the Cardinals continued their preparation for the "Run for the Roses" is after the Louisville team finished in the NIT. It went like this: they took on teams from the Big Ten, Pac 10, Southwest, Big East, ACC, Missouri Valley, Big Eight, Metro Atlantic, Mid-American, Ohio Valley, SEC, Sun Belt and WAC conferences along with a major independent. And you might want to add to that a very demanding Metro Conference schedule.

I defy anyone out there to duplicate the toughness of that

schedule. I have said in previous articles the Cards played nine of the country's top 20 teams, some more than once, including three of the top six teams in the nation. No other team does that.

What does all this prove?

Simple — they've been tested all over this country, in different arenas under a lot of different circumstances. I think they are "travel tough" and "game tested."

The Louisville basketball team reminds me of the old-time fighter in the circus — the guy who traveled with the circus and took on all comers in a bare-fist fight until the best man won. I've been with this team every step of the way and there were a lot of times that I got just plain tuckered out.

These guys have taken on all comers. Looking back, it seems it was always travel a day, play a day, travel home a day, be home a day and start all over again. I've seen these guys take the court without much emotion and they appeared to be dragging. They would find themselves behind the 8-ball and the game would usually be either an important conference game or a national TV game. They had to shift gears even though the old body was saying, "No, not again." But they shifted anyway.

This makes a person reach down and get something he didn't know he had. It's called "performing under adversity" or "going against the grain." It pushes a person to heights that were beyond him. It doesn't always have a happy ending but with each effort a person becomes stronger within himself.

For sure, these Cardinals are travel tough and game tested. They are a proud bunch. I think they feel like a group of Marine recruits that have just completed a tough training course in the jungle — a course that tested their intestinal fortitude and determination. I think another term for it might be "gut check."

The Cardinals have been in 11 different states that include Ohio, New York, Tennessee, Mississippi, Florida, Kansas, North Carolina, Virginia, Illinois, Texas and South Carolina. This team has played teams from the north (DePaul from Chicago) to the south (Florida State from Tallahassee), from the west (UCLA from Los Angeles) to the east (St. John's from New York).

There are a lot of ways a coach can approach a season. Some coaches take one game at a time and make the current game equally as important as the rest. These coaches are the ones that put the priority on the won-loss record.

Some coaches believe that losing is contagious so they go for the win at all costs. A lot of times, these coaches are in job trouble or they just think they have to win them all. They believe the theory, "Win this one tonight and we'll worry about the next one when it comes around." If that means playing only five people, then that's what they do.

The other school of thought is to get as many players as much game experience as possible. Put as many players as you can into tough situations. Give them a chair and whip, push them into the cage and tell them to handle those lions. If you don't, the lions will handle you.

There were a few times this season when the lions handled Louisville. The freshmen were put into tough situations and did not respond very well, most in the early part of the season. It was a price that needed to be paid. Whether or not it will prove to be worth it will be answered when the Cards enter the tough NCAA Tournament.

Tournament time is always a very special time. It is a time where a season can become a success. For example, look at the Auburn Tigers of last year.

Coach Sonny Smith had already turned in his resignation, effective at the end of the 1985 season. His team had struggled and the pressures on Smith had been tough. Tournament time came around and so did the Auburn Tigers. They rolled through the SEC Tournament and well into the NCAA Tournament. Coach Smith was urged to remain at Auburn, which he did. I'm sure there was a little "money talk" going on, too. Let's just call it a "rags to riches" story.

It can also go the other way. A team might have been super successful then "Bingo," out they go in the first round of the NCAA. A lot of times this will really put a cloud over what had been a great year.

Last year's Georgetown team is a perfect example. They did make it to the finals, but losing to Villanova put a great big blemish on what had been a great year.

Most coaches love the feeling of tournament time. It's a chance to really make your mark — a shot that will be heard around the world. It's sorta like an exhibit at the state fair, except this exhibit will be seen by most everyone in this great country of ours. You, as a coach, are thinking, "Here is what I have. This is what I've been working on all winter. Is it going to be good enough to win a blue ribbon?"

Tournament time is a mysterious time to both coaches and players. You think you know how different people will react to various situations, but there is never a way to really know. Sure, your juniors and seniors have given you some idea about how they they will deal with this "now or never" situation, but the guppies . . . well, that's something else.

It was just four years ago that North Carolina and Georgetown were playing for the national championship. It went down to the final few seconds of the game. Georgetown was bringing the ball up court with a chance to win when a player named Freddie Brown just blanked out and threw the ball directly to James Worthy of NC. Worthy raced to the other end of the court and "roto-rootered" the ball for the clincher.

Even when you watched it you couldn't believe it, but it did happen. It was a devastating blow to this young man. I remember watching coach John Thompson go directly to the player and gave him a hug that simply said, "That's OK, Freddie. We all make mistakes."

As fate and the man upstairs would have it, two years later Georgetown returned to the NCAA final game and won the national championship. It was Freddie Brown who played a big part in that accomplishment, and it was Freddie Brown who went directly to Coach Thompson and gave him a hug that simply said, "Thanks, Coach, for giving me another chance."

These are the kind of theatrics that tournament time makes possible. It's a time for thrills and chills. It's a time for fun and new clothes for the ladies. It's spring time, a new beginning. It's party time for the many loyal fans that follow their team to wherever.

It's a time to test yourself against the best of the rest. Tournament time is a time to see just what has been accomplished during the long winter months of hard travel and hard work. It's a time to renew old acquaintances and make new friends.

It's also a time to cheer and celebrate. It's a time for some to be in pain because of a loss. Most basketball fans are hearty souls and can weather any storm. They will celebrate to honor a win and most likely celebrate to ease the pain of a loss. Whatever, it's a terrific time, win or lose.

The bottom line of all this is that the Cardinals have done all the things that had to be done in order to prepare themselves to face whatever challenges lie ahead. They have been in a lot of tough situations in the past few months. They've played tired and sometimes with pain. They've had their basketball family problems off the court, but worked it all out. They've paid the price.

This is not hearsay. I've watched it with my own two baby blues. Now it's just a matter of taking the court and giving it their best effort for 100 percent of the time they are on the floor. Hopefully, they will get a little luck along the way.

But I promise you they are travel tough and game tested. There is no bluff to the Cardinals. They will have to be beaten.

Just like the little cowboy who went outside only to find the rear-end of his horse painted yellow. He stormed back into the saloon and said loudly, "Whoever the coyote is that painted the rear-end of my horse yellow, step forward." This huge, ugly and dirty cowboy stood up, all 6-6 of him, and said, "I did, Shortie. You got a problem?" The little cowboy meekly replied, "No, sir, I just wanted you to know that the first coat was dry."

The Cardinals are not ugly or dirty, but they know how to stand tall.

Springtime in the Rockies — basketballs are in bloom

reprinted from SCORE**CARD**
(Mar. 22, 1986; Vol. 3, No. 30)

Flowers are not the only things that bloom in spring. NCAA Tournament time is also "bloom time" for the college basketball world. It's a new beginning and a new enthusiasm

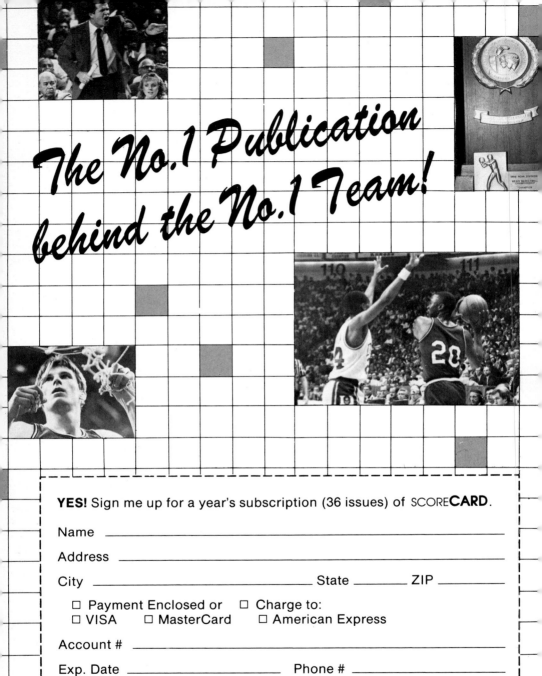

The No.1 Publication behind the No.1 Team!

YES! Sign me up for a year's subscription (36 issues) of SCORE**CARD**.

Name _____

Address _____

City _____ State _____ ZIP _____

☐ Payment Enclosed or ☐ Charge to:
☐ VISA ☐ MasterCard ☐ American Express

Account # _____

Exp. Date _____ Phone # _____

Signature _____

Mail to SCORE**CARD**, The Falsoft Building, 9509 U.S. Highway 42, P.O. Box 385, Prospect, KY 40059, (502) 228-4492

Enclosed is my $26.25 (for Kentucky residents) for a full year's subscription of SCORE**CARD** or $25 for non-Kentucky residents. Canadian and Mexican rate U.S. $34. Surface rate to other countries U.S. $57. Air mail U.S. $85. All subscriptions begin with the current issue. Please allow up to three weeks for first copy. We do not bill.